YOUR DESTINY

UNLOCKING THE
IMPOSSIBLE PROMISES OF GOD

IVAN & ISABEL ALLUM

Highlands Publishing

CONTENTS

INTRODUCTION

Have you ever wondered about the meaning of life? What is my destiny? Why do I exist? These are some of the greatest mysteries of life. Since the beginning of time men have been searching for the answer. The search for destiny is what drives most people to do what they do, and the lack of it, is the greatest cause for dissatisfaction, frustration, depression, suicide, mid-life crisis, etc. There is something in the heart of man that will never be satisfied until this question is answered. That is when deep calls unto deep. Men try all kinds of things to find this satisfaction, which is like a hunger that nothing takes away. Some try drugs, alcohol, addictions, work, education, money, power, etc. People have ideas of what will satisfy them and strive to obtain it only to be greatly disappointed when they get there, as the answer can only be found in the heart of God.

Everyone experiences this at different levels throughout life. We both have experienced it, but also know what it is like to find the answer and have that deep hunger satisfied. Finding the answer also brought rest to our lives. That is the place where peace and contentment comes to us, where our identity is found, and all things come together. There is nothing in life that compares to knowing what you were born to be, why you exist, and attaining it. When you experience this, everything in life changes, rest comes to your soul and success to your life. Yet, it seems so impossible and, in the kingdom of men, no one can achieve this. But, we do not belong to the kingdom of men. We are foreigners in this land (1 Peter 1:17; 1 Peter 2:11). We belong to the Kingdom of God. A Kingdom where everything is possible because our Father is the KING of Kings and LORD of Lords and nothing is impossible for Him. His word is incontestable and as His children we have access to all His resources and to the fullness of His Kingdom. God acts according to His realm of possibilities and, therefore, His promises and offers are "big" and impossible according to the minds and resources of men. He is a BIG God who thinks big and talks big and we must learn to think like He does in order to walk through His impossible promises and fulfill our destiny.

God is supernatural and everything He does and says is supernatural. Therefore, our destiny is also supernatural, but it is possible to live and fulfill it in a very natural way just like Jesus did. He lived a very supernatural life in a very natural way. That is why we can only attain our destiny through Him and in Him. In this book we want to share with you how to find this answer and possess your destiny. We want to show you the easy way to get there. Jesus said, "My yoke is easy and My burden light" (Matt. 11:29-30). Yet, very few people have discovered this. The world has shown us the hard way of doing things. In the ways of the world we learn ambition, competition, striving, confusion, and only a few people ever achieve success. This way has come into the church and we have accepted it as normal. However, Jesus made a way for us so it can be simple and possible. As children of God we have access to another realm and have to learn to live there.

Here we will share our journeys into our promised land, and the stories of what we have seen God do as we have ministered to others. This is really a testimony to the transforming power of our Father, to His greatness, His goodness, His undying love, and His Kingdom. We want you to realize that it is possible for ordinary people to live the extraordinary lives that they were created for. Like Peter, we too are eye witnesses of His power and of the transforming glory He brings to our lives (2 Peter 1: 16-18). We have experienced this power and are living a life we were not raised for, a life that was impossible for us. Today we live to make our Father famous and we will do it till the end of our days. We are fulfilling the destiny God created us for and we know, without doubt, that He is longing for all of His children to live their kingdom life and receive their kingdom identity. May your ears be open to hear what the Spirit of the LORD has to say to you!!!!

SECTION ONE

THE NAMELESS AND FACELESS GENERATION

We are entering into an amazing season. It is the time that the prophets of old spoke about but could not even imagine. We have heard of this for years but did not understand its reality. This is the hour when the Kingdom of Heaven is coming to earth and is becoming a reality. God is taking the mystery away from it. This is also the season of the regular people when we all get to participate in the glory of God and make Him famous.

In early 1994, I had a vision in which I saw a multitude of people walking down a street. It was a narrow cobblestone street. There were old buildings on both sides. I noticed that everyone was holding a lantern. The shape and size of the lanterns was exactly the same and their brilliance was identical. No one was bigger or brighter than another one. The light of the lanterns was such that I could see even the smallest crack on the road and on the walls of the buildings. It made everything completely clear and the hidden things became noticeable. However, there was one thing I could not understand. In spite of the brightness of the light in all those lanterns I could not see the faces of the people carrying them. I could see their silhouettes, but their features were hidden behind the brightness of the lanterns.

At that moment the LORD spoke and said, "What you see right now is the army of people who will carry My glory throughout the streets of the nations of the world. I am preparing a generation that will be the carriers of My glory, which will be so strong and powerful that it will shine in the darkest places. The whole world will see My glory

3

through them. However, no one will know or recognize them. They will be so hidden by My glory that no one will know who they are but, everyone will see ME when they look at them. This is the "nameless and faceless generation".

At the beginning of the year 2000, while I was flying from Brazil, the LORD spoke to me and said, "The season is now coming when the ministries of men are coming to an end. The time has come for the restoration of the ministry of Jesus back into the church and on the earth and along with it, the Kingdom of Heaven will come back to earth.

About 15 years ago the LORD spoke through a prophecy that went around the world and said that He was raising a nameless and faceless generation. Many people responded to that calling and soon after began to experience fires, brokenness, stripping of identity, reputation, ambition, pride, etc., etc.

Many of these people had not done anything to cause that to happen. They were loving and serving the LORD, but the storms began. The LORD caused that to happen in order to prepare a generation without name and face, a generation that He can trust, and to whom He will entrust the ministry of His Son. This generation has paid a high price, has died and lost it all, and now will gain it all. They have endured much but will receive something that no other generation on earth has received before, "the ministry of Jesus".

The ministry of Jesus is a ministry of love, sacrifice, service, humility, and intimacy. It is a ministry of power but the power that comes from intimacy with the Father. "I only do what I see the Father do" He said (John 5:19). He came to make the Father known and to release His Kingdom on earth. The Kingdom of His Father flowed through Him in a natural everyday way. Like when the woman with the issue of blood touched His garment and He said, "Virtue (or power) has gone out of me" and she was healed (Luke 8:46). The Kingdom that resided within Him came through Him like Peter's shadow (Acts 5:15), and He did not do anything for that to happen. He just walked with the Father in such intimacy that those who met Him met the Father through Him, like the man who said, "Whether He is a sinner, I do not know; but one thing I do know, that though I was blind, now I see." (John 9:25).

Almost 20 years ago, we were in Costa Rica and the LORD spoke to us and said, "I am going to give you a ministry that is going to be like the wind. When the wind blows no one knows where it comes from or where it goes, but everyone can feel it passing through the land. That is the same way it will be with you. No one will know who you are, where you came from, or where you are going, but just like with the wind, everyone will know that my Spirit passed through the land when you came". We heard that and said, "OK LORD. Here we are!" At the time, we did not know what that meant as we had never heard anyone say anything like that. About a year later, the prophecy of the nameless and faceless generation God was calling was given. We heard it and knew right away that this was what the LORD had told us the year before. Now we had a name for it: "nameless and faceless." However, we had no idea what we were getting into.

The next 10-15 years were very difficult and during those years the LORD allowed us to go through situations that we could have never imagined. We went through hotter fires than we could endure, or at least it felt that way. We were so broken that we did not know if we could ever be put back together again. We lost everything that had any value to us. The LORD stripped us from much pride, reputation, ambition, recognition, identity, and much more. Doors that should have opened, closed before us for no reason and could not be opened. People who should have helped us and believed in us, turned their backs on us. Our finances crashed, and nothing worked out for us. We died a very intense, long, and painful death in every area of our lives and could not find a reason for it. We were being faithful, were serving the LORD, and were giving more than we could, not just financially but in every area of our lives. That made it even harder because it did not make sense.

We faced seasons of discouragement, anger, disillusionment, and both of us experienced a season of depression during those years. It was very hard and we could not understand why. We continued doing all we could to deal with the issues of our hearts. We were trained counselors and, for many years, had helped people get healing, so we knew better and helped each other deal with our issues, plus sought healing and ministry for our hearts. Thank God we took turns being down and discouraged because when one was down and weak the other one was up and strong (Ecclesiastes 4:9-10). Many times even the LORD felt far away but, in spite of it all, we knew that there was a destiny for us. We had promises from God and He kept saying that He had not changed His mind. It was a choice to believe Him and not let the vision die. We had nothing else to hold onto but God and His promises and, like Peter, we too said, "LORD, to whom shall we go? You have words of eternal life." (John 6:68).

It was a constant choice to not be consumed by the circumstances around us and to look beyond, fixing our eyes on the LORD and the impossible. We were hurt, rejected, and misunderstood by many people and it was a great challenge not to harden our hearts and become bitter, but we kept choosing forgiveness and focused on the hearts of people and not on their ways. We realized that our destiny did not depend on what people did, or on their choices, but on our response to all those situations, so we worked on keeping our hearts right and found people we could trust and be accountable to. No matter what, we were not willing to lose our destiny. In the midst of all these things we were ministering and ministry was increasing. It seemed that our journey was bringing good fruit to the Kingdom of God. We gave ourselves to serve in the best possible way we could, and refused to entertain the thought of walking away.

Many things happened during those years. We learned much and were transformed. With each death new life came to us. We entered into a life we never knew before. When that season came to an end we were different people with changed hearts and a character that was useable by God. God then began to work more and more and His favour began to be noticed in our lives. However, by then we were in a place where all those things did not matter anymore. We honestly did not care to be recognized, or for reputation. We had died to all ambition and striving. We had entered into the rest of just being children of God. We had entered into 'sonship' and that revelation transformed us. We found a different knowledge and revelation of God and knew Him in a different way.

Then the LORD came to us and said, "You are now ready and I can send you out and release you to go and do my work. Now I can send you to the nations and open doors for you because all ambition is gone and now you only have vision. While you had vision with ambition I could not release you but now I can trust you. Now you are useable in my Kingdom and, indeed, His glory began to fill our lanterns and His light began to shine through us.

SONSHIP

In the world we learn many things that bring destruction to our lives. We both came from difficult backgrounds where we learned to strive for acceptance and found value in the things we did, not in who we were. We actually were not too happy with who we were, but learned to perform in order to fit in. We had become like the elder son of Luke 15:11-32. In that story, we see a father with two sons who are very different and who have two very different stories. Let's talk about the youngest son. He was bold, strong, adventurous, and unwise. He made a big mistake and blew his inheritance and, in his eyes, had also blown his sonship. We see this when he prepares his speech for his father in verse 18. This boy thought he had lost it all, even the right to be called his father's son. However, we see in verse 20 that when the father saw him he ran to meet him and showered him with love and acceptance. Then he brought him into his house and threw a party for him. Here we see the love of the father for his son. He loved him not for what he did but for who he was. Sonship cannot be earned or bought. It is given to us by the Father. Sonship is a birthright and here the father demonstrated that. However, there are many who have lived their lives without this understanding. Our parents were not perfect and therefore, their love appeared to be conditional upon what we did. Because of this, there are many in the church who believe they have blown it with God and think that it is too late, but just like with this child, your heavenly Father is waiting for you to come back home. He and His house are waiting for you because He never gives up.

Then there is the eldest son. In verse 29 we see his heart: He gets angry and complains because of what the father is doing for his brother. He is also upset that, even though he was always there working hard for his father, he never received any favour from his father. This son did not know sonship either. He was always with the father but he only served him. He worked for him but did not have relationship with him, and did not know his heart. He was working like a slave trying to earn his father's favour and had never bothered to get to know him and to become his friend. If he had done that, he would have known that ALL the father had was his and he could have enjoyed it.

He did not have to earn it, it was his. He could have enjoyed all of it instead of getting upset that his father never gave him anything. He was filled with ambition, jealousy, and self-righteousness. His brother on the other hand, encountered sonship when he came to the father. He had lost it all: name, reputation, finances, and recognition, all that he knew and was important to him. He blew it, but he came back and realized that all that his father had was still his. He was welcomed back into his father's house as a son. He was healed, restored, and what he found was greater than what he had lost. Yes, he suffered the consequences of his wrong actions, but his sonship did not depend on what he did but, or on who he was. We know from experience what that encounter is like and how it transforms you. The revelation of sonship changes us forever.

When we don't understand sonship we work for God and try to earn His favour. We are like the eldest son, and are trying to earn gifts, anointings, and ministry. We get filled with ambition, striving, jealousy, and self-righteousness. We compare ourselves with others and have a list of the things we do to please God, which give us the right to feel the way we do. We have a slave mentality and keep track of our labour so we do not get less than we deserve, and we get terribly upset when we see others who do less than we do, who in our eyes have not earned as much as we have, pass us by. I remember that feeling. I remember seeing others overtake us and saying to the LORD, "What is wrong? I have been working for You. I am faithful, do not miss any meetings, do everything the pastors and leaders want me to do. I give, and serve the people, I counsel, and am on all these committees. I pray so many hours a day and read the Bible for this long each day, I do, I do, and I do. And here is this person who comes out of nowhere, has not done hardly anything, has not worked as hard as I have, and You turn around and give them what belongs to me. You anoint them and open doors for them. You raise them up and make them known. They don't deserve it. They have not earned it like I have."

Every time that happened I was jealous, angry, hurt, and bitter, which caused ambition to rise within and made me strive to make a way for people to notice me, to recognize me, to make myself known, and make the gift in me known. I was full of pride, and selfishness, and tried to promote myself, but doors did not open. It was a slow death for both of us but God did not give up and continued dealing with us until we learned and were able to rejoice when others got their break.

There are so many in the church who are the way we used to be, people who have the 'elder brother' mentality. We encounter them everywhere we go. It is sad because we know the pain this causes in their lives. I remember one time we were somewhere doing a day seminar for a group of international pastors and leaders. Some people came from far away to attend the seminar. They were also prophetic people whom we loved dearly. As the day went on and I was teaching my session, one of them asked for the microphone to share something but went on and on, and, suddenly, it became evident that this person wanted to show off their prophetic gift and be recognized by all the people in the room. Then a sense of competition, ambition, and striving came from them. I recognized what was going on and I remembered what it was like to be there. That used to be me. But now it did not matter. I would have gladly let them have the spot light. I did not need to be recognized any more. It was a wonderful feeling of freedom and I realized that the fruit of that death had brought life for me and for those we teach and minister to.

There is something else that happens when we encounter Sonship. When you are a son or a daughter you realize that ministry is 'the Father's business' and, as sons and daughters, you get to partake of it. We get to take care of the Father's business. As Jesus told His mother, (Luke 24:9), He was not about His own business but about His Father's. Unfortunately, there are many in the church today that make ministry their own business and, in doing so, build their own kingdom and try to spread their own fame. They get filled with ambition which, at the end, brings great destruction to them and to those they encounter along the way.

When you are a son or a daughter you have the right to partake in the family business. In the natural, when a father has a business he teaches his sons and daughters how to do what he does, so that when they grow up they can take over the business. He wants to trust them and entrust them with the inheritance. The dream of all fathers is that their children will be like them. It is no different with God. God wants His children to learn His business and be like Him. Our Father has a huge business and there is room for us all in it. As sons and daughters it is our birthright to partake of it. Jesus said, "It gives your Father great pleasure to give you the Kingdom" (Luke 12:32). Therefore, there is no need for competition, jealousy, or ambition. There is much work to be done and there is something for everyone to do.

When we understand this principle and revelation our approach to ministry completely changes. For instance, those who make ministry their business run it their way, and by doing that, they misrepresent the Father and keep people away from Him. Then there is the way Jesus did it. He only did what He saw the Father do and He did it in like manner (John 5:19). For instance, Jesus not only saw the Father heal someone but He watched how He did it, and then He did exactly what He saw His Father do (imitated the way His Father did it). This is a key to releasing the Kingdom of Heaven on earth. We need to know what the Father is doing so we can do it, but that is not sufficient, we must also pay attention to how He does it so we can do it in 'like manner'. A long time ago the LORD said to us, "I am happy that you are doing what I want you to do, but there is a problem. You are doing it your way not my way and in doing that, you are only bringing me a harvest of 20 – 40%. I want you to learn to do it my way because if you do it the way I do it, then you will bring me a harvest of 60, 80 & 100%." That began a new journey for us.

We had to take a step back and watch Him do it. Jesus said, "Come with Me to the fields of My Father and watch Me do what I see My Father do. Pay close attention to what I say and how I say it, to what I do and how I do it and then imitate Me and you will see the Kingdom of My Father come down to earth". Have you ever heard in town when there is a business that has been there for a very long time and everyone loves it? The owner is a wonderful man who deals well with people, is honest, fair, kind, his products are the best and therefore, the reputation of the business is great. Then the owner dies and his son inherits the business. However, the son is not like the father. He learned the business and can run the store, but he does not run it as his father did. His ways are different and then people say, "Oh that was a great place when the father had it, but now his son has it, and it is different". The son has kept the name of the business and the reputation of his father, but word gets around that the business has changed and people stop coming.

That is the way it has happened in the Kingdom. The LORD told us a while ago that His heart was grieved because there are many who talk and teach about 'The Father Heart of God' and have made it a cliché to open doors for themselves because people want to hear about it, but they do not carry His heart, the revelation, and impartation. They only have knowledge of the teaching, but their lives do not reflect what they speak about. They simply talk the talk that opens the doors.

Another day the LORD spoke to us and said, "I am going to open doors for you to travel to all the nations of the world to build my Kingdom, but I have a condition for you. I will open them and give you great favour, but I will not allow you to teach someone else's teachings, and I will not allow you to teach from books or another person's revelation. You must only teach what you live. Everything you teach must come from your personal journey and experiences. It must be your personal revelation. I want you to be real and let your lives be the message that brings the teaching forth. Your teachings will be used around the world but you will birth them first so that impartation can flow from you and My power can be released". We realized that we had a lot to learn and then began to pay attention to our lives and our walk. We started letting the Father teach us the way, and change us.

We have spent thousands of hours ministering to people from all over the world and from all kinds of journeys. But, in reality, we have spent all those hours watching the Father minister to them and seeing how He deals with them and with every situation He encounters. We pay close attention to His ways, His heart, His reactions, to the way He handles sin, brokenness, hardness, fears, loneliness, rejection, pride, etc. We watch His mannerisms, His eyes, His responses, and so on, so we can learn and do it 'in like manner'. As a result, very slowly, we are becoming more like Him.

Once we were doing a conference somewhere in Europe and we both prophesied over people for 13 hours straight with only a 20 minute coffee break. When we finished someone asked us, "Oh my goodness, how can you do that? How can you prophesy over people for all those hours and keep smiling and even look refreshed?" My response was, "Oh dear what are you talking about, we didn't just spend that time prophesying. We spent thirteen hours watching Jesus reveal the Father to these people; hearing Him talk; hearing His voice; feeling His heart, and His love. We just spent thirteen hours working with Jesus in the fields of our Father and getting to know Him closer and deeper. Trust me, we are not the same people we were. We have received a new impartation of His heart and His love, and being this close to Him we are learning His ways. We just hung out with Him for thirteen hours straight without interruption, how amazing and divine can that be?"

For many years we did it our way and it did not quite work. We got tired and got burned out, plus people's lives were not really being changed or impacted in a noticeable way. Then through that we had a powerful encounter with the Father in which we learned that ministry is not about us but about Him. It is not about making our gifts and abilities known but it is about making Him and His heart known. It is not about us being recognized but it is about making Him famous and releasing His Kingdom into the hearts of each person we encounter. We realized that prophesying is not about 'giving words' to people but about sharing His heart with them so they can find Him, see Him, be drawn to Him, and discover who He really is, so they can trust Him. It is not enough to do His business; we must learn to do it His way.

EXPERIENTIAL TRUTH

God's plans are so different and what He wants to do in us and through us is beyond our comprehension. Many times we are so afraid that God will pass us by that we actually become the hindrance to His great plan for our lives. For most of us that was the story of our lives. Some of us were passed by, were rejected and/or neglected. Others, were used and abused, alone or abandoned and there was no one to take care of us. Therefore, we learned that we had to take care of ourselves and sometimes push, shove, and do whatever we had to do in order to make a way. Then we come to the LORD and we learn the truth that God is not that way. That He loves us unconditionally and will never leave us or forsake us. We read it, we hear it in sermons, people around us tell us that over and over and we believe it in our heads, however, our hearts have yet to find that out. The problem is that there are three kinds of truth we all have. There is the knowledge of truth, the revelation of truth, and experiential truth. They are all very real, powerful, and affect us in different ways. The knowledge of the truth is in our heads, the experiential truth is in our souls, minds, and emotions, and the revelation of the truth comes from our hearts. There is a gap between the head and the heart and the experiential truth resides in that gap. The only way to change this and close that gap is healing the soul through experience. Experiential truth cannot be changed through knowledge. Our hearts need to have an experience, as only experience can replace experience.

This is something that causes much frustration in our walk with the LORD. We read Scripture. We memorize it and repeat it. We hear it, but somehow our hearts and emotions tell us otherwise. Everyone tries to convince us of the truth but the heart cannot be convinced that way. When the experiential truth changes then the revelation of truth comes to our hearts and becomes real. And as a result, healing and freedom come to us. Unless this happens we go through life struggling because we know the way it should be, we know what the Bible says and what the preacher says. We know it in our heads but our hearts and emotions do not agree. Every time we face situations that deal with those issues our hearts remember the experience we had in that area, and our experiential truth tells us that this is the reality and dictates the way we feel and react to the situation. Thus, many struggle with confusion and even condemnation in their Christian walk.

That was my experience. I had a very difficult and traumatic childhood. My father was a severe alcoholic and my mother was very angry and abusive. My father loved me and was present but was not reliable. He was a 'good drunk' (he always came home with a treat for me, listened to my mother yell at him, and 'slept it off'), but he was not a provider. We could not count on him to take care of us. My mother struggled tremendously to make ends meet and to feed us. She came from a very horrible background with much abuse and rejection and had deep wounds in her life. She was a very angry woman who took her anger out on me. I was the baby of the family, the youngest of four daughters. My oldest sister was 23 years older than I was, so she left home shortly after I was born. My other sister was 12 years older than I was, but she was not around much and she left home a few years later. My sister Lucy was only two-and-a-half-years older than I was but when I was six she went to live with my oldest sister and her husband out of town. Therefore, I grew up pretty much as an only child with my alcoholic father and my abusive mother.

Things were very difficult for me, and there was no one to help me. I could not go to anyone. We had no relatives so I was alone with them. I do remember my father protecting me from my mother's abuse sometimes, and even as a little girl I found refuge in him. My mother still hurt me when he was home but it was a little better than when I was alone with her. My mother was always very angry and I never knew when I was going to 'get it'. I suffered tremendous physical, mental, and verbal abuse. She would unleash her wrath on me for no reason at all. No matter what I did, even if I pleased her she still hurt me. Things were even worse if I did something wrong of course. More than anything I wanted to please her but all my attempts always had painful endings. Sometimes she hit me just because I was there. I was terrified of her and never knew what to do. I was a bother and burden to her and was always in the way. She never ever smiled at me and only talked to me when I was in trouble or to tell me what to do. She smiled and laughed with others but never with me. She always had a frown on her face when she looked at me. I did not understand why she did not like me if I tried really hard to be good for her. I believed it was entirely my fault and that I could never do anything right. I also learned very well that there was no mercy if you made a mistake. I would have to pay over and over and over for every mistake I made. She kept account of all my wrongs, and never forgave or forgot anything, so I learned to survive.

She was always very happy to see my sister Lucy and used terms of endearment when she talked to her or about her. Lucy only came to visit us for a weekend once every 3 months. I figured that Lucy was her favourite but I never resented that because I knew it was not Lucy's fault. It was not until I was an adult that I realized that the reason why she acted that way was because she had 'lost' Lucy and suffered greatly for that. Due to our great poverty she had to send Lucy to live with my oldest sister when Lucy was so young. I can only imagine the pain she lived with. Of course, as a child I did not know that.

Then my dad died when I was ten years old. It is a long and painful story and even though I knew in my head that he did not choose to die, that he had a severe heart condition that took his life, I still felt abandoned, and attained an orphan spirit. I felt that he had just left me alone at my 'mother's mercy'. Now, for sure, I had no one to help me at all. I later got another Dad but he was a sexual predator and we could not trust him. He tried to molest my two other sisters but, by God's grace, he did not molest me but he sexually harassed me in many other ways. He made holes in my bedroom walls to watch me get dressed and undressed. I found him watching me several times. He also made holes in the bathroom ceiling and used to climb up there to watch me in the shower. That was very upsetting but there was nothing I could do. I used to cover up the holes but he made new ones. I also had to be very careful around him because he tried to grab me and touch me as soon as he came close, and he would make comments that made me feel very uncomfortable. Therefore, my image of a father was not good and my image of a mother was even worse. I had no hope and no help.

I was never allowed to cry or express any emotions. My mother hated that and hurt me even more if I did it. Out of fear I was a very good child but because I could not release my emotions I slowly became very angry and bitter. I hardened my heart and built walls that no one could touch. As time passed, the bitterness turned to hatred. I was cold, and evil began to enter my heart. My sister gives testimony of this as she suffered greatly around me. I took out a lot of my hatred on her. Without healing the abused becomes the abuser. That was true with me. I treated her so badly that twice our next door neighbors called the police on me. My eyes were filled with that bitterness and hatred. I used to have a look that could reduce anyone to a puddle of nothing. No matter how confident they were, one look from me could strip them from it all and make them feel worthless. I have photos which captured that image. They clearly show the hatred in my eyes and face. People used to be scared of the look in my eyes. I never ever smiled and had a permanent frown on my face, which I enjoyed. I had a huge chip on my shoulder and wanted to make others pay for it.

Because of the hardness of my heart and the hatred in me I am sure I would have literally killed someone if God had not rescued me. Today I have wrinkles around my eyes, 'laugh lines' as some call them, and I love them. I have them because God healed my heart, set me free, and taught me to laugh. These wrinkles are a sign and a wonder of the power of a God who can change a heart of stone and turn it into a heart of flesh. Many times people say that they see Jesus in my eyes and every time I hear that, I remember what people used to see in my eyes once upon a time. Our God is indeed an awesome God and surely nothing is impossible for Him.

Life went on and I came to the LORD when I was 18. I got saved supernaturally. I was a very strong Catholic and down there Catholicism is very different than in North America. The rule was that if you were born a Catholic you died a Catholic. I had zeal to serve God since I was little, and, since we were very devout Catholics, I gave myself wholeheartedly to the religion and rituals we had. Thus I became a strong Pharisee. We hated born again Christians or 'the followers of Jesus", as we called them. We were taught in our church that they were deceived and were deceiving everyone who listened to them. We believed that we Catholics had the truth and were the only ones going to heaven. We were favoured by God and anyone who left our faith was going to hell. Therefore, we had to stop those followers of Jesus. They were hurting our people, and since I had so much hatred in me I was happy to hate them and persecute them in any way I could. I thought they were the scum of the earth and had to be stopped. I passionately despised them.

Then one day, as I was minding my own business, I ran into Jesus, the real thing, and He personally led me through a sinner's prayer. (I will share the whole story in another book). I had no idea what it all meant as no one had ever preached the true gospel to me. However, I repeated every word after Him. Then the next day, as I was alone, a very bright light came from heaven, and covered me. I was powerfully filled with the Holy Spirit that night but, I did not know what had taken place. It was not until two weeks later that I found out what happened those two nights. This was taken as high treason by my family. They pressured me in many ways and put me through different tests, in order to force me to deny Jesus, but I never did. I kept choosing Jesus in spite of it all, regardless of the price I had to pay. As a result, I was disowned by my whole family, beaten even worse and, one night, my mother tried to kill me because I refused to deny Jesus. That night the LORD promised me that if I stuck it out He would be with me forever and I would serve Him for the rest of my life. He also promised me that He would save and restore my family.

The church I went to after this experience was very legalistic. I learned many good things from them but there were many things that were not so good. They knew the God of the Old Testament. Their God had no mercy, was mean, and literally 'killed people'. They taught me that the best thing was to stay away from Him. Jesus was fine, and the Holy Spirit was OK, but God was a different story. Once

my best friend fell into immorality and the church immediately condemned her. They threw her out of the church and excommunicated
her. The pastors had a meeting with me and explained to me how the
judgment of God was going to come on my friend and they said that
if I had anything to do with her that same judgment would fall on me.
Therefore, they told me that I had to cut her off from my life so God
would spare me from the judgment that was coming. I, of course,
believed them. I did not know any better, so I did as they told me even
though it was very painful.

Then a while later my friend, her baby, and the baby's father died in a
major car accident. The pastors of the church said that, "It was God's
judgment and He had killed them". They told me that it was good that
I listened to them or God would have killed me too. They used this as
an example to bring the fear of God into our lives. We were terrified of
God the Father and none of us wanted to have any dealings with Him.
Of course, this only confirmed what I knew. My experiential truth at
home had taught me what to expect and, as we know, our parents,
especially our fathers, form the image we will later project onto God.
Based on this, trusting God was out of the question for me, and this
only showed me, beyond the shadow of a doubt, that I was right and
God was much worse than my parents because He was all powerful
and could do anything He wanted and would literally kill you (just like
He killed my friend). I had learned basically the same rule at home.
I could not be myself and paid badly just for existing. One thing was
for sure: "It was not good to be me". It was actually very painful to be
me and I spent a great part of my childhood and adolescence wishing
I was someone else. At church I learned that it was the same with
God. You had to do whatever He wanted regardless of anything else
and you could not make a mistake. Once again existing was not what
mattered. No one knew who I really was, not even me.

I later married Ivan and came to live in Canada. The full story is in
another book, currently being written. Ivan was like a son to John
and Carol Arnott. He got saved at 16 years of age with John at his
church and from then John and Carol took him under their wing and
opened their home and lives to him. They literally loved him back to
life and healing. When we got married John and Carol took me into
their lives in the same way and loved me. We lived with them for the
first four years of our marriage. John and Carol are amazing people
and it was only God's great mercy that brought me into their lives. I

cannot imagine what our lives would have been like without them. God used them to change and transform us. They knew how to love and were able to truly love us with real unconditional love, something I had never seen in life. Through them God literally changed our lives. Who we are today is a credit to them and to their hard labour of sacrifice as they loved us, believed in us, taught us, and imparted their hearts into us. They allowed God to use them to bring the Kingdom of Heaven into our lives.

There is one thing that people do not know about them. We hear people say how the outpouring that took place at TACF in 1994, made John and Carol who they are. That is not true at all.

John and Carol were the way they are today back then when no one knew their names. They were ministering the Father's love and living it. They poured out their lives and spent endless hours healing the brokenhearted. They were teaching the Father Heart of God to as many people as they could. They were loving people back to life day-in-and-day-out. That, I believe, is the reason why God chose them to release the amazing move of His Spirit in 1994. They were doing back then what they are today. The only difference is that now they are doing it on a much larger scale. They were faithful in little and God entrusted them with much.

When I came to live with them, I came with the idea of God I explained before. I 'knew' God, or at least that's what I thought. Carol used to talk about the heart of the Father and I would think, "Oh lady, you really do not know God. You are so lucky I came to live with you because I can teach you how God really is, and how you have to deal with Him, so He will not kill you." I used to tell her how 'mean' God could be and how I had proof of it. After all, He had killed my friend. I buried her. No one could tell me otherwise because I lived through it. I had full blown experiential truth. Carol used to cry telling me about the Father's love and I could not figure her out. I was convinced that the reason why I came to Canada was to 'save the Arnotts from the wrath of God'. These people did not know how to treat God, and I had so much to teach them. My mission was to convince them that I was right about God. Ivan tried to tell me about the Father's heart and His love too, but he did not have any success either. Carol and John would take any chance they got to tell me their version of God.

Then it happened. I had an experience that changed everything. Someone (from the States I believe) gave John a lovely shirt. It was beautiful and very special. It was also very expensive. It had blue and white stripes. John loved that shirt. He wore it very often. It truly was his favourite. One day John and Carol were away doing a conference and I went upstairs to do laundry. I found that Carol had left some laundry in the machine. It was washed and had to be dried. I was not sure if it all could go in the dryer or not, so I decided to place it on the counter while I washed my load. A while later I came back to check on the laundry and to my horror I found that Carol's wet green sock had touched one of the white stripes of John's shirt and now the shirt had a green spot on it.

I cannot express the fear and terror I felt inside at that moment. I had destroyed John's shirt, 'The Shirt', and now I was in trouble. I panicked and decided to try to fix it. I made a mix of water and bleach and dipped the green spot in it. A while later I came to check and the green was gone but I discovered that the white stripe was actually off white, which meant that now there was a white patch on the off white stripe. This was not good. I thought of dipping it in tea, but figured that I would make a bigger mess and realized that things get worse when we try to 'cover up our sin'. I knew I could not replace the shirt and, at this point, everything I knew about authority figures came to face me. Everything within me told me that things as they were would come to an end. I had done what in my eyes was the worst possible thing I could do to John. I had destroyed his favorite shirt and now I had to pay for it. I had never known mercy, grace or compassion. I always paid for everything, even things I did not do, and even God was merciless and killed those who crossed Him, so I put the shirt away and waited.

The next two days were agonizing waiting for John and Carol to return. When they came home I waited until John went out and I went upstairs to see Carol. I knew she would be kind and would help me. I wanted her to tell John for me because I knew she would intercede on my behalf. I told her what happened, and explained to her how it was an accident. I apologized over and over promising to buy John another shirt. Carol just looked at me with eyes as big as saucers, put her hands on the kitchen counter and said very slowly, "Oh no, not his shirt". She then told me that she would explain it to John. For the next week I managed to avoid him. I kept track of his going out and his coming in. I listened for the sound of his footsteps and the sound of his voice. For a whole week, we lived in the same house and never saw each other. I thought that was pretty amazing. Then Sunday came and we went to church. I also managed to avoid him there and kept an eye on him at all times to make sure I would not run into him. We were having a potluck lunch after church and I was busy visiting with people and for a minute lost track of John's whereabouts. Suddenly I turned around to go to the food table and as I turned John Arnott was the last person on the line and he was looking at me. My stomach froze as we had eye contact and at that moment I knew I had to face him. I could not turn around and pretend I had not seen him. I braced myself and walked towards him.

As I got close John said to me, "I heard you did laundry". At that moment I began to blurt out a speech filled with explanations and apologies that I had rehearsed for a whole week in case I ever ran into him (somehow I was hoping to avoid him forever). As I was talking his eyes filled with the deepest and most amazing love I had ever seen and, at that moment, he cut me off. I was halfway through my great speech when he put his plate down, grabbed me by my shoulders, looked very deep into my eyes and said, "Everything is all right honey, because it is you and I love you!" Then he pulled me towards him and gave me the biggest and strongest hug I have ever felt. It felt like I went right into his heart and at that moment, as I went in, I met the Father Himself. It was a completely supernatural experience because as John held me tight into his heart I went right into the Father's heart and looked into His eyes (the same look of love I had seen in John's eyes just seconds before). As we looked into each other's eyes the Father opened up His arms and said to me, "Everything is all right honey, because it is you and I love you". He pulled me into His arms and, for the first time in my life, I experienced the Father's love and His embrace.

At that moment for the first time in my whole life it was good to be me. That was the thing that made everything alright. That is what John said, "Because it is YOU, and I love YOU!" He loved me more than his favourite shirt. He did not punish me and did not cast me away as I had expected. Instead, he embraced me and showed me the Father's heart and there I received His love. The Father also said that

He loved me for the same reason. For the first time in my whole life I was safe and I was loved, and the only reason for that was, because 'it was me'. Imagine that!!! Right then I knew that I was not a bother to the Father and was not in His way. I no longer had to pay because I existed. I could enjoy life. Being me was no longer a cause for pain and sorrow. From that moment on, being me became a cause for love and today I can say that it truly is a good thing to be me.

At that moment I also knew that I had been lied to, because the God I had just encountered was not hard or mean. As I looked into His eyes I knew that He had not killed my friend. He was a perfect loving Father who is merciful and kind. I knew that He was not like my parents and I could trust and love Him forever. At that moment I also knew I was His daughter and realized that He loves me more than life. I am indeed the apple of His eye. It was not head knowledge but full revelation alive in my heart, my soul, and body. I received the revelation of 'Sonship' and a deep impartation of His perfect love. Right there and then, my experiential truth was replaced with a new and powerful experience that could not be contested by man or demons, and with it a new life opened up to me. Now I had access to my Father's house because along with His heart, He gave me His Kingdom.

SECTION TWO

THE KINGDOM OF GOD

Our revelation and understanding of God is very personal and different from one another. It determines what we believe, what we receive, and what we teach and minister. Ministry flows from the Father and we minister according to the revelation of God we have. That is why we see two people ministering in the same area but in different ways. We represent God as we see Him. Therefore, if we think God is harsh and judgmental we will minister with that edge, but if we think He is loving, kind, and abundant, that is the way our ministry will flow. We also have different realms of limitation. Our limitations are based on many factors such as culture, personal experiences, family, finances, education, etc. Our realm of limitations determines our abilities to believe, expect, give, receive, and the possibilities available to us. Unfortunately, we have learned to project these limitations on God and hold Him prisoner in that box.

This is actually something that hinders God from doing all He wants to do in us and through us. I grew up with incredible limitations due to culture, family, and finances. The ways of the land and the possibilities available to my parents taught me what was possible. This happens to all of us and we come to the LORD believing that He is like our parents and that His Kingdom is like our country/culture, and home. We do this subconsciously and it is very hard to break. We may have all the knowledge of the truth about God but not revelation of the truth. Again, this is an area in which we must be aware of our experiential truth. I remember one of my experiences in this area happened when God started to call me to full-time ministry.

I had a very good job with a good salary, and I was in a position where I was needed in the company. Ivan was already in full-time ministry and I was part-time. I was actually getting tired and stressed out by burning the candle at both ends. I knew God had created me to serve Him and that one day I would take the step of faith and leave my job to trust Him fully in the area of finances and provision. However, every time I thought of it my soul would go into turmoil and fear. I knew God is faithful and had experienced some amazing financial miracles, but I was terrified to have to trust Him full-time. Something inside of me would tell me, "Sure He has come through here and there, but He will not permanently do it for your everyday needs". This was very difficult for me because I knew God is faithful and true, and He will never leave us or forsake us. I knew all that the Bible and the preachers say. Yet, I felt this need to take care of myself, which was at an emotional level not at a rational level.

People kept asking me, "How much longer? When are you going to leave your job and trust the LORD?" I could not tell them that somehow deep inside I could not trust God in that area. A few times I mentioned it and people with good intentions gave me big lectures about the 'truth' and how God would be faithful. I knew that well in my head, but my heart did not know it and was afraid. The funny thing is that I could believe for others. I had no problem believing that God would come through and be faithful for Ivan and our daughter Amanda, but not for me. The reason was that my experiential truth was in charge of my reactions and responses. It was unconscious. It was written on the tablets of my heart, and imprinted deep into my soul.

As a child I grew up in a third world country with many limitations. We lived in great poverty and need. My father was not a provider for our family. As I said earlier, he was a severe alcoholic and, although he was present, we could not count on him. My poor mother suffered so much and worked around the clock, even when she was sick, in order to keep us alive. However, there were a few occasions when I had a great need for something and my dad managed to come through and provide for that particular need, but he never provided on a daily basis for us, so I knew since I was little that I had to take care of myself. Throughout the years I had seen the faithfulness of God. He was always present, but without realizing it, I had believed the lie that just like my dad, God was present and would come through sometimes for big things, but I could not count on Him for my everyday provision. Therefore, I had to take care of myself.

I had no idea what was behind this feeling. I did not know it was a lie or ungodly belief. It was the way it felt inside in my soul and heart and it was a familiar feeling. Thus I struggled with the knowledge of the truth and my inability to walk in its revelation. It was not until the LORD revealed clearly the lie and its source that I was able to deal with it, and believe not only with my head but with my heart. Next I had to work in changing my mindsets of fear and replace them with new thoughts of His faithfulness, provision, and unfailing love. (Later we will share more about the changing of the mind). It was then that I was able to take the leap of faith and obey Him, and a new experiential truth was written in my heart and emotions as the Kingdom of God was manifested in this part of my life. My realm of limitations changed tremendously and I can truly say that God has been faithful and has taken care of all our everyday needs.

This syndrome is a big hindrance in the fulfillment of our prophecies and in walking in our destiny. We subconsciously place limitations on God and believe He can only do what we believe and expect from Him. We forget that He is not limited. He is all-powerful, mighty, sovereign, LORD of Lords, KING of Kings. He has unlimited resources and can do anything He wants. He offers us things according to His possibilities and resources. I know that if I were the daughter of the Queen of England, I would have a completely different realm of limitations. I am sure the children of Donald Trump have a much broader realm of limitations as they know and have experienced their father's resources, and they expect accordingly because they know what he is capable of doing. We have a much greater Father who has no limitations at all. Even the greatest and most powerful person on earth has a ceiling of limitations but not our Father. This is very difficult for us to fully understand, but it is a key to unlocking our destiny. We must know Him as He is.

We have seen many times with the prophetic, that people only expect to receive prophecies that agree with their personal realm of limitations and within their possibilities. Many people hear 'impossible' things spoken over them and dismiss them. Sometimes they do this without realizing it but other times they do it intentionally. We have been trained to believe only what we can see and what is possible for us to attain. We must understand that God belongs to a different realm. He is supernatural and all He says and does is supernatural. That is the reason it is impossible to attain His promises in the realm of men. They come from His Kingdom, a kingdom that is not from this realm (John 18:36). The problem is that we do not understand what the Kingdom of God is and try to figure it out with earthly mentality. This is impossible to do. God's Kingdom is not human or earthly, and therefore, we cannot reason it out with our human mind no matter how smart or how brilliant we are. We actually must be simple like children in order to enter into God's Kingdom (Matthew 18:3).

The Kingdom of our Father is very, very easy to attain and is accessible to us today. Jesus said, "The Kingdom of God is at hand" (Mark 1:15). It is here today and as children of God we have the ability to live in it enjoying all it has to offer. In life we have learned to make all things very complicated and through religion we have done the same thing in the church. I know 'complicated' and used to do 'complicated'. I did it in the world and in the church. I became a Pharisee and everything became works-based. That is what religion does to us. I loved the LORD and wanted all He had to offer and, therefore, I strove really hard to attain it, not knowing that it is our Father's good pleasure to give it to us. There is absolutely nothing complicated about God. He is amazing and, in many ways, is a mystery. His mind no one can understand, but His heart and His Kingdom are very easy to understand and possess.

I used to hear that scripture in Matthew that says, "Seek first the Kingdom of God and all these things will be added unto you" (Matthew. 6:33). I read it many times and heard many talk about it, but I could not really grasp it. "Seek the Kingdom", they said, but 'the Kingdom' was very abstract to me. What exactly was I supposed to seek after with all my heart? I asked many and no one could explain it to me. They just said, "The Kingdom, seek the Kingdom", so I figured that it meant to attend every church meeting and event, to participate in every single program the church had, and to do all they told me to do. I did it with all my heart, thinking that it was 'the Kingdom', but in time I realized that it was not fulfilling me and nothing was really being added unto me. Then one day the LORD came and gave me the answer. He said, "What you are doing is not what I mean by that. Relax, because I am the Kingdom. The Kingdom you are searching for is found in My heart. Seek My heart with everything in you as if your life depended on it, and when you find it you will possess My Kingdom and everything else that is found in it".

What an amazing and easy revelation that was. Finally I knew what to seek and I sought it with all my heart because my life indeed depended on it. I found the heart of the Father and entered into His Kingdom. After that, "all other things have been added unto me". The LORD spoke again and said, "Now that you have this, things will change for you because, 'My yoke is easy and My burden is light.' You no longer have to do 'complicated'. It is simple and easy. If at any time following Me is complicated, and doing what I want you to do is hard then you are NOT doing it My way. You are doing it man's way, because My way is easy and light". I realized that being a Christian and living for and serving the LORD can actually be fun and greatly enjoyable. The LORD then gave us a mandate to make things simple and accessible to others so they too can possess His Kingdom and all that it contains. Therefore, a big part of what we do is making complicated things simple.

One of the problems we have is that we listen to too many voices and many times forget to listen to the voice that matters the most. Jesus is our teacher and He has all the answers we need. Men have come with theologies that confuse many. In the Bible days, every teacher or rabbi had their particular teachings and ways of doing things, their doctrine was called 'their yoke'. They used to have students who followed them and who became their disciples. These students had to learn his teachings well, had to do things the same way their rabbi did, and then he would choose the ones who 'got it' and give them his 'yoke', so they would continue teaching it and passing it to others. It was very hard to accomplish this because their teachings and ways were filled with the rules and regulations of men as they were based on the law. Then Jesus came and when He chose His disciples He said, "Come to me, all you that are weary and are carrying heavy burdens and I will give you rest. Take my yoke upon you, and learn from me; for I am gentle and humble in heart, and you will find rest for your souls. For my yoke is easy, and my burden is light" (Matthew 11: 28-30).

Jesus came to take away the heavy yoke and to bring us into freedom and joy. Yet, we tend to fight this, because there is a need within us to feel important, plus we have believed the religious lie that we have to work hard and earn it. Plus, we have 'grown-up' and have adult faith. Jesus said that we have to be like children to enter into His Kingdom, and one thing is certain, children are not complicated. They understand simple things. The moment you make things complicated you lose them. Childlike faith is not complicated either and does not require explanations the way adult faith does. No wonder Paul also said that, "God uses the foolish (simple) things to confound the wise" (1 Corinthians 1:27). It is not easy to become simple, but we know from experience that it is possible. We both have experienced the freedom of this revelation and know that our Father's greatest desire is for us to enjoy the Kingdom and all that is in it.

KINGDOM MENTALITY

In order to enter into the Kingdom of God and to possess it we must have Kingdom mentality. Most people are trying to understand God and His Kingdom through earthly mentality and that does not work. The mind of man cannot comprehend the things of God. These things are not earthly. Jesus said that His Kingdom is not of this world but of another realm. (John 18:36). Therefore, it is pivotal that we learn to think according to that realm and for that, we must attain Kingdom mentality. I remember praying for a long time asking God to "give me the mind of Christ". Scripture says, that we must have the mind of Christ and must renew our minds (1 Corinthians 2:16; Romans 12:2), so I thought that if I laid hands on my head and prayed God would snap His fingers and give me the mind of Christ. Then one day the LORD said, "Stop wasting your time because it is not going to happen that way". I said, "Why not? The Bible says that we must have the mind of Christ so, give it to me, I want it". He replied, "That is not the way. If you want to have the mind of Christ, then you have to learn to think like He thinks and believe as He believes. You must replace your thoughts with His and slowly you will get His mind". Wow! That never occurred to me.

It is very easy to find the mind of Christ. Scripture is filled with it. Jesus had Kingdom mentality and that is why He could access all the Father has to offer. Jesus thought according to the ways of heaven not the ways of man. He knew His Father and all that was in His Father's house. He knew there was healing in the Kingdom of His Father and therefore, He was able to reach it and bring it into the kingdom of men. Power was a reality to Him because it was real in His Father's house (Kingdom). When we learn to think this way, all things will become possible to us. The best way of dealing with this is by being filled with the Word of God. God's Word is alive, very alive. All throughout our Christian life we hear pastors and preachers telling us to read the Bible. Reading the Bible is actually a burden to many. They do it out of religiosity to "meet their dues" but don't really get anything out of it. For a long time I did not realize the importance of Scripture.

God's Word is alive and has real power in itself, which can transform our lives. We must know Scripture but also be filled with it. It has life. We don't always have time to sit down and read the Bible, but we know that we need the Word of God in us daily so we have the Bible on CD and listen to it as we are busy doing things around the house or driving. I had a powerful experience that proved the effectiveness of the word of God in our lives. We had gone to do a conference in Europe and I only took one CD which contained the writings of Paul. For days and days I listened to it over, and over, and over until I felt like Paul was a close friend. Then one day on the way to a meeting the enemy sent a dart my way. There was a lie that the enemy used to tell me throughout my life that triggered areas of insecurity in me. It was a struggle because every time this particular thought came, it would weaken me, and would throw me into insecurity and fear. Normally I had to fight my way out of it for at least two days.

Then this particular day on the way to the meeting, with the eye of my spirit I saw this arrow coming from the outside and into the right side of my head, into my mind. It was that particular lie from the enemy. As I saw this arrow coming through, suddenly, I felt something arise from deep within my being, from my belly upwards. Immediately, I heard the words of Paul from Scripture speaking the truth regarding that particular situation. I saw the Word of God arise within like a wall and intercept the lie halfway in, and immediately the arrow stopped and fell to the ground. That was the very last time I had to deal with that lie. It was defeated forever, and I did not have to do anything about it. I did not have to fight it or struggle with it. The Word of God, which is alive within me, arose in my moment of need and set me free. The battle was won forever. I realized at that moment the reality of that Scripture that says, "The truth will set us free" (John 8:32). I also understood why it is so important to fill ourselves with the Word of God. All that truth within us becomes a reality that transforms us and sets us free.

The Word of God is supernatural just as God is supernatural. It comes from and conforms to His Kingdom, and therefore, carries power from heaven and reveals the mind of Christ. To acquire the mind of Christ what you must do is identify your thought patterns. You will be amazed at what you find. We get so used to thinking the way we do that we do not realize that most of our thinking is influenced by the accuser and not by the Comforter. We have thinking patterns or mindsets of defeat, rejection, loss, etc. For instance, a common mindset in many is, "I am a failure and cannot do anything". Once you identify that thought then find out what Jesus has to say about it. What is the truth from Scripture about that matter? Scripture says that, "We can do all things through Christ who strengthens us" (Philippians 4:13) and, "We are more than conquerors" (Romans 8:37). This is the truth that defeats the lie. Now all you have to do is every time you find yourself in a situation when the thought of defeat rises up, you simply tell yourself, "That is not true. Perhaps in the past it was but not now. Today I can do all things through Christ who strengthens me because I am a conqueror". You will need to tell that to yourself over and over and over until eventually it becomes part of you and replaces the mindset of defeat. You must give yourself time for this change. Remember that you have had those old thinking patterns for many years and they are ingrained in you. That does not change overnight. Be persistent because slowly you will notice that, when facing a challenging situation, your reaction becomes one of victory and possibilities as the mind of Christ starts taking over different areas of your life. All we have to do is replace one thought at a time (not the whole mind at once) with the thoughts of Jesus and, in doing this, we renew our minds constantly and obtain Kingdom mentality.

Another way of obtaining Kingdom mentality is through the prophecies spoken over us. They come from the heart of the Father and His Kingdom. These prophecies say things about us that reflect God's mind for us and our lives. So, by listening to our prophecies regularly, we will come to experience faith arising in us because Scripture says, that faith comes by hearing God's Word (Romans 10:17). That applies to the written and the spoken Word of God. As you listen to your prophecies and choose to believe them, slowly you will start thinking of yourself in that context and your mindsets will start changing. You will start seeing yourself through God's eyes and the impossible becomes possible as you are transformed by the creative power of the Word of God. You may have a mindset of failure, but you have a prophecy that says that God is going to use you and raise you. Now you have a personal thought (Kingdom mindset) from God's mind about yourself and your life, so every time that mindset of failure comes up you can simply say, "Well, that is the way I used to think (or the way things used to be), but now I have a prophecy that says God is going to use me and raise me up. I am useable to God. He has a place for me in His Kingdom and He is making room for me." Do this time after time, and slowly you will see that the thought of failure disappears and a new belief about yourself comes along with expectation, and you become a conqueror as you obtain the mind of Christ. Again, we do this one step at a time. Like the saying goes, "You move the piano one inch at a time and before you know it, it is on the other side". Take each prophecy and find God's mind about you. Then start replacing your thoughts with it.

I remember when I first married Ivan and came to Canada. I was born and lived in Costa Rica all my life until then. I lived and behaved according to the ways of Costa Rica. I thought as a Costa Rican, behaved as a Costa Rican, cooked, ate, dressed, etc., all as a Costa Rican. That was my identity and all I knew. I came to Canada, which was completely different in all aspects. Everything was different: the language, behaviour, weather, food, clothing, etc., and I did not fit in. I was here but I did not belong. Nothing was familiar, and life here was very uncomfortable. I consciously knew that, but subconsciously I wanted it all to be the 'familiar' way. It is part of the natural behaviour of men to seek that which is familiar to us because familiarity brings comfort. I thought that the ways I knew were the right ones. I remember going to the grocery stores. The shelves were full of things and others around me were getting loads of stuff but there was nothing in them for me. I could not comprehend the way they lived. Ivan introduced me to something called 'macaroni-and-cheese' and told me that it was sort of a 'staple' in North America. I could not believe that was a meal. Ivan would take me to restaurants but there was nothing in the menu for me. It was so frustrating. I was hungry a lot in those days and in my mind I thought that there would never be anything for me to enjoy. Oh how I longed for our Costa Rican rice-and-beans…

Then one day my mother-in-law, bless her heart, gave me something called 'long underwear', which would help keep me warm on the cold winter days. I came from a tropical country and had never ever seen or heard of anything like that. I could not imagine wearing it. In my country we did housework in a particular way and to me that was the only way. We used to scrub our laundry. Our mothers said that washing machines only helped us soften the dirt but did not wash the clothing, so we had to scrub it all by hand after it came out of the washing machine. Especially our white socks, we scrubbed them really well to make sure they were whiter than white. Then, in Canada, I found out that they did not have scrubbing tubs and their laundry room consisted of two machines side by side, one to wash and one to dry. I was horrified and found myself many times scrubbing our socks in the bath tub. It was very hard, but for me it was the only way and it was my way. Life was not enjoyable in this new land. People said that it was better than living in a third world nation, but I could not see how. There was nothing for me to eat. I did not have proper clothing for the weather and was not comfortable with the layers of clothing Canadians wore. I could not shop, or take care of household chores properly. I could not enjoy anything.

Then one day after much pain, frustration, and prayer I realized that my problem was that I was trying to live in Canada as a Costa Rican and that was not going to work. Canada and Costa Rica are very different countries with completely different cultures and lifestyles. The only way I could possibly live in this country and enjoy it would be to let go of my Costa Rican mentality and attain a Canadian mentality. I had to let go of my Costa Rican ways and adopt Canadian ways. But, before I could behave like they did I had to learn to think like they thought. It was not easy, but slowly I began to learn the ways and mindsets of Canadians and then everything changed. I learned to eat like Canadians eat and then, there was plenty for me to buy in the shelves at the grocery stores. I learned to dress like they dress and found the beauty and joy of Canadian weather. Life became easier as I relaxed and found out that washing machines do wash the clothing, and vacuum cleaners clean the carpets. Just by changing mindsets I could enjoy all this country had to offer. Suddenly, as my mindsets changed, my behaviour changed too and Canada became a land flowing with milk and honey.

The same thing happens with the Kingdom of God. We are born and live in the kingdom of men. A kingdom ruled by the devil, which has his identity and his ways. In the kingdom of men no one wins. As soon as we are born labels are placed on us and that becomes our identity. We are dumb, ugly, fat, a failure, too tall, too short, etc., etc. Then we see the ways of those around us and our family, and their ways become our ways too. We do not question it. That is just the way things are and therefore are 'normal' for us. It is sad but real. We get saved and Jesus gives us access to the Kingdom of God, but we come in carrying all our ways and mindsets from the kingdom of men and we expect them to function there, because that is all we know and what is familiar to us. The voice of the accuser is second nature to us and we have taken it as our own. But now, in God's Kingdom things are different. This is a Kingdom ruled by God and it has His identity. God is love, mercy, grace, righteousness, power. He is a perfect father who loves us more than life itself. He is light and victory. There is abundance and provision in His Kingdom, life, health, and so much, much more. Of course, coming from where we are coming from, these things are foreign to us and subconsciously we reject them.

Then God speaks and gives us offers, but we cannot understand or believe them. We see the shelves of heaven and God's provision, but really, there is nothing accessible for us there because we are looking at it through earthly mindsets. We see everything through that grid and nothing changes. We continue living life as we know it and do not obtain the abundance that God has for us. Rejection continues, as well as fear, failure, poverty, etc., and as a result, many become frustrated and disillusioned. This has caused many to walk away and never find the destiny and life Jesus died to give them. We must learn to obtain Kingdom mentality and let go of the ways we have learned all our lives in the kingdom of men. It is possible to do it. It takes time, yes, but once we own this key we can use it day after day to unlock these doors. We know it is possible because we have lived through this, and by using this key our lives have been transformed. Once you have Kingdom mentality you begin to change from the inside. It happens naturally. You start seeing things through the mind of Christ and your grid changes forever. Faith rises causing unbelief and doubt to go away. Suddenly, the voice of the Comforter becomes familiar and all things become possible. Certainly the Kingdom of Heaven is at hand.

This key is very important if we are to understand prophecy and access our prophetic destiny. Prophecy comes from the heart of God and reflects who He is. It speaks of things that do not fit the realm of men. It does not make sense to our human understanding and becomes 'foolishness' to many. Prophecy is not about telling people what they had for lunch yesterday, for breakfast this morning and what color of pajamas they will wear tomorrow. That is simple revelation and psychics do that all the time. A psychic and a prophet can both easily give revelation to people although they receive it from very different sources. However, the greatest difference that separates them is that even though both can give revelation only one has the ability or power to reveal the heart of God to others and to release the Kingdom of heaven into their lives right there and then, giving them a hope and a future. When we prophesy we must focus on the Father and His heart, which is the place from where all good things flow. He is the only one who knows the heart of men. There is a big difference when we learn to draw from His heart and not from the gift. If we minister out of the gift we simply give information that reaches the head, but when we minister from the Father's heart, we reach the heart of men and connect their hearts with the heart of God. This is what we should experience when we receive prophecies. Prophecy simply reveals and facilitates an encounter with the heart of the Father.

When we understand this, everything changes. Scripture says in Jeremiah 29:11, "For I know the plans that I have for you, declares the LORD, plans for welfare and not for calamity (to bless you and to prosper you), to give you a future and a hope". 1 Corinthians 2:9 also says, "No eye has seen, no ear has heard, and no mind has imagined what God has prepared for those who love Him." (NLT)

These two scriptures hold the essence of the heart of prophecy. Prophecy that flows from the heart of God reveals those good plans to bless us and to prosper us and the hope and future we so need. Prophecy indeed opens our understanding and makes us aware of the things that we have never seen, heard or imagined. That is why it is pivotal to know the heart of God in order to prophesy, to receive prophecy, and to walk into the fulfillment of prophecy.

SECTION THREE

RUNNING THE RACE

Prophecy is one of the most wonderful gifts the LORD has given us in our journey on earth. It is a great source of life, refreshing, and encouragement. I cannot imagine living without it. I liken prophecy to running a race. Hebrews 12:1 talks about running the race set before us. We know what running is all about. We all have run at one point or another in life. When I was young in high school and decided to become an athlete, it was a short-lived venture, but I learned a few things. I remember starting the race. It was fun and exciting and the finish line did not seem far away at all. I took off with great force, being sure that I could win without problem.

In my ignorance, I did not know how to really prepare for the race and soon found out that things were not as I expected. I had to run up and down hills in the heat of the summer and, shortly after running up the second hill, I began to feel this pain down my throat and chest, then an intense pain started in my legs, and I began to slow down. At this point, I looked and noticed that the finish line had 'moved further away', and slowly it became unreachable. Great discouragement overtook me. I felt defeated before actually losing the race. However, I knew I had to finish and was determined to keep on going. At that point there is one thing that can really help: fresh water. A drink of fresh water or even better, a bucket of fresh water thrown at you brings great refreshing and makes a world of a difference. Nothing compares to that. It also takes the pain of the throat away and refreshes the body to continue. The bucket of fresh water on you takes the heat away and enables the body to continue running, but as time goes on, the dryness, the pain, and the discouragement return. The

35

only hope the runner has now is that someone else who is watching the race will pour more fresh water as he passes by.

We have learned that this is exactly what our Christian life is like. We meet Jesus and feel like 'Superman'. We are a new creation and take off running, unprepared for such a great race. We do not really know how weak we are, and how difficult the race will be, especially when the enemy starts placing hurdles on the road. It is a hard race to run and discouragement is one of the first things we pick up. It is here that prophecy comes in like that drink of fresh water that goes into the heart and brings life once again, like the bucket of water it encourages us to make it till the end. There is nothing more wonderful and welcoming than a word from the LORD when we feel hopeless and the finish line keeps moving further away from us. We have experienced this many times and are so grateful to that wonderful crowd of witnesses around us that poured that fresh water on us as we passed by.

Prophecy, of course, does not replace hearing God for ourselves and never will, but it is a source of life and encouragement as we run the race set before us. We all need to hear someone say, "Well done, you can make it!" "Keep on going you are almost there". "Turn here, change that, and you will get there", etc. Most of the time we get so caught up in the challenges of the race that we cannot see what is ahead. This is one of the reasons why we need each other. There is no one on earth, no matter how mature, spiritual, or anointed they are that does not need the rest of the Body to make it to the finish line.

FULFILMENT OF PROPHECY

Prophecy is a big part of our lives and we certainly can give firsthand testimony of the transforming power it has. We both have seen all the prophecies that we have received come to pass and therefore, we know, without a doubt, that prophecy can be fulfilled. We cannot imagine a life without the fulfillment of prophecy. It must be greatly discouraging and frustrating. We were very surprised to find out that the amount of people who have not walked through the fulfillment of their prophecies is greater than those who have. God never intended for it to be this way. Our desire is to share with you some of the keys that will make this possible for you. We pray that, as you read this book, the ears of your heart and your understanding will be open so you too can say, "I have walked through the fulfillment of God's promises over my life". We are going to share with you our journey and also firsthand accounts of what we have seen God do. As stated in 2 Peter 1:16: "For we did not follow cleverly devised tales when we made known to you the power and coming of our LORD Jesus Christ, but we were eye witnesses of His majesty. For when He received honor and glory from God the Father, such an utterance as this was made to Him by the Majestic Glory, 'This is My beloved Son with whom I am well-pleased,' and we ourselves heard this utterance made from heaven when we were with Him on the holy mountain. (For we were not making up clever stories when we told you about the power of our LORD Jesus Christ and His coming again. We have seen His majestic splendour with our own eyes. And He received honor and glory from God the Father when God's glorious, majestic voice called down from heaven, 'This is my beloved Son; I am fully pleased with Him.' We ourselves heard the voice when we were there with him on the holy mountain. NLT).

We do not give second or third hand information or stories, but we talk about what we have seen and witnessed in our journey.

Understanding prophecy is very important. We have found much confusion and misunderstanding in this area. There are many mindsets of men, tradition, and religion that hinder the fulfillment of prophecies, and, as usual, men have complicated simple things. The Father is not pleased when we make His Kingdom unattainable.

There has been a strong belief regarding prophecy that has made people believe that it is only for a few elite people who are above the rest. This was said and done out of pride by people who wanted to be special. The sad thing is that in doing this much damage was done in the church at large, and a great fear of the prophetic was released. Our heart is to bring some basic understanding in this area because we perish due to lack of knowledge (Hosea 4:6). There is also a great lack of understanding of who God is. Recently the LORD told us that one of the problems He has with His children is that most of them operate out of concepts but not out of reality. When we have concepts we think we 'have it', but unless we have the experience behind it, we really don't. Many people have concepts of God. Faith is also a concept for many. Most of us know what faith is and can explain it. We may have even experienced it to a certain degree, the least getting saved. However, we are not always willing to believe God. Therefore, we are still living out of the concept but not the reality.

We hope that by the time you finish reading this book you will be willing, able, and have the courage to move from concept to reality, so you can possess the land that our Father has set apart for you. The promised land is a reality not a concept for some day in the future.

SECTION FOUR

RECEIVING AND DISCERNING PROPHECY

It is very important to know how to receive prophecy, therefore, we want to give you some keys to help you receive and discern it correctly, so you can collect 100% of the harvest intended by the Father. The correct response to prophecy is very important. We must understand that prophecies are offers from the Father but are not absolutes. One of the things that has hindered the release of prophecy greatly is 'Christian fatalism' that says, "If God said it, then it will come to pass no matter what". That is not true at all. Yes, God does not lie and does not change His mind. He will do what He said. However, the greatest responsibility in the fulfillment of your prophecies is you and your response to God's offers. Your choices will determine the next step God will take. We are sons and daughters, not slaves; therefore, we have free will and make choices, which God respects. He is a perfect father not a dictator.

We compare the receiving of prophecies with the parable of the sower. As we prophesy, we often see the ground on which the seeds fall and can usually tell if they will bring fruit or not. In Matthew 13:4-8 we read about four kinds of soil:

a) And as he sowed, some seed fell on the path, and birds came and ate it up: These are the ones who listen to the words given to them but do not understand it. Therefore, they do not do anything about it and, shortly after, doubt and unbelief come and steal it away.

b) Some fell on rocky ground, where it had little soil. It sprang up at once because the soil was not deep: These are the ones who

39

receive it with joy but do not nurture it and, as a result, they do not go deep and they wilt away when facing difficulties because they have no roots.

c) Some seed fell among thorns, and the thorns grew up and choked them: These are the ones who hear and accept it but focus more on the cares and circumstances of the world, which choke and kill the words.

d). But some seed fell on rich soil, and produced fruit, a hundred or sixty or thirty fold: These are the ones who receive the words, believe them, nurture and invest into them so they grow roots and produce the fruit they were sent to give.

We must prepare the soil of our hearts so the seeds can grow, be safe, and bear fruit. These are some of the ways in which we can prepare our hearts:

HOW TO RECEIVE PROPHECY

HUNGER AND EXPECTATION: Scripture says that if we ask our Father for bread He will not give us a stone but He will give what is good to those who ask Him (Matthew 7:7-11). This is pivotal for us as prophetic ministers. As we travel and minister around the world we can see the difference it makes when we go somewhere where there is hunger and the people have been asking the Father to feed them. The heavens open up and the Father satisfies their hunger. One of the lies people have believed is that those who come to minister carry a special anointing that makes it happen. We hear this a lot and feel very sad, because this is not true and has caused many to fix their eyes on people and their gifts and not on the LORD and His heart. All good things come from the Father's wonderful heart. He is the source. When we go somewhere to minister we count on the hunger of the people and on them asking the Father to feed them. We know, as we live and breathe, that the Father will feed them. We are 100% sure of that. We have never seen Him leave His children hungry and can share endless stories about it. We have complete confidence in His faithfulness and His abundant generous heart. We know that if

His children ask He will not deny them. But we also know that we do not carry it and we cannot make it happen. It is between the Father and His children and we have nothing to do with that. Our part in this is only that we have access to the Father's heart and to the heart of men, and we are willing to love and serve them both. That is the only thing we have to offer. We are able to reach and grab what the Father wants to give them and deliver it into the hearts of the children. We cannot produce anointing or release from heaven. It is like the waitress at the restaurant. She simply receives what the chef prepares and delivers it to the table. The chef prepares according to the request of the customers, not of the waitress. She simply is the delivery person in between. Her part in it is that she has access to the kitchen and to the table. Therefore, you must have a hungry heart and attitude. Bring your request to the Father and place your expectation on Him, not on the vessel who delivers. Remember, it is between you and your Father and He will always satisfy the hungry hearts.

YOUR RESPONSE: As we said before, prophecies are offers from the Father for His children. Recently the LORD said to me, "I have a problem with My children. Many want their prophecies fulfilled but they are not responding to My offers. I am waiting for them to say 'Yes' or 'No', so I can do the next thing. Tell them to simply answer me". I was shocked when I heard this, as it is so very simple and it makes perfect sense. As with all things, when someone offers us something we must say "Yes, I accept" or "No, thank you" and then they act accordingly. Why should it be different with God? Yes, He knows what you are going to say, but He wants you to say it so you take ownership of your response. When I make an offer to my child I always wait to hear her answer. I do not scoop the ice-cream until she says "Yes I want it". As children of God we have the same option to say, "Yes" or "No". If we say, "Yes", then God starts moving things in order to bring it to pass. But we can say, "No". It is OK. If you say, "No" God is not going to be angry with you and will not turn His back on you. He is not like our earthly parents and is not like us. He is a perfect father and loves us with perfect love. He will never leave you nor forsake you. If you say, "No" your Father will still love and bless you. For instance, if I offer my daughter a day at the beach and she says, "No, thank you" I will not leave her unprotected and unloved. I will still make sure she is safe, has a good time, and I will take care of her in whatever she does. However, she will miss out on a wonderful day at the beach and on all she could have enjoyed if she had come. It is the same with God. If we say, "No" we will miss out on amazing adventures and incredible things, but He will still bless us and be with us. Please consider the prophecies you receive and answer Him. He is waiting for your response.

HAVE AN OPEN HEART: You must believe God will speak to you because God always has something to say. It is important to expect, knowing that His heart is for you, not against you. We must be open to hearing what He wants to say. A big hindrance in receiving prophecy is that, many times, we have an 'agenda' about what we want God to say and are not open to what He wants to say. His priorities are many times different from ours. We both know what it is like to receive prophecies that we did not like at the time, and that were not what we wanted to do. Our first reaction was to reject them and say that it was not a word from the LORD. Yet, we knew deep inside it was Him, so we chose to receive it each time, and God was faithful to do what was necessary to change our hearts and bring it to pass. We must come to Him with an open heart, knowing that He is God and knows all things. We only know in part and therefore, we must trust Him. Other times people get disappointed because the prophecy did not speak of the obvious. I was prophesying over this young man and he was very disappointed at the end because I did not say that he was musical. I knew he wanted to hear that, but the LORD told me, "He already knows that. It is obvious. I want to talk to him about things that are deeper in his heart". I explained that to him and immediately his attitude changed and he was able to receive the things the LORD wanted to tell him.

FAITH AND OBEDIENCE: Faith is pivotal for the fulfillment of prophecies. Hebrews 4:2 says that, "The word they heard did not profit them, because it was not united by faith in those who heard it". Faith is pivotal when receiving prophecy. Scripture says that, "Without faith it is impossible to please God" (Hebrews 11:6).

Recently the LORD spoke to me and said, "There is another problem with My children. They do not believe me. Many want me to fulfill their prophecies, but the problem is that they like the prophecies they receive but do not really believe them. I do not fulfill prophecies because people like them, I only fulfill them when people believe them".

Then He said, "Everyone has the concept of what it is to believe but they do not have the reality of it. Again, that is because most of them are living out of concepts only". I was really surprised to hear that so I began to pay attention and, sadly, realized that it was true.

Let's talk a bit more about concepts in the Kingdom. In the world we have concepts about everything. I have a full concept of what it is like to travel to the moon. I have read the experiences of astronauts and I have seen documentaries and movies about it. Therefore, I can explain to anyone what it is like to travel there with great understanding and precision. Yet, I do not have the personal experience and that makes a big difference. God is looking for people who believe Him, not out of concept but in reality. The kind of believing He wants is like when a woman receives a marriage proposal. She believes and begins preparing for the wedding. She does not wait to see if it is true. She believes and acts on it, or when someone invites you over for dinner on Friday night you believe them and prepare to go to their house that night. By the same token, when I invite someone to come to my house for dinner on Friday night and they say, "Yes," I believe them and start preparing for it. Then on Friday I make the dinner and expect them to show up. I do not wait to see if they show up before I start cooking.

God is looking for people like Abraham, who believed God and did something about it. He was willing to risk it all because he believed what God told him, even if it did not make sense. Many people think that to believe God we must first understand what He says. Not at all. Understanding is not a requirement to believing. Faith does not come from the head, it comes from the heart. Faith is the result of a decision, not the other way around. Many people are confused as to how faith works. They expect to first have the manifestation of faith and then they will act. They think that they have to produce it. It does not work that way. We cannot produce faith. For faith to come first we choose to believe and as a result, faith arises in our hearts because the Holy Spirit empowers our decision to believe God. I do not understand many of the things God says, but I believe every single thing He says and He has never let me down. Ivan and I have experienced this first hand. We will share one story with you to illustrate how faith works.

Hebrews 11:1 says that, "Faith is the assurance of things hoped for, the conviction of things not seen". (The NLT says, "Faith is the confidence that what we hope for will actually happen; it gives us assurance about things we cannot see"). Here we see that there is something we first believe in, or hope for. Something has been said or offered to us first. We believe it and, as a result, faith comes to our hearts. Scripture says that faith comes by hearing the word of God (Romans 10:17). First we hear then faith comes.

I remember when the LORD told us to get married. That was a complete work of choice, faith, and obedience. Ivan and I never dated. We were an arranged marriage. Arranged by God that is. We were not even attracted to each other when we got engaged. Our engagement was an absolute act of obedience to what the LORD had spoken to us and to the commitment we had made to obey Him. It is an amazing but long story. However, I will summarize it for the illustration and will share the long version in another book.

Ivan and I first met three years before God brought us together. We saw each other briefly a year later, but we never really connected with each other or became friends. We were not attracted to each other at all and would have never ever, in a million years, have considered each other for a relationship. We would have never thought of going on a date as we both actually greatly disliked some aspects of the other. Then one day almost two years later, the LORD spoke to me very clearly, through a dream, and said, "I want you to marry Ivan because I have called your lives and your destinies together. If you marry Ivan I will use you together to build my Kingdom throughout the nations of the world. I want you to do this for me, not for you. If you do this for me, I will give you a supernatural gift of love from heaven that will join you both forever."

I knew God had spoken, so I had a choice to make. Marrying Ivan was not something I would have ever thought of doing, but for the Father and His Kingdom I was willing to do anything in the world. I had not heard from Ivan in almost two years and did not know really what had happened to him. For all I knew, he was already married or in a relationship. However, God had spoken and I had to respond. I said, "Yes Lord, here I am. I will do it. For you I will do anything. Today I choose to marry Ivan and serve you with him for the rest of my life. I will build Your Kingdom with him and go anywhere You want me to go. Please do all that is necessary to make it happen." At that moment, I was 'engaged' to marry Ivan, but my promise of marriage was to the LORD. I have to admit that it is the flakiest thing I have ever done in life. I did talk to two people, as I greatly believe in accountability.

Anyway, I decided to believe. Once I made the decision to believe God, the Holy Spirit responded and gave me the confidence that what I expected would come to pass, and that gave me the assurance of the things God had promised to do, which I could not see or imagine at the moment. In other words, faith arose within me as a result of my decision to believe God. Then, as a result of this, hope became expectation. This is an important key. For instance, a woman hopes to have a child one day, but once pregnant she stops hoping and starts expecting her child to be born. Hope turns into expectation. The same is true for us. We hope, but the moment God gives us the promise we do not need to hope anymore; we now begin to expect the fulfillment of that promise.

Now, like Abraham I acted on it. After responding to the LORD I started aligning my life according to the direction I was now going. I began to prepare for what the LORD said would happen. God also started to work and, through a series of amazing heavenly ordained circumstances, He arranged for Ivan to come to Costa Rica. Suddenly, Ivan was coming to arrange a mission trip for his church and was going to stay for two weeks, and since I knew some English, he asked me to translate for him.

Two weeks before Ivan was due to arrive, I was out of town helping someone and the phone rang. It was my former boss. He was now working for a different company and had a job for me. It was the job of my dreams, and literally the job I went to college for, plus it was with a new American company in my country, that paid really well, I would have been set for life if I took the position. It was very difficult to get a job there because no one ever left and my former boss told me that he wanted me for this position and he had already hired me. He did not know if I was working or not at the time, but was sure that I would accept his offer as it was literally a once in a life time opportunity. Everything was set and he wanted me to start on Monday morning. He said that all I had to do was call the Human Resources office and officially accept the job, but this was just a formality. It was now 4:45 p.m. on Friday afternoon and the office would close in fifteen minutes.

Was I willing to keep my eyes on the promise and not be distracted by the chariot of fire that came? I had no time to think as it was almost 5:00 p.m. Did I really believe God? If I believed God, then I did not need that job because I was going to marry Ivan and leave with him. Again, I still did not know if Ivan was married or not, and I did not have any attraction towards him nor feelings about marrying him. All I had was the confidence of what God had spoken and of the things that were to come. Then, of course, the enemy stepped in and said, "But what if you are wrong about this Ivan thing. You have nothing to back up what you think God told you. All you have is just a dream. However, you have this job in your hand, your dream job and it is here now". I heard that, considered both options for a minute, and then the faith that had been released within me as a result of my decision to believe God arose, and I remembered my promise to the LORD. I decided that indeed if I believed God then I would not need that job because soon I would leave the country as Ivan's wife and would go to build God's Kingdom with him, so I picked up the phone, called the office and turned the job down. I aligned my life accordingly and prepared for what was ahead.

Ivan arrived in Costa Rica not knowing God's plans for him yet. He had no idea he was going to marry me. On his second day there the LORD came and spoke to him audibly and said, "Ivan I brought you here because I want you to marry Isabel". This was a big surprise to him but he believed God and said, "Yes LORD here I am. I will marry her". The next morning the LORD sent an angel to confirm the message and to give him the time for the proposal. I actually saw the angel. In the natural this was crazy. First, proposing to a woman he barely knew, and who was not even his friend, plus he was not attracted to me. He had just turned 22 years old and had nothing. He was doing a pastoral internship at the church and his income was $50 a week. He had no other natural resources to marry a woman from another land, take her, and support her. Yet, he did not consider the circumstances that surrounded him but focused his heart on the fact that God had spoken, and, as such, He would make the impossible possible. As Ivan chose to believe God, the confidence of what the LORD said would happen arose in him (faith was released by the Spirit). So that day, within an hour from the angel's visit, Ivan proposed and I said yes. We both had complete confidence in what the LORD had said. However, it was like a business transaction and we could have shaken hands on it because there was no emotion or attraction whatsoever between us. It was 100% obedience to what the LORD had spoken to both of us.

As we did it, we fixed our eyes on what the LORD had said would happen, what He promised to do with and through our marriage. He promised that we would serve Him and build His Kingdom and that became the reason for our obedience. He also promised to give us a supernatural gift of love that would join us forever. Therefore, even though we were not attracted to each other, we had confidence that God would fulfill His promise. And He did! Right after we "shook hands" on the engagement, Ivan left with my pastor for a three day mission trip to the mountains, which had been pre-arranged. During those three days the LORD released the gift of love He promised. When Ivan came back from the mountains we looked at each other and we loved each other with such a deep and strong love, that it was as if we had been together forever and ever. It was the most supernatural thing ever. That was back in 1987, and that love has continued to grow between us throughout the years.

Then, just as promised, God began to use us together to serve Him, and to build His Kingdom locally and throughout the nations of the world. We live to make Him famous and this has taken us to amazing experiences. His faithfulness has been greater than we expected. It has now been 20 years since we 'shook hands' on that engagement and we have never ever regretted it. We both can say honestly and truly that if time went back, we would do it all over again. We believed God and, as a result, He gave us the confidence that what He said would come to pass, and today we are living the things He promised, which, back then, seemed impossible and we could not imagine. He has been true to His word and has gone the extra mile for us. Obedience is indeed better than sacrifice.

Many people criticized us and said that what we were doing was not from God because it was 'outside the box'. People cursed our marriage and said that it would fail. It did not make sense to the minds of men. Scripture tells us that the things of God are craziness to the world. We need to be 'silly' in the eyes of the world, in order to believe the outrageous things the LORD tells us. Most of the time, they are so impossible that, like Sarah, we must just laugh (Genesis 18:12).

BELIEVE GOD: It saddens the LORD that His children do not believe Him. He is such a perfect father and is love. He is almighty and sovereign, yet, we are the most important thing in His world and our wellbeing is His main concern. If we could only understand this, how different things would be. We would not have trouble believing and trusting Him. Our lives and ways would be so different and we would be able to live and move in His supernatural realm of miracles and power as we walk through the impossible. Abraham indeed received an amazing and completely impossible promise (Genesis 15: 4-5). Every time I think of it, I am amazed to read how he simply believed God and acted on it. Verse 6 says, "Then he believed in the LORD; and He reckoned it to him as righteousness". Believing God made him righteous. We have this idea that righteousness is one of the hardest things to achieve, yet here we see that it is actually simple. One of the ways to be righteous is to believe God. Obedience also produces righteousness. So, if you want to become righteous before the LORD, start by believing Him and walking in obedience. I promise you that these two things will keep you on the straight and narrow path and out of trouble.

We all want to please God and believing and obeying Him make Him very happy. When we please God, His favour comes on us and, when God's favour is on us, He blesses all we do and we prosper in all things. It is amazing how very many children of God live without the favour of God in their lives. Trust me, if you believe God His favour will become evident in your life. This is a key to walking in our prophetic destiny. One of the problems people have with believing God is that they do not really know Him. We know a lot about Him and hear much about Him and His ways, but few people actually invest into knowing Him deeply for themselves. We all have concepts of God and live out of them. Many times our concepts of Him are based on someone else's opinion or perspective or on our earthly experiences. To trust someone you have to know that person well. We do not trust strangers or acquaintances. We trust people whose hearts and character we know. Many people think that knowing someone's ways is the same as knowing them. That is not so. Most frequently the ways of a man and his heart are two different things and we must learn to separate their ways from their heart. Yet, most of the time, we do not invest into getting to know their hearts or even finding their hearts. We get caught up in their ways, but the ways of a man are circumstantial. They are determined by their journey, their hurts, their lack of healing, their sins, etc., and they can be changed as healing, love, restoration, and freedom come to them. However, the heart of man was created by God and that is the place where life flows from. The real man is found in his heart not in his ways. God placed eternity in the heart and His plans are deeply in there. That is why prophecy from the Father's heart is so important. It reaches the heart of man.

We can only say that we know someone when we know their heart. Most people say that they 'know' their parents; however, what they know are the ways of their parents. Proof of it is when they are alone with their parents. After talking about the turkey, things become awkward because they do not have anything to talk about. I used to think that I knew my mother. Then, after the LORD did a work of healing in our lives and restored our relationship, I actually began to know her. She started sharing her heart with me and for the first time I knew who she was. We became friends and I realized that she was a very different person than who I thought she was. I found out that her ways and her heart were two different things and I now can say that "I know my mother". Being your parents' child does not mean that you know them. The same is true when it comes to God. Most people think that because they get saved and are His children they know Him, but most of the time that is not true.

As I shared before, once I did not know God the way I do now and therefore, I did not trust Him. I knew Him through His ways and the ways others presented Him to me. But I did not know who He really was and how He was. Because of my upbringing I had a distorted concept of authority figures. There are many in that situation and the Father wants to give you all your very personal experience and encounter with His heart and love so you can know Him as He is and then you can trust Him and believe whatever He tells you.

There is a story we love. It is found in 2 Chronicles 20. King Jehoshaphat was facing trouble and needed direction from God. The LORD sent the answer through the prophet. King Jehoshaphat heard the message and believed it. I greatly admire him because what God said did not make sense, but he did not rely in human reason but in faith. He trusted God. He summoned the people and told them what the LORD had said, then, he told them in verse 20, "Listen to me, O Judah and inhabitants of Jerusalem, put your trust in the LORD your God and you will be established. Put your trust in His prophets and succeed" (trust in the LORD your God and you will be able to stand firm. Believe also in His prophets and you will succeed). As we read the rest of the story we see how God came through for King Jehoshaphat and gave him complete victory. He trusted God and believed the words of His prophets.

Hebrews 11: 32-34 says "What more shall I say? I have not time to tell of Gideon, Barak, Samson, Jephthah, of David and Samuel and the prophets, who by faith conquered kingdoms, did what was righteous, obtained the promises; they closed the mouths of lions, put out raging fires, escaped the devouring sword; out of weakness they were made powerful, became strong in battle, and turned back foreign invaders" (NIV).

Scripture says that by faith great and mighty things are achieved. By faith the heavens open and God is revealed into our lives. We too can say that by faith we have seen miracles and power happen in our lives. By faith I married a stranger and left my home and my country, to come to serve the LORD believing the promises God made. By faith, Ivan, being a young man with no possibilities or resources, took a wife from another land, brought her to his country, and started a new life believing the promises God made him. By faith, we received the fulfillment of every one of those promises. By faith, we left profitable jobs trusting the promises of God to build His Kingdom. By faith, we planted churches and started ministries against all odds, and with only God standing with us. By faith, we have bought buildings, houses, financed Kingdom projects, sent people to overseas missions, raised others into ministry, paid people's debts, have given cars away, fed multitudes, have had miracles of multiplication of food like the feeding of the 5,000 in our house, have seen angels, helped angels, have been helped by angels, have walked through the supernatural promises of God, and much more. These are just a few of the things we have done by faith and we can truly say that God has been faithful to everything He has ever said. He has been more than good to His word. Through this all, we can also say that we know Him better each day.

PATIENCE: Another important thing we need to understand, in order to receive our prophetic promises, is patience and timing. These two things cause much frustration when it comes to prophecy. We have noticed two common responses to prophecy. Some people expect it to happen immediately and lose faith when it takes time. The other is feeling overwhelmed and not able to cope with what they have heard. We must understand timing as we interpret the words of the LORD. God's timing and ours are usually different. Scripture is filled with examples of how timing varies in this area. David is a great example of someone who had to wait to receive his promise. He was anointed king by the prophet but the realization of it in the natural took years. There are many reasons for this, and we will talk later about them in detail. Caleb is also a great example of someone who believed and had to wait for his promise to be fulfilled. Prophecy confirms, affirms, and creates. A mindset many have is that prophecy only confirms or affirms what the LORD has already spoken. Yet, we see that God speaks of yesterday, today, and tomorrow. The tomorrow is very important to the LORD and He wants to reveal it to us.

CALLING VERSUS COMMISSIONING: It is important to also understand that prophecies reveal callings in people's lives, but do not commission them. Many people confuse calling with commissioning and this causes much frustration. They can't understand how come if they received a prophecy saying that they are going to pastor, no one is giving them a pulpit right away. We must understand the difference between calling and commissioning. The apostle Paul was called in Acts chapter 9 but was commissioned in Acts chapter 13. There were many years between his calling and his commissioning (some who know say that is was 17 years). The reason was his character. Our character and preparation are very important. We have found that many people think that receiving a calling from God or having it revealed, endorses their current character. One thing has nothing to do with the other. Not understanding this causes many problems for people and for the leaders.

When Paul was called he was Saul of Tarsus, a persecutor of the church, and a murderer. God revealed his calling, which was not in accordance with his character. God had to change and transform him, so his character could match his calling. God was not endorsing his current character when He called him. For instance, the fact that someone realizes that his calling in life is to be a mechanic, does not qualify him to get under the hood of my car. That would be dangerous and would get me killed. In order to trust him I want to make sure that he has completed his training and has graduated. It amazes me that people expect it to be different in the Kingdom of God. In God's

Kingdom the bar is even higher because we deal with the hearts and lives of people. Character is much more important than gifting and calling. One of our greatest concerns is leaders who choose people according to gifting and not character.

A few weeks ago as I was with the LORD, He said, "Many people are so focused on building their gifts and ministries that they are not paying attention to their characters. This is a big problem because for me to build, I need and am looking for people who invest in their character not in their gifting". He then spoke that Scripture in Psalm 127:1 that says, "Unless the LORD builds the house, they labour in vain who build it".

He said," Many in the church at large right now are building "houses" (ministries and gifts) that I am not building and soon it will become evident because what they are building will not last. Tell my children that if they invest in their characters, I will invest in their gifts and I will build in them and through them. Tell them that I need them to develop a character that I can use to build, a character that is good for me. I do not need their gifts to build, but I need their character. I will not give increase and release because of a great gift. I am not impressed by their gifts. It is their hearts and character that I look at. Remember I see beyond what men see, because men see the appearance, but I see the heart and I cannot be deceived."

SECTION FIVE

THE PRISON OF GOD'S WILL

There is something that we call 'The Prison of God's Will'. Joseph's life illustrates this prison. He was a young man with a great calling, but right after the revelation of his destiny, everything went wrong. Things did not go as expected but instead they went the opposite direction. He went through a journey that transformed him. In this time, the enemy rose to steal his destiny, but God used it to make him the man He had called him to be. Many times we go through this same journey. God always uses it for good and, at the end, we find ourselves exactly where we are supposed to be. We both have experienced the Prison of God's Will.

I remember when the LORD called me to serve Him. I was a very proud, arrogant, and hurting 18 year old. Yet I had an amazing gift, which was given to me when I was in my mother's womb. I was born a seer and the prophetic was a part of me all my life. It was one of those sovereign decisions of God, so for me, being prophetic was God's choice. One day I was with the LORD and asked Him to show me the plans He had for me. As I say elsewhere, when I was six years old, God had shown me my future in a vision. Now I wanted to know more detail and explanation as I was too young the first time to fully understand what I saw and heard.

So as I asked Him, He opened up another vision and I saw my future. I saw things that were 'too big to be true'. I saw myself serving the LORD in a big way, standing behind pulpits around the world ministering to large crowds, teaching and ministering to spiritual leaders from all over the world, men and women of great stature. I saw myself traveling around the world and saw God's power, signs, and wonders taking place. It was absolutely amazing. I got very excited because, at that time, I dreamed of being famous and being recognized. I wanted identity. The LORD was standing next to me as I was seeing this vision and after a few minutes He asked me, "Do you want this?" I was surprised He was even asking me that. I looked at Him and said, "Of course I do. I am perfect for it". We both looked at the vision again and then with a deeper and softer tone of voice, He asked again, "Are you sure you want this?" In my great pride and ignorance I could not see past my ambition and I thought He wanted me to respond with a 'serious' tone of voice, so in a deeper and softer voice I said, "Yes LORD, I want it." He looked at me in a profound way and said, "Very well then." Little did I know that the road ahead would not be at all what I had anticipated that night.

I thought that since I already had the gift in me I was further ahead than most and, surely, room would open up for me immediately. In my mind I figured that my pastor would probably move aside and hand me the pulpit. I was very excited and went to talk to him. I told him that God had revealed the calling on my life and now I knew what I was to do, and I was ready to start. Being a man of experience he said to me, "I am very happy that you know what you are called to do. That is wonderful. However, you need to slow down a bit and learn much before you can be released. Otherwise, you are going to crash badly and the consequences will not be good for you and for others around you. Apply yourself and learn. I assure you that when you are ready, God will make sure doors open for you." I was very upset to hear that, because in my mind I was ready and God had spoken clearly that He wanted me to do those things. What was wrong with this man?

I believed God and kept talking to Him about His calling on my life and kept asking Him to do it. The LORD began to work and, if someone had shown me what the next 15 years of my life were going to be like, I probably would have run the other way. At that time I was in college, studying for a big career in business, and my dad had made plans for me to get me a job in the government, as he had high connections there. I was also working and making lots of money. I actually made more money than most people I knew and was very proud of myself. I had become very self-sufficient. Suddenly, one day the LORD said to me, "I want you to give up your career and follow me". Because of my background, degrees and careers were very important to me at the time. My family had come out of great poverty through education and hard work and their careers had become their identity and value. I come from a family of intellectual overachievers so I had been raised to believe and do likewise.

The thought of giving up my career was very hard and I fought it for a year but the LORD said very clearly that I had to give it up if I wanted to follow His calling. "I have a different kind of training and education for you. I will teach you things that no one else can teach you. You must join my school and then your destiny will come", He said. So, I finally gave in and left my career. My family did not take this kindly and things got hard for me at home. They could not understand how a young, healthy, and intelligent girl would give up her life for 'religious nonsense' as they called it. They were not Christians at the time, so they could not comprehend the journey I was on. Day after day they would try to talk me out of it. My oldest sister, who is like a second mother to me and a woman of high intellect and success, would daily tell me, among many other things, that I had become a waste to society, a parasite, and now I would certainly never amount to anything.

Day after day I would endure their many insults, without being able to defend myself or explain the reason behind it all. Since I had no money, I had to do something to live and my family allowed me to take over all housekeeping work in exchange for my room-and-board. At the same time, I began to do an informal internship in the church for no pay, which began to teach me what to 'live-by-faith' is all about, certainly a very humbling road to walk on. I did the housekeeping work at home in the mornings and did church work in the afternoons and evenings. I helped in the church, doing anything and everything that was necessary. I spent much time with the pastors and leaders learning from them, did administrative kinds of work, and helped people in the church with whatever was necessary, from practical things, to counseling and ministry. I also went on mission trips to the mountains and, in very hard conditions, helped build churches and houses for the poor.

One day, the mother of one of the poorest families in the church and probably in the town became ill. She was pregnant and had to be in bed. They had several children and were in great need of help, so the LORD told me, "I want you to be a maid for them". Now, where I lived being a maid was the lowest of all jobs and everyone looked down on them. It was a disgrace to have to do that kind of work. I could not believe the LORD was asking me to do it. It was bad enough that I had to keep house for my family. However, the LORD said, "Go and serve them". I hated it but I went. Then the same thing happened to another of the poorest families, and the LORD said again, "Go and serve them too in the same manner". Then a third family, and again the LORD said, "Go and be a maid for them too". So there I was being a maid for the poorest people I knew. I had grown up in great poverty too, but my family had come out of it and things were different now, so as a result we had followed the ways of the land and became very proud and arrogant. The rule seemed to be that as soon as anyone came out of the great poverty of the country, pride filled their hearts causing them to forget where they came from, and they would look down on those who were still stuck behind. No one gave a helping hand to others in a worse situation than they were in.

So there I was, serving people who were way poorer and very needy. I had to do all their work, scrub their floors and dirty diapers by hand, cook and tend to the kids, etc. I distributed my days through the week, going from one house to the other. I tried to keep it from my family but they found out and things got even worse for me at home because I was embarrassing them. To make things worse, I was doing it all for free so I had to keep silent and take it without protest. Inside I was struggling with the same feelings. My pride could not take it. I remember scrubbing messy diapers by hand (no rubber gloves either) and thinking, "How can it be that I am here doing this for people who are less than I am, people with no education and no possibilities. I have this and that; my family has this and that. We have degrees and success, a nice house, and had maids up until I left my career and took over the housekeeping". In my great arrogance and ignorance I despised those families. I remember also thinking, "My goodness I have this amazing calling from God in my life. I have this incredible gift in me. I am more special than all of them. I have an amazing calling and will probably become famous and rich too, and God is forcing me to do this. What is wrong? Why? How could this be if I was called to be this and that?" I could not get past the pride in my life and for weeks just kept going around the mountain in circles.

Finally, one day, the LORD spoke to me in a way I understood. Among many things He said, "Isabel, it is not about your gifting or calling, but it is about your heart. If you cannot learn to serve those who, in the eyes of the world are considered the least, then no matter how great your gift and calling are, you will never ever be able to serve me". I heard that, and something broke inside of me. I knew what He meant and I repented with all my heart. Then I said to Him, "LORD, I now understand, and I choose to do this. I choose to serve these people. I give you back the calling you offered me and the gift you gave me. You no longer have to bring it to pass. I choose to give it up, in order to serve your people. I want to do this and will be happy to do it for the rest of my life, if you so wish". At that moment, the most amazing thing happened. My heart was changed and God filled me with abundant love for those families and great joy as I served them. I served them with all my heart and loved it. I looked forward to going to their houses, and constantly reminded the LORD that, if He wanted, I would be happy to keep doing that forever. When other families needed help, I volunteered to be their maid for free and rejoiced in serving them. I found such fulfillment that I felt like Billy Graham after doing a great crusade. Actually, one day as I thought of that, the LORD said to me, "I am as pleased with you as I am with him because you both are doing what I am asking you to do, and you both are serving my people".

I did that for about four years as the need arose in the church and, when I look back, I can truly say that those were some of the best years of my journey and, if time went back, I would gladly do it all over again. The relationships that were formed remain as strong today as they were then and the fruit of it is eternal. One day, many years later, when the LORD began to release us into public ministry, Ivan and I came back from doing a big conference somewhere where we saw God do amazing things in the hearts and lives of people, and the LORD came and said, "Can you tell me what I am raising you to be?" I thought about it and gave Him what seemed to be the obvious answer. Then He said, "No, you are wrong. That is not what I am raising you up to be. I am raising you to be a maid to my people. I want you to serve them. I want you to carry a bucket and a towel and wash their feet. The only reason why I will use and anoint you is because my Bride needs servants to prepare her for the coming wedding. It has nothing to do with you. It is because of my Bride that I raise people up. She needs servants." Then He said, "Do you remember those years when you used to scrub those floors and diapers?" I said, "Yes, of course". Then He said, "I want you to know that your ministry did not start when anointing began to come to you, or when doors began to open for you. Not at all. Your ministry began back then, all those years ago, when you learned to serve my people with a glad and grateful heart".

Many other things have happened since the years scrubbing floors and diapers. That was just the beginning of preparation. The LORD has taken us through great fires and brokenness. We have very often been taken to the potter's house, where the Father has changed us forever (Jeremiah 18:2). The journey has been long and hard. The price has been very high. Sometimes higher than what we wanted to pay. But I remember when, years later, a prophet came to our church and said to me, "The LORD says that the season of your commissioning is here because finally your character has caught up to your calling. Now you are safe and therefore, I can trust you and release you." The amazing thing is that, by then, I did not care anymore about recognition, position, identity or anything else. Ambition had been burned out of both of us and we just wanted to serve and love people. In looking back, we are so grateful God made us wait and learn. I know that if God had released me back then, I would have destroyed myself and many others along the way. I would have built a kingdom for myself not God's Kingdom. I am so grateful that my pastor had enough wisdom not to run with gifting, but to look for character as well. There are many leaders that get taken by the gifting in people's lives and release them before time.

The worst thing that can happen to a man (or a woman) is to be released before they are ready and, when this happens, their lack of maturity and character causes great trouble and sorrow for their soul and for others. We remember years ago watching others pass us by. It was hard especially when they arrived later and suddenly, without any difficulty, because of their gifting, doors were opened to them. We asked the LORD, "Why?" and He said, "The preparation for your calling and destiny is intense and I need to do much work in your lives, so you become people who can endure the race till the end. Do not fix your eyes on what men can do for you and do not expect them to open doors for you. I am the one who is preparing you and I alone will create a door for you when you are ready".

Days began to pass and turned into weeks, weeks into months, months into years and we kept pressing in and trusting in the LORD.

We learned to serve, love, and heal God's people and that indeed is the greatest gift God has given us. The greatest motivation behind all we do is the strong passion that the LORD has given us for His Bride. Because the Father hid us away until our characters were ready, we have been able to endure many tests, and are further ahead in the race, looking at the goal set in front of us.

It is so important to have patience for His plan. There are many who quit ahead of time because of lack of patience. As we go around the world ministering we see people with unfulfilled callings who live in frustration and disappointment, and others who have dropped out of the race because the process got tough. They got called but never commissioned. Hebrews 6:11-12 says, "Our great desire is that you will keep on loving others as long as life lasts, in order to make certain that what you hope for will come true. Then you will not become spiritually dull and indifferent. Instead, you will follow the example of those who are going to inherit God's promises because of their faith and endurance" (NLT).

PAYING THE PRICE

God's Kingdom works like this: God calls us and waits for our response. Those who respond then start the training and preparation. The price is high and many get discouraged along the way. For instance, if I had all the resources and means in the world, I would make an offer to my daughter. I could say to her, "I want you to become a brain surgeon. I want you to succeed and have the best there is. I will provide and open all the doors I can for you. I have the means if you want it". If she says yes, then I will begin to provide all she needs for it, but she has to do the work. She has to study and apply herself. She has to pay the price, as her marks would have to be excellent to enter into the required universities. Many times when her friends are playing and having fun, she will have to study and work hard. It is possible that she may decide to quit and have fun with her friends, or do something else, perhaps something less demanding. If she does that, then no matter how much I want her to become that successful brain surgeon and how much I can give her, it will not come to pass. It is her choice and she has to pay the price.

During our journey there were many times when the fires seemed too intense and the price too high. We saw others having an easier time and enjoying themselves and many times we wanted to quit. We are so grateful that the LORD kept us and has sustained us this far, and we trust He will continue doing it till the end, when we reach the goal set before us. It is easier to quit but, from personal experience, we can say that it is truly worth paying the price and enduring the race. When you are ready the LORD will come and choose you from among the many that have been called. Many are called but not all are chosen to be commissioned. Many drop out of the race before the end and blame God for their disappointment. We know many who have received callings like ours but have not made it past being called and who will remain called forever, unless they choose to follow the process that will get them ready to be chosen. Being called is not enough.

One thing about God is that He never gives up and never gets disheartened. It is impossible to cause God to give up hope. No matter how many mistakes we make along the way, He is a redeemer and our destiny is redeemable. Perhaps you received a calling from the LORD but you did not know what you had to do about it, or you knew but chose to drop out of the race, or you rejected it at the time. Whatever the circumstances have been, it is important to know that God does not change His mind and does not lie (1 Samuel 15:29). Therefore, if you still want to live the calling God has given you, you can now respond to His offer. Yes, it may be later than God had originally planned, and perhaps you now have some baggage that you did not have before due to the detour you took and the choices you made but, at the end, God will turn it all into good for you and will even cause your mistakes to become weapons to fight well in His battles. God's character does not change because of circumstances. He will never change.

Once someone said to me, I am not sure about this prophecy stuff. A while ago this man came and prophesied over some people. He prophesied over this man that God had called him to be a pastor and how powerfully he would be used by God in evangelism and other things. Yet, after a while, he left the church and got into alcoholism and all the things of the world. Therefore, they said that the prophecy was not from the LORD because if it had been, then it would have come to pass no matter what, and this young man would now be a pastor. As I heard this, the LORD spoke to me and said, "That is not true. I did call that young man and made him a great offer. I offered him a wonderful destiny but it carried a high price tag. He liked the prophecy but when it came time to respond and be prepared he was not willing to give up all the things he liked, the cares of the world suffocated the seed and he chose another path. However, I will never give up on him and, if at any time he decides to accept my offer, even if it is many years from now, I will still do as I offered, and will take him to his destiny. Unfortunately, he will have to deal with many unnecessary things because of the baggage he has been collecting."

I heard that and was amazed at the character of God. That was not what I was used to seeing in the world. God is 100% faithful and He never fails. He sees our hearts and acts accordingly. That is why many times we see Him do things that are not according to the deeds of men. His mercies are new each morning and His love remains till the end. He keeps no record of when He has been wronged. How different from our ways and the ways of our parents. How different perfect love is!!!

SECTION SIX

MOTIVATION

The motivation of the heart is more important than the gift we have. This is what determines what God can do with us and through us. If your driving force is identity or pride, God will close doors for you. I know well what that is like. Many, many years ago, I had very bad motivations in my heart. I was so full of pride that I used the gift for my advantage. I used it to show off and to make myself known in the eyes of men. I wanted recognition and knew that the gift I had would give it to me, so I prophesied out of pride and used the hearts of people for my ambition. Then slowly, in time, things began to change around me and, instead of release, doors began to close. Opportunity was taken from me and I was passed by. I could not understand what was happening as there was so much opposition all around me.

I thought it was warfare and began to do battle against it. I called on intercessors to fight the enemy away from me. Then, after much warfare, the LORD came and said to me, "You might as well stop all you are doing because it is not going to work. Yes, there is much opposition against you right now, but it is not the devil that is against you. It is ME. I am the one who stands against you and who is opposing you from all directions because I oppose the proud but give grace to the humble. Your heart is so full of pride that I have to stop you. You are of no use to me like this. Remember, you cannot warfare Me away. There is only one way out of this and that is through repentance, brokenness, and humility, because a broken and contrite heart I cannot deny".

Then, a few days later the LORD spoke again to me in a dream. In the dream the Father himself came and said to me, "You are a spoiled brat and you are angry because I am not giving you your way. The only reason why you want Me to open doors for you is because of pride and as long as that is your motive I will NOT do it. Deal with your pride and give it up". I was speechless after that and knew that I had to give in and let Him deal with my heart. It was not an easy journey. The fires were hotter than I anticipated and the visits to the potter's house more intense (Jeremiah 18:2). Oh how I wish there would have been someone who could have told me these things back then. At that time there were no fathers for the prophetic as there are today. I remember growing in the prophetic and not being able to find a mentor who could have told me, "I know. I have been there and understand. Let me teach you the way to get there".

However, we are grateful for our mistakes and the journey we have both lived, because it is out of that journey that we are able to help others grow. A long time ago, when the LORD began to send us out, He said, "I am going to send you all around the world to minister, teach, train, equip, and impart into my people, and I am going to open doors that no one can open. You can go all over and brag as much as you want but only about one thing. In my lack of understanding I thought, "Wow aren't we special? Most people get told that they cannot brag about anything and the LORD is giving us permission to brag". "What can we brag about LORD?" I said, "I have a list of things and can give you some suggestions". The LORD said, "There is only one thing you can brag about and that is your mistakes. You can go all over the world and tell them openly about every single mistake you have ever made and teach them how to do it right. That way they will go further than you have in a much shorter time".

So, God has used our mistakes for good. We have made every mistake you can think of, every mistake you have heard and will hear about. For many years now we have been teaching God's people, all over the world, to hear God's voice, prophesy, and live a prophetic life in the natural and the supernatural realms, and one thing that is very helpful is that no matter what people tell us, we can look at them and say, "We know and can help you". We understand their mistakes and know the way out. We have not yet found one single hindrance that people have run into that we have not dealt with before and so we are able to help them move to the next level. Certainly all things work together for good for those who are called by Him (Romans 8:28).

One of our greatest desires is to save people many years in their journey. We want to see those that we mentor rise up and go beyond us, accomplishing at least twice as much as we will ever do. We have learned that when we have humble and teachable hearts God can give us ears to hear and eyes to see, so we can learn from those He sends to mentor and teach us, thus learning in a short time what took others years to learn. So, stay away from pride and examine the motives of your heart in wanting to minister but also in wanting to receive God's promises. We remember, back then, wanting God to fulfill His promises so others could see how special we were. We both wanted identity and this was a way of getting it. Remember that it is impossible to deceive God because He searches the hearts and nothing is hidden from Him. When God sees that the motivation of your heart is to serve and love others as He does, He can trust you and release you.

People always ask us, "How can we grow in the prophetic quickly and move to the higher levels?" There are, indeed, many things that can be done in the natural to help us do things better and grow in our ability to use the gifts God has given us, yet the greatest key is to become someone that God can trust. When you develop a character and a heart that God can trust, He will release into you without limit. When He knows that no matter what you know and what you see in the hearts of His people they are safe in your presence and you will heal them and love them as your own, He will open the realm of revelation, wisdom, and understanding without limit. He will give you access to the depth of the heart of man and His heart. Love is God's language and the key that turns His heart. Learn to love His people with God's love and you will see heaven open up in your life. God is looking for people He can trust.

So the sooner we deal with our heart and its motivation, the sooner God can bring release and give us the amazing things He has promised us. Believe us, we have walked this walk and know what it is like to have God oppose us. There is nothing worse than that. But we also know what it is like to be restored and set free and, even though the journey has been difficult and painful at times, we do not regret any of it as God has been transforming us and the fruit of it is good for Him, good for us, and good for His people. May you have ears to hear what the Spirit of the LORD wants to say to you today!

SECTION SEVEN

TIMING AND INTERPRETATION

One of the things that causes great chaos in the church is the lack of understanding regarding the interpretation of prophecy. There are very many factors to consider when we hear prophecies spoken over us. Here we want to address some of the most common hindrances, in order to help you change your views and cooperate with God in the fulfillment of your prophetic promises.

A big obstacle to receiving prophecy is that, as soon as we hear it, we figure out exactly how and when it is going to happen. We all do it and become greatly discouraged and disillusioned when it does not happen the way we thought and expected it to happen. We must keep in mind that God's ways are not our ways and His thoughts are not our thoughts. Understanding this makes all the difference when receiving prophecy. We hear what God says and want it to make sense to us. We try to figure it out and, to make it worse, we hold God to what we think it means.

We have received promises from God that did not make any sense, plus they were completely impossible. Therefore, there was no way of reasoning them. They were out of this world, and others around us tried to discourage us from believing them because they did not make any sense.

We knew that, but also knew God could do anything and, when others questioned us about the feasibility of them coming to pass, we could not give answers or explanations. It was not up to us to explain God's ways, just to believe Him. We must stop trying to figure out the ways in which our prophecies will come to pass and let God be God. I remember once some friends received a prophecy that said, "I see you laying hands on a globe of the world. God is going to use you to literally minister to the nations of the world and you will lay hands on them and impart into them." Immediately they thought that God was going to literally send them to minister to all the nations of the world. They did travel to some nations but the fulfillment of that word came when, years later, they became the directors of an international ministry centre and people from all over the world went there. They literally laid hands on the nations and imparted into them. God fulfilled His word, but not quite the way they thought.

Another time, we prophesied over someone and said that God was going to use him as a leader of leaders and a pastor of pastors. He became very excited but, immediately, began to figure out how the prophecy would be fulfilled and set his eyes on it. A couple of years later, he came to see us and was even more excited to report that God had fulfilled that particular word in his life, but not the way he had planned or expected. He had been asked to come to an international school of pastors and leaders to be a small group leader, which meant that, for the duration of the school, he was a pastor to those pastors and a leader to those leaders. He said that as he was there ministering to his group of pastors and leaders, the LORD spoke to him and said, "Do you realize that right now you are a pastor of pastors and a leader of leaders?" At that moment, he remembered his prophecy and understood God's plans. He then noticed that if God had not pointed it out to him, he could have missed the realization of the fulfillment of that prophecy, simply because he had fixed his eyes on his idea of how it would come to pass. This happens a lot. As we teach people they look back and realize that many of their prophecies have come to pass, but it was not in the way or time they expected.

THINGS YET TO COME

God speaks of the things that are yet to come. Again, we must keep in mind that these are offers from the LORD and, as we are learning, their fulfillment depends greatly on us. We must understand the heart of God. He wants us to know the plans that He has for us because He wants us to have a hope and a future. He wants us to have vision. Once I heard this lady say how upset she was about prophecy, because this prophet had given her a word that said that God was going to heal her from her depression and would completely deliver her from that terrible bondage. She said that she did not have depression when the prophecy was spoken and had never had depression in her life yet, within a month of receiving the prophecy, she fell into a terrible depression, and she blamed the prophecy for causing it. As I heard it, the LORD spoke clearly to me and said, "That is not true. I knew she was going to be attacked by depression and I gave her the promise of healing and deliverance before it happened so that when it came, she would have a life-line to hang on during the storm".

Another time, we heard from a couple of missionaries who received a prophecy about how God was going to do great things in and through them in the country where they were ministering. They were very encouraged by the prophecy. About a year or so later, a great hurricane came to that country. They got burned-out and decided to go back to their home country. They returned defeated, discouraged and, of course, questioned the prophecy they had received. As we heard their story we clearly understood what had happened. The LORD gave them great promises for the land where they were ministering before the hard time arrived so that, when the storm came, they could have a life-line to hold onto and stick it out. After the hurricane that land would have been a great harvest ground for the Kingdom because the people were broken and, usually, that is when they are open to hearing from God. However, they decided to leave because of circumstances, not because God had changed His mind. There is a big difference between God saying "Go", and the circumstances making you go. We must be careful not to make decisions based on circumstances and then blame God for it. They heard the prophecy and formed their idea of how and when it would happen. They did not understand how to deal with prophecies, and how to process them ahead of time and they quit before the race ended.

God is faithful and is a perfect father. He knows what is to come and wants us to know that He is aware of what is happening. He always gives us the hope to carry us through it. It is like the time when our airplane caught on fire in midair. We had just finished a very intense week of ministry in England and we were exhausted. Our flight was delayed for hours, which made it worse. Finally we boarded the plane and, as I was sitting, the LORD said to me, "There is going to be trouble with the plane when it is in the air." I heard that and said to the LORD, "Thank you for letting us know and please help us. As a personal request, I would really appreciate if we do not fall on the water. I am so tired and do not feel like getting wet". We were not worried at all because we knew that He knew. He was fully aware of what was coming and, knowing that, made all the difference. We decided to rest on the flight and sure enough the landing gear caught on fire when we were flying over the ocean. Many people were understandably distraught, but we both enjoyed complete peace and rest in the midst of the storm and, at the end, everything worked out just fine.

I remember a long time ago people began to prophesy financial blessing over us. That seemed to be the topic of the hour for us. Shortly after the prophecies began, everything caved in our lives and our finances crashed. Many people said, "It is because of those prophecies", but we kept hearing the Father say, "No, I knew this would happen and did not want you to be in despair. Therefore, I gave you the promise of blessing so you can get to the other side. Keep your eyes on the promise and not on the circumstances. This storm will pass and I will bless you". We held onto those promises as everything else left us. It was the worst financial chaos of our lives. Everything was out of control and all we could do was survive. There are few things that bring discouragement like financial chaos and we were in the thick of it, but those prophecies kept us above water. Then in time, Jesus 'woke up' and stopped the storm (Matthew 8:25). He began to redeem and restore and we certainly made it to the other side with amazing stories to tell about the faithfulness of God.

Many people are afraid that a 'wrong' prophecy can curse them. In other words, they have a fear that if someone makes a mistake or misses it, that word will curse them. That is not true. That is simply a mistake. This is the reason why we need to learn how to properly discern and judge prophecy. Later we will talk more about this.

God is God and knows best. Be open to His ways and listen to Him closely. Revisit your prophecies and look at what the LORD has done in your life. See how He has brought things about, which you did not notice before and discover where He is leading you. Remember that God loves small beginnings. When we hear prophecies, often God is speaking of what is to come and shows us the finished product. However, most times, we think that is where it begins. God first makes an offer and waits to see our response. Then He takes us through small beginnings, which train us and also reveal the issues of our heart such as pride, ambition, etc. As we deal with them and choose God's way, He brings increase, and eventually, when we are ready and the time is right, we will see the great endings God has planned. We have both lived through this and know how important it is to invest the one talent we are given. Recently we heard the LORD speak about the importance of stewardship in the Kingdom. He referred to the parable of the talents in Matthew 25:14. Then He said that He is not going to waste talents anymore and, therefore, has begun a redistribution of talents in the Kingdom. May you have ears to hear.

CONDITIONS

We need to pay attention to what the LORD is saying, in terms of conditions. Many times prophecies have conditional words where the LORD says, "You must do this" or, "If you do this, then this will take place". This is just an example of a conditional word: Once we were at a meeting where a pastor and his wife, whom we knew, received a word from a prophet whom we greatly respect. The LORD said to them, "Son I have given you the oversight and I want you to take it. Daughter to you I have given the insight take it. The oversight belongs to your husband. Take the places I have given you and I will raise you and establish you". It was a powerful word but it carried a big condition: "Take the places I have given you". They were very excited about the word and the promise given, but did not pay attention to the condition attached to it. They continued doing things as they were doing before and expected God to fulfill the promise. Time went by and, of course, God did not release it. Instead doors closed for them. It was not that the prophecy was wrong, not at all, God was waiting for them to do what He required in order to open up the doors to the next level, where He wanted to take them. It is amazing how things like this can cause our promises to remain unfulfilled. Again, it is important to listen to everything God speaks and pay attention to what is required of you. Then be diligent and do it.

ALIGN YOUR LIFE
WITH YOUR PROPHECY

Another important thing is to align your life according to the prophecies given to you. That is a big part of seeing your prophetic offers fulfilled. For instance, if God says that He is calling you to be a pastor, and you say, "Yes" to His offer, then you must align your life accordingly and start making decisions and changes that will get you there. It would be good for you to talk to your leaders, to see how they can help you. Then, you should probably go for some training and equipping, and get involved in whatever ministry can be offered to you in order to start learning. If God says that He is sending you to the nations, then you must prepare for travel and for a life with some level of instability (the kind that comes from moving around as God leads and the inconveniences it entails, etc.). You have to do your part so God can say, "OK he is ready, now I can do the rest and open doors for him". Remember God is looking for stewardship and investment. One thing is for sure, God could have called you to be a pastor, but you are not going to become a pastor, a prophet, a teacher, or a missionary by sitting and watching Oprah on TV. Many people think that it is going to fall from the sky and they will be transformed overnight like Cinderella. You must invest and God will bring dividends your way. It is important to position yourself in the place of availability so when God calls your name, you can say, "Here I am LORD, send me".

I remember when God told me I was going to live in North America and from there I would to go the nations. I was young, but I figured that it was important for me to study like Paul told Timothy. I began to prepare for the work I was called to do. I learned English because I knew that was going to be very necessary and, when the time came, I was ready and could communicate and be active in the plans God opened up for me. Also, in a vision, I saw I was going to marry an English-speaking man, so knowing English became very handy in that area as well.

Some friends received a calling from the LORD to go to Norway as the next step in their journey in three years. They heard the prophecy and said that the LORD had actually been speaking to them about it. They received it with excitement and joy, and responded to the LORD saying, "Yes, we will go". Shortly after, the LORD arranged a contact for them with a church in that country and it looked like things were coming together for when the move came. Time went by and they began to lose sight of the goal, mostly due to circumstances. We watched as the years passed and as time got close they said, "Well we do not think we can go to Norway because we do not have connections, and nothing is lined up, and there is the language, which we do not speak, so we do not see how it can be feasible in the near future".

As we heard this, we realized that they received the prophecy three years before and God really confirmed it. They knew it, but they did not prepare. They did not align their lives accordingly. They did not plan a strategy to be ready when the time came. There were several things they could have done during that time, which would have positioned them in the place of availability for God to open doors for them. For instance, it would have been great for them to learn the language during that time. They could have pursued the connection the LORD gave them in order to develop a relationship with them and, perhaps, could have gone to visit them and their church, which would have helped greatly. Through different circumstances one of them was allowed to work in Europe, which meant that they would not have had a problem establishing themselves in Norway. It would have worked out well if they had been diligent in preparing for it but, unfortunately, when the time came, they were 'lost' in what to do. They had time to prepare but did nothing and, somehow, expected that when the time came God would have everything lined up for them.

We met Ron and Kim Cipcic of Grand River Church in Grand Rapids, Michigan at a Leaders School of Ministry in Toronto and prophesied over them. We gave them a very strong directional prophecy that would change their lives forever. Among many things the LORD told them to plant a church and not wait. Some of the blue prints for their church were also revealed. It was a 'now' word. By the look on their faces they seemed to be taken aback, to say the least. However, they chose to believe God and responded to Him appropriately. They began to seek the LORD for further details. They did not waste any time and soon knew the location where they were to plant the church and began to prepare.

In a few months they moved to that other city and began their church plant with less than a handful of people in their living-room. In no time, they had to move out of their living-room because people kept on coming. Since the beginning, they have had one of the most successful churches we have ever seen, and it continues to prosper. The growth has been phenomenal and they are radical for the LORD and His Kingdom. They are making a huge difference in their city, their region, and further beyond. They are training and equipping people for the work of the Kingdom and God is investing greatly in them. As we see and hear what the LORD is doing, it is clear that the Kingdom of God is advancing. They have been, and are, a great Kingdom investment, which brings great dividends to our Father. How we wish many more people were as courageous as they have been, and would take hold of their destiny, regardless of the risk or circumstances. We constantly hear them say that it is worth it. They are a great inspiration to us and a living example of what we believe and teach.

CREATIVE WORDS

Another thing that confuses a lot of people is when they receive words that do not fit at that time. As said before, there is a wrong belief that prophecy only confirms what God has already spoken and, therefore, we should discard any words that are not confirming, which means that new words and directional words are not from God. This is a lie and the enemy has used it for years to confuse people. Prophecy affirms, confirms, and creates. There is a powerful creative element in the word of God. God is a God of yesterday, today, and tomorrow and, therefore, He is not limited in knowledge and understanding. Thus prophecy speaks of the past, the present, and what is yet to come, the future. We see, throughout Scripture, how the LORD revealed His plans to His people and those who obeyed and followed Him certainly prospered in all their ways

We always pay attention to the new things God speaks, because we know God will create and will transform us in order to bring it about. Future words are also big, sometimes they seem too big to be true, which makes them even more exciting. We love the impossible promises of God and have seen Him do amazing miracles to bring them about. We will actually talk more about this in a later section. However, we must pay attention to the new words that God gives us instead of writing them off, because they do not make sense or don't seem to fit. That is fine, they are not for today. They are for tomorrow and will make sense and fit then. As with all things, we must inquire of the LORD and seek His counsel and wisdom, especially when it comes to new directive words. If we receive a brand new directive word we simply put it on the shelf and talk to the LORD about it. If necessary, we wait for confirmation, knowing that God is always faithful in repeating Himself.

I remember this one time we were in a meeting. I looked at this lady and her husband and immediately I saw them boarding an airplane to go on an overseas mission. I was talking to her later and mentioned it to her. She got really angry and told me clearly that it was not a word from the LORD because God had only called them to minister in Canada and not outside Canada. She then turned her back to me. I did not push and simply walked away. I know I am not infallible so I am open to correction. Two weeks later, she was standing at the front of the church with her husband. She said that, the night before, they received an unexpected call from a prominent leader who asked them to go to a far away country on a mission trip for a few months. They had been chosen for this project because they had expertise in the related field.

She was in tears asking the people to pray for them so God would tell them if they were supposed to go on this trip because they had to give an answer in a couple of days, and they were not expecting this. I thought to myself, "If she had only kept that word I gave her two weeks ago 'on the shelf' now she would have known what to do". God told her ahead of time so she would be prepared when the invitation came and avoid much aggravation and stress. It was a new word but it was from God. They did manage to sort it all out and went on their trip and did what God wanted them to do. Bless them! The thing is that they did not have to pack and go just because of getting that word for the first time, but if they had inquired of the LORD about it, He would have confirmed it clearly. We have seen God do that time and time again.

Once, many years ago, we received a letter from someone with a prophetic word that said, "The LORD says, choose a car, any car you want and I will give it to you as a token of my love for you". We read it and were not impressed because we had a wonderful car we loved, and had just spent a lot of money making it better. We expected it would last us many more years. That word was completely new, did not make sense, and did not fit our plans or thoughts. So we figured that this was just one of those 'flakey' words and literally threw the letter in the garbage can, and forgot about it.

Exactly a month later, I was hit at an intersection by another car that had run the red light. My car was completely totaled and the insurance company gave us only a fraction of the value of the car. So there we were, with no car and no money to buy another one. Suddenly, we remembered the word we threw in the garbage and greatly repented from rejecting it. We asked the LORD to please redeem it from the garbage can. So, armed with the prophetic word, we set off to look for a car. We found one and asked the LORD, "How much do you want to pay?" He gave us an amount that was over two thousand dollars less than the asking price of the car we chose (excluding taxes, and the amount He gave us had to cover the price and the taxes), so we knew that dealing with the sales people would be a challenge. The salesman was very keen on selling us the car, until I told him the amount I wanted to pay taxes included. He laughed and said that it was impossible. I told him to call his boss because I was going to buy it.

The boss came and I gave him my offer. He laughed as well and said that it was impossible for me to buy that car for that money so we began to negotiate. He was adamant that I could never get the car for that price, and I kept insisting that I was only going to pay the amount I had offered. Isabel got tired of the going back and forth and left, but I sat there for over two hours talking with this man. He came down a bit at a time but not close to my offer. He was getting really agitated, but I was very relaxed as I had a prophecy from the LORD saying that He would give us the car we chose. How could he or anyone else fight that? He could argue but not win and I knew that, so I decided that I could sit there all day if needed.

Finally, I think he realized that he was not going to win and he came down to his limit. I said, "No sir, this is the amount I am paying. Not a single penny more". He became very, very angry and turned away. He walked away a few feet and suddenly stopped. At that moment, I saw his shoulder blades flinch back, as if he had been hit on the back. The Holy Spirit got him, I knew it, and so I smiled and waited for him to come back. He did, and as he turned and walked towards me his countenance changed. He had a nice soft smile on his face and said to me, "Congratulations Mr. Allum, you just bought yourself a car. However, I do not want you to ever come back to my lot. I don't want to do business with you ever again".

God was faithful to His word and, of course, He provided for it just like the prophecy said. We have many more stories about how 'new words' have transformed our lives forever. It is exciting to see what God does when we are willing to believe Him for the impossible things of tomorrow.

WORDS OF WARNING

Another thing that people often dismiss is a word of warning. Scripture shows us that God reveals the schemes of the enemy ahead of time so we can spoil them and be one step ahead of the enemy (2 Kings 6:9). He also reveals His plans. He always alerts us before He deals with something in our lives or in our midst. God is faithful and says that He will not do anything without first revealing it to His servants the prophets (Amos 3:7). Many people are afraid of words of warning and take them as 'negative' words. They are not negative, warnings are a good thing. There is nothing worse than being unprepared and taken by surprise. God always reveals the way out and gives strategy for victory, so there is no way of losing when He is on our side. We have many stories to illustrate this, but will share one that shows exactly what not to do.

A few years ago we were ministering at a large gathering of pastors and leaders. We prophesied over one married couple who pastored a nice church, full of vision, and moving into their destiny. We had done a conference in their church the year before and prophesied over the people individually and over the church corporately and they really and truly 'got it' and began to apply themselves to the prophetic words received. Things began to change and the Kingdom began to advance in their midst. It was amazing and we were delighted at seeing a whole church being transformed and entering into their destiny. When we saw them, a year later, they were very excited and had even more vision as God had been doing powerful things in their midst and many prophecies were being fulfilled.

We prophesied over them again and the prophecy said that there was an attack coming against them and the church. A spirit of control and division had been released against them and would attack first the leadership. The purpose of the attack was to divide the leadership and then the church, and by doing that, their destiny would be delayed, if not stolen by the enemy. The prophecy also gave them instructions as to what to do to prepare and overcome, and then it spoke of what God would do with them and through them after the attack. They were grateful for the word and left. Nine months later we were doing a conference somewhere else and they came back to see us. This time the news was not so good. They had just resigned their position in their church and the church had suffered a split. They said that every time we had prophesied over them they would write down the prophecy and start responding, praying, and aligning their lives accordingly.

This last time, however, they were really busy because things were really going well at church and they were moving forward. There was much to be done, so they put the tape in a drawer and decided to write down the prophecy another time. Time went by and they forgot. Later on, when things had blown-up really badly, they remembered that prophecy and remembered that it said something about an attack. They got the tape out and heard everything described in detail. They said that if they had written the prophecy, as they always did, then they would have shared it with their leadership and their intercessors and would have prepared. The devastation caused by that attack was awful, but it could have been avoided because, through prophecy, God revealed the plans of the enemy ahead of time.

God used Jonah to bring a word of warning to a whole nation that was not listening to Him. God, in His mercy, spoke to them and gave them an opportunity to change their ways. They listened, responded well and God spared them. We have seen the effectiveness of words of warning many times in our personal lives, ministry, in our church, and in the lives of many around us. We should not be afraid of them and must understand them for what they are.

THE SOULISH AND
THE SPIRIT REALMS

God is faithful and true and does not lie. However, there are situations that cause much frustration as many people are upset because, they say, "God did not do what He said". There is much confusion in giving and receiving words from the LORD and many people take it lightly. This is a big concern for many pastors and leaders. Here we want to address some of the problems we have seen in this regard.

The first thing we have to know is if it is the LORD speaking. This is pivotal not only when we prophesy but also when we receive prophecies. We need to be able to recognize the voice of the LORD when He speaks directly to us but also through others. This is the most confusing thing for most Christians. Is it the LORD or not? We all go through that but there are ways of clearing this up and moving forward. Scripture says that His sheep hear His voice and follow after Him (John 10:3). Being able to discern His voice in the midst of a million voices will keep us safe from deception, fears, and frustrations.

First, we want to talk about a few of our pet peeves in the prophetic, which contribute to a lot of this confusion. One of them is people who believe that everything is prophetic. This is not true. Not everything is prophetic in life. Sometimes things happen because they happen. Sometimes the bird drops a 'wet gift' on your head, simply because you are standing underneath when he had to go to the bathroom. Sometimes a butterfly flies into the house because the window is open. Yes, there are times when something like that can be a message from the LORD. , but I am talking about people who have no balance and find absolutely everything to be prophetic. Things like these cause people to distrust the prophetic and, honestly, who can blame them? Here is where wisdom and discernment are very important. It is prophetic only if it is spoken by the LORD and produced from heaven. It is pivotal to inquire of the LORD before we make assumptions.

SYMPATHY WORDS
OR WORDS FROM THE HEART

Something else that is a huge problem is prophetic people who think that because they are prophetic everything they think, feel, sense, say, and perceive is prophetic. Good heavens, that is so not true either. No matter how prophetic you may be, you do not live and walk 100% in the spirit. Everyone makes mistakes. I remember one time we attended a prophetic conference and the speaker, a well known prophetic voice made a comment from the pulpit. The person sitting next to me said to me, "Do you think that that statement was prophetic or just a comment from him?" At that moment the speaker's wife who heard the question interrupted us and said, "Oh no, everything he (her husband) does, says, thinks, feels, smells, tastes, senses, etc., etc. is prophetic. He is 100% prophetic and so is everything in his life, you can be sure of that. We were really taken aback by that statement as only Jesus was and is infallible and perfect in hearing everything from the Father, and doing only what He saw the Father do. We are all learning to be more like Him but the reality is that no one is there yet. Pride causes people to believe that about themselves, and that leads to deception and control.

We also get very worried about people who claim that the LORD tells them absolutely everything they do and say. Most of the time, we find that people who believe this have issues with accountability, pride, and are not teachable. Many times these are people who have had issues of rejection and relationship issues, and find that if they attach the phrase, "The LORD told me", people have to hear them and accept what they say. Somehow this gives them endorsement, and identity. Also, this keeps them from responsibility, as they blame God for all they do. It does not work that way. God constantly gets blamed for countless things He never said or did.

We know God is a father not a dictator. He created us in His own image and has given us brains, will, emotions, wisdom, understanding, personalities, and allows us to make choices. He gives us freedom. Yes, He wants to be involved in our lives and participate in everything we do, but as a father. We see that with our own children. At the beginning we tell them everything they have to do and say, and lead them very closely. We teach them our ways and put them into their hearts and minds but, as they grow up, we allow them to make choices and have initiative, yet we remain close in order to help them, protect them, guide them, and give them advice if they allow us to be part of their lives and choices. As parents, we trust that we have taught them well and that they will follow in our ways and teachings. Scripture says, "Train up a child in the way he should go, even when he is old he will not depart from it" Proverbs 22:6. We know well what happens if we are controlling. Nothing brings more destruction to a family than controlling and manipulative parents. God is not that way. He is a perfect father. He wants to help us and show us the best way of doing things. His love endures forever and, no matter what happens, He will never leave us nor depart from us. He is always willing to speak, to help, and to intervene on our behalf, but He also wants to see us grow and become all He created us to be. His Spirit will always help us and lead us to all truth, but out of love not control.

A big problem of the prophetic is people who lack maturity and teaching and, therefore, are not able to separate their own opinions and perceptions from the voice of the LORD. That is a key to accessing the release from heaven. I remember once, a long time ago, a ministry contacted us for prophetic advice on a big purchase they were going to make. I read the message they sent describing the situation and, immediately, I felt good about it. I waited a day or so before answering them but every time I prayed I felt good about it. So I went to send the answer to them, which was going to be, "Go ahead and do it. It feels good. It is good". Just as I went to do it, the Holy Spirit said to me, "How about you take a minute and ask the LORD about the answer you are going to send?" I was really surprised to hear that, but did it. I asked the LORD and immediately a vision opened up in front of me. I saw three things that were hidden from them, which were very wrong. I was shocked and said to the LORD, "Do you mean to say that I was wrong?"

He replied, "Yes. You made an assumption, based on what you felt, and thought that it was good, but did not inquire of Me. It was good with your spirit, but it was not good with Mine. Even when you prayed, you had already made up your mind about the answer and, therefore, you were not open and objective to My answer." Ouch! I was speechless and learned a huge lesson. There is a big difference between my personal perception and the word of the LORD. We must set aside our ways, opinions, and perceptions, and become completely objective to what the LORD has to say. The problem is that since we learned that it is easy to prophesy and that we can all do it on different levels, there has been lightness in the minds of many and the word prophecy, or prophetic, is lightly attached to anything. People have forgotten the importance of inquiring of the LORD for everything, especially before giving a prophetic word. Inquiring of the LORD has never gone out of style. There is one thing that we both are very aware of as we prophesy. We prophesy over thousands of people each year all over the world and, every time we prophesy, we know as we live and breathe, that we have to give account to the LORD for every careless word that comes out of our mouths (Matthew 12:36). We do not take it lightly as we know the great responsibility of speaking on the LORD's behalf.

We have also found that there are more 'sympathy' words given in the church as prophetic words, than true words from the LORD. This is sad, as God does not fulfill those words, because they are not His. They come from the hearts and emotions of men but not from the heart of God. Sympathy words are so common because people's emotions and hearts get deeply moved by situations and desires, and they do not take the time to consider that it may not be God speaking. That is why it is so very important to work closely with the LORD, so we can learn to understand and separate what comes from Him and what comes from us. Many mistakes in the prophetic are made because of this, which have caused great confusion, disappointment, and frustration in many, including pastors and leaders.

For example, a lot of these sympathy words are given regarding health issues. It is very common for prophetic people to give words of healing and life that are not coming from the LORD. People are moved by their emotions as they are praying and, knowing that God heals and that He is healing, they go ahead and prophesy that the person will be healed and/or live. Then the person dies and everyone gets angry with God because He did not heal the person as He said. Their pain doubles now as they are not only dealing with the grief caused by the death but also with the disappointment and betrayal they feel from God.

Yes, we pray for healing and always will because we know God heals. Of course we do, but we are slow to prophesy healing out of assumption. We only do it when we know, beyond a shadow of a doubt, that the Father has spoken it. One of the greatest mysteries in our time is, "Why is it that God does not heal everyone?" That is a question that only God can answer. Many have tried but no one has been able to give the absolute answer. Maybe there isn't one, as God deals with each case individually. We do know that He heals and have seen Him heal many, as well as ourselves, so we will continue praying and believing, but when we prophesy we do not assume anything. We inquire of the LORD for every little detail and only say what we truly believe the Father is saying.

We have seen these 'words from the heart' given for all kinds of situations; like people going into business, relationships, finances, trips, ministry, marriage, buildings, babies, etc. It is scary and happens everywhere constantly. Once we were in a large conference ministering to pastors and leaders of a large organization. During our time with them an announcement was made that a property they owned had to be sold. They were sad to hear the news and decided to pray together about it as they did not want to lose this property. As we heard the prayers we realized, very quickly, that their emotions were being stirred and we knew that any minute a sympathy word would be given. Sure enough, in a few minutes the first person 'prophesied'. The prophecy given said to hold onto the property and the vision that they had, because the enemy wanted to steal it from them, but God said that He was going to let them keep it, and not to be discouraged because victory was at hand, and so on. Immediately, a second prophecy was given along the same lines, and then the third one. They were all very excited. We were standing at the back as this was going on and separately both of us inquired of the LORD about the situation and He told us both, "They are going to have to sell the property and will lose a lot of money in the process because I never told them to buy it to begin with. I was never in on this". Sure enough, a few months later, they sold the property and lost a lot of money, just as the LORD had told us.

Again, people asked, "What happened to those prophecies spoken that night and other occasions when people gathered to talk and pray about it?" The answer is simple; those words did not come from the LORD but from the hearts of the people. They were so moved and overwhelmed by their emotions and/or desires and could not be objective enough to separate themselves from the voice of the LORD. It is important to understand that, in most of these situations, the hearts of the people giving those words are in the right place, they just do not know the difference. Yes, there are also times when people, who have issues of control and manipulation, will use prophecy to get their way and push their agenda. That is why we need to know the voice of our LORD clearly.

Another time a friend of ours was going to do a business deal and gathered with his friends. They were moved in their hearts and really wanted him to do well and succeed, and soon the prophecies came saying to go ahead because God was going to bless him. We heard these words and knew immediately that they were not from the LORD. We had inquired of the LORD with a completely objective heart, not letting our emotions influence us, and heard the LORD say otherwise. This fellow decided to go ahead with it because of the encouraging words he received but things did not turn out as expected because God was not the source of those words. They came from the hearts of well-intentioned people who loved him, but who lacked the maturity in the prophetic to discern properly.

Once, a long time ago, we were in a church where the leaders really wanted a particular ministry to join them. They had been praying about it and finally that man contacted them saying that he was seriously considering moving to that city and joining their church. We attended some of the meetings with the leaders and, as they prayed together about it, people began to give prophetic words about how God was bringing this man to them and the things that would happen when this man came. I inquired of the LORD and He said, "No, I am not bringing him here. He is going to move but I am taking him to this other part of the country," and He gave me the name of the city where he would go. I shared this with the leaders but they did not receive it well because it was against what they wanted and what they believed God was telling them.

The next day, one of the pastors came and shared a dream she had the night before confirming that this man was coming to join their team and the things God was going to do. I knew that it was a dream from the heart, but they could not hear it so I did not say anything else, as we never push any words we give. We have also learned that sometimes speaking God's word will not make us popular, especially when it is against what others are saying and what they desire in their hearts to do. However, we are not interested in tickling people's ears and will not give words so people will like us. No matter what happens, our responsibility is to honour the Father and be true to what He says.

About three months later, the pastors contacted us and said that they had just heard from that man who was supposed to come, and he said that even though he originally was planning to come to them, the LORD had spoken to him very clearly and told him to move to another part of the country and to a particular city, which happened to be the place I had told the leaders three months before. This man did not know the word I had given the leaders stating the direction where God would be taking him. The pastors told him afterwards and he was very encouraged. He and his family moved there shortly after.

We have learned that there is wisdom in being slower to speak and in standing in the counsel of the LORD, inquiring of Him for everything, never trusting in our own understanding. We know how easy it is to make mistakes and how dangerous that can be. We are very concerned with prophetic people who always have something to say. We want to clarify that we do believe that God can speak constantly about any and every thing and that the closer we are to Him the more tuned we become to His voice and can hear Him more and more, as there is no limit on how much one can prophesy. However, when we see people who rush to put their word in, every single time and are not willing to wait and let others do it, we get concerned, because many times they do it to show off and if that is the case, then it is very easy to speak out of the soul and not the Spirit.

THE SOUL AND THE SPIRIT

To avoid this, we need to understand how our soul works and how our emotions influence us. Understanding this will make a big difference in discerning the source speaking to us. It is very easy to discern the voice of the accuser, just by the fruit of it, which is discouragement, fear, insecurity, death, etc., and it pushes us away from God. The problem is discerning the voice of God and the voice of our soul. Our soul usually talks to us about our own desires, tells us what we want to hear, and makes us feel good. That is why it is hard to discern between these two. We are going to share some of the keys we have learned through the years in this area. These keys can be applied when we prophesy and also when we receive prophecy. We need to be wise when we receive prophecy because sometimes the person giving the word may not even realize that they are tapping into the soulish realm (being influenced by their emotions, their heart, opinions, perception, and/or knowledge) as they speak.

It is important to know that prophecy is never endorsed by the styles, attitudes, behaviours, or manifestations of the person prophesying. Once we had a situation when someone wanted something particular done in the church, which was not according to the vision of the church, and would have caused a big detour and many problems. As a leadership, we had been praying about the situation and the LORD clearly spoke to all of us and gave us the opposite direction. One night, we had a meeting and someone came to us before the meeting and gave us a prophetic word that, in essence, said that God wanted us to do the particular thing she wanted done. We thanked her for sharing but told her that we had been praying and the LORD had spoken to every one of us, individually, saying to do exactly the opposite. She did not say anything but later in the meeting she began to manifest very strongly (shaking and bending over) and proceeded to prophesy the very same word that she had given us before the meeting. One of the leaders went over and very gently told her again what we had told her earlier, and that we believed that her word was from her heart and not from the LORD. She became very upset because she delivered the word while manifesting and said that because of that we had to accept it as a word from the LORD. Then a group of people, who saw her manifesting, said that they believed the LORD had surely spoken because she was shaking when she gave the word. We tried to make them understand that the fact that she was shaking did not mean that the word was from the LORD. We told them that we knew the word was not from the LORD and why, but they were completely stuck on the manifestation and could not hear what we were saying. This started a wave that eventually led to a church split.

Another time, we had a situation with a group of intercessors and, while manifesting, this lady prophesied that God wanted us to do something that was completely against Scripture. We confronted the situation and stopped what was going on, but this lady prophesied a second time while manifesting and shaking even harder, and emphasized the word she had delivered before. We again said, "No, because it is contrary to Scripture and harmful to others." She got really upset and stormed out of the room saying that we had to believe because she was manifesting 'under the spirit' when she 'prophesied'. The group of intercessors was shaken because most of them had believed what she had said because of the manifestations. We then proceeded to explain to them that manifestations do not endorse prophecy as a definite word from the LORD, and that we have to test all words regardless of how they are delivered. They were so caught on the manifestation that they missed the fact that the word being given was unscriptural. Lately we are finding this more and more. People do not know Scripture and, therefore, believe all sorts of things that are not from God, whether they are said in a sermon or in a prophetic word.

A while ago, this lady from our church came to us and said that she was at a big conference where someone with a major international ministry had taught a particular thing and our friend wanted our church to do what was taught because, at the conference, they said that God's great blessing would be released on any church that would do it. I heard that and immediately said, "Well, that teaching sounds good and I can see how many would like it, but it is not scriptural and, therefore, we cannot accept it." She was shocked and said, "But so-and-so said it. How can you say it is wrong?" We do not care who says what. What we care about and always want is to make sure that what we hear, learn, and teach is scriptural. We always tell the people in our church to make sure that they do not believe everything we say just because it is us. We want them to study the word so they can challenge us or anyone else who is teaching them, if they feel that what they are hearing is not correct, like the Bereans who went home and researched everything that Paul taught them, to make sure it was correct (Acts 17:11 NIV).

Fill yourself with the Spirit and the Word. These two are pivotal in knowing and discerning the voice of God. Scripture tells us that the Holy Spirit leads us to all truth and walking in close fellowship with the Him will keep us in the truth and away from confusion and deception. We must know the Word of God well and have it running through us constantly, as this is another way of discerning His voice when we prophesy and when we receive prophecy. A rule-of-thumb is that prophecy never, ever, contradicts the word of God no matter how anointed the word is, or what manifestations take place. It is amazing how many people do not read the Bible and yet they want to be used by the LORD. It is dangerous to want to minister if you are not filling yourself with the Word of God. It is scary to receive prophetic words if you are not studying the word of God. Remember that God's word is a light unto our feet. (Psalm 119:105). Paul told Timothy, "Be diligent to present yourself approved to God as a work-man who does not need to be ashamed, accurately handling the word of truth" (2 Tim. 2:15).

This is pivotal for anyone who wants to work with the Holy Spirit building the Father's Kingdom on earth. The Word of God has some-thing we call 'pulse'. Remember IT IS ALIVE. The pulse of Scripture resonates in our spirits and, once we learn to feel it, we can hear and feel it when people preach, teach, share, and prophesy. The Word of God is the same and carries the same pulse, whether it is written or spoken. In time, when you hear someone speak, you will hear the pulse of God's Word in your spirit and will know it is God who is speaking. It is really amazing!! When you combine the Spirit and the Word of God you have dynamite inside and that is a combination that will explode. They are both weapons to fight the good fight and will get us safely to the end of the race. They are here to help us. They are for us, not against us. The greatest thing is that they will keep us on the straight and narrow path, free from deception.

We know a man who fell in love with a woman who was not a believer and had a challenging medical condition. He really wanted to date her and so one day he came and said that the LORD told him that He (God) wanted him to date this unbeliever and that, as a result, this woman would get saved and would also be healed from her condition. He said that God told him that this was the woman he was going to marry. We said to him that according to Scripture we could not agree with that statement because the Bible is clear about unequal yokes and I know, for a fact, that God does not contradict Scripture. He became very angry and said, "How dare you insinuate that I did not hear from God?" He went on to date this woman and things did not go as he expected. The relationship ended but, again, he came and said that the LORD told him not to give up but to continue loving this woman because she was the one he was going to marry and soon she would also be healed. Again we told him that we did not believe it was the LORD speaking to him but his own soul (heart). Once again, he was angry and carried on with some sort of relationship with her, while waiting for God to fulfill His promise. However, she died unexpectedly and then his questions began.

The first thing was anger towards God because He did not do what He had promised. This man had invested many years of his life in this relationship because he had a promise from God, and now God had betrayed him. It was devastating. He was angry, left the church, became bitter, and went into depression. People tried to tell him that he had made a mistake and it was not God who had spoken to him, but, perhaps out of pride, he could not admit that he had not heard God. This is sadly a good example of someone who acted in the soulish realm and tried to satisfy the soul, instead of focusing on the voice of the Spirit.

We must first learn to know ourselves. How do we react to situations? How do our emotions work? Are we people who are moved by our emotions or are we able to understand how our soul works? Many people are so used to satisfying their soul, and investing in keeping it happy, that they miss what the spirit is saying. King David discovered this and learned how to deal with his soul. He was able to discern when the soul was stirring and would talk to it commanding it to, "Trust and bless the LORD" (Psalm 42:11, Psalm 103). David did not try to satisfy his soul that was in turmoil, but took charge of it by staying focused on the spirit. The spirit is always willing and ready to please the LORD but in the world we learn to satisfy the soul. The soul is truly fickle and very demanding. It wants satisfaction quickly and pushes until it gets it. That is why people are in such a mess. They have learned to do whatever it takes to satisfy their soul, but the problem is that the soul is never satisfied. The moment it gets one thing, something else arises and we can spend our whole lives catering to it. King David learned to listen to the spirit, discerned the difference between the two, and made choices accordingly. The soul is self serving, but the spirit is God serving. There is a great conflict between the soul and the spirit and we must learn to separate them by teaching the soul to follow the leading of the spirit.

I remember once, a long time ago we were going through a difficult situation and the fire was very hot. It was so strong that, at times, it felt that we could not survive it. One day, I was in the backyard working on a project when I felt the presence of the LORD and my spirit arose and spoke to Him. Suddenly, without thinking, I heard myself say, "LORD, please do not stop this trial until you are finished, and this jewel is in the crown. Please do not cut it short but let it continue until the end, until you are satisfied". I heard that and my soul reacted and shouted inside of me, "Are you crazy? How can you say that? Don't you know how much pain this is going to cause me? I do not want this. I do not want more pain. Make it stop." It was fascinating for me to hear the exchange between the spirit and the soul, but I knew that my spirit was responding to the LORD and, therefore, knew something that my soul did not know, so it was up to me to make the choice and I decided to follow the spirit instead of satisfying my soul. I stood up and said, "No, I want this. I agree with my spirit. It may not be good for my soul but it is good for my spirit and it is good for my God". Then I said out loud, "LORD, I agree. Please do not stop this trial and this fire until you are finished, and the jewel is in the crown". At that moment the Holy Spirit came and gave peace to my soul.

You see, we must teach our soul (mind, will, and emotions) to submit to the spirit; otherwise our lives would be a roller-coaster. We have been Christian counselors for over twenty years and, many times, when we are helping people, I ask them, "What would it take for things to change?" And, usually, the answer tells me that they are listening to the demands of the soul and not the spirit, and that is the filter they have when ministering but also when receiving ministry. This is very dangerous in the area of prophecy and that is why it is so important to receive inner healing, on and off, throughout life. We have never known of anyone who is completely healed and the reason is because we get new wounds along the way, all the time, and need to keep our hearts right.

SECTION NINE

UNDERSTANDING DREAMS

God also speaks to us through dreams. The Bible is filled with examples of how God spoke to Kings, Pharaoh, Joseph, Daniel, Joseph the husband of Mary, and many others. He has continued talking to His people in that manner through the ages. We both have had many dreams from God that have changed and defined our lives and we are great believers in this powerful revelatory anointing. However, there is a great misunderstanding in the area of discerning and interpreting dreams, which has led many to great disillusionment and frustration. We often hear people say, "The LORD told me this or showed me that in a dream", but many times it was not God who spoke through those dreams, and we know for a fact that God does not fulfill dreams that do not come from Him.

We have heard people say that all dreams are from God. That is not true. There are three sources of dreams: God, the devil, and ourselves. The majority of our dreams occur during REM (Rapid Eye Movement) sleep. This is a physiological function that happens during the night and is very important because without it people die. In simple terms this is what REM is: In our computers we have something called the hard drive in which we store all the information we want to retain. However, there is only so much room in the hard drive and every so often we have to clear some clutter, by deleting some unnecessary files, otherwise the hard drive would crash. The same thing happens with our brain. Our brain stores everything we do, see, sense, smell, experience, etc., in 'files' like the computer's hard drive and during REM sleep it de-clutters by getting rid of some of those unnecessary files.

91

Some of these dreams may be stored memories or events; others are just bits and pieces of different things that don't make sense. Have you ever had dreams that are completely 'crazy' and do not make sense? In those dreams different things mix together. They jump from one thing to another, and you see places and people you do not know. All those things are actually stored in your brain. Those faces and people you see are people you have seen at different times on the street, on TV, magazines, newspapers, stores, etc., etc. Every single thing we see gets recorded in our brain and stored away. Our brain has a powerful archiving ability and much space, however, it gets full and when that happens our psyche gets rid of them, it throws them out, thus those weird random dreams.

During REM sleep you may also dream of events you have lived or seen in the past or that day, which are also stored in the brain. Sometimes, out of the blue, you dream of something that happened many years ago and you had not thought of for ages. Suddenly, they are in your dreams. You may dream of things you heard as that is also stored there. You see, REM is very powerful and interesting, but it is a completely physiological process, which means that those dreams are not from God. It really is fascinating to see how our body works. What complexity and perfection! Only God could create something that powerful. Therefore understanding REM sleep is very important because God does not speak during REM. Dreams from God happen before, or after, REM sleep, so do not waste time trying to understand or interpret them. These dreams mean nothing. Many times I wake up remembering lots of dreams but I just know that there is nothing behind them. There is no substance from the soul or the spirit. They do not awaken anything in me so, by now, I know that those are REM. Most of our dreams actually are this kind, so when we wake up in the morning we need to pay attention to what kind of dream it was and just let these ones go instead of trying to spiritualize them.

DREAMS FROM THE HEART

Then there are the dreams of the soul or of the heart as some call them. This is when we dream of matters that are concerning us, that are relevant to our current life and circumstances. This is common and these dreams are not from God either. Very often the desires of our hearts come up in our dreams. Regularly people go to bed and dream about the things they were talking about that night. I remember this situation that came up in a particular church we were helping. A lady in the church was accusing her husband of flirting with other women, but no one else in the church had noticed anything unusual about this man. The wife was getting really out of sorts and decided to have a talk with her pastors. They had a meeting about it in the early evening, then when the pastors got home they talked some more about their meeting with that lady and reviewed the issue. That night the pastor had a dream that this man was flirting with his wife, and he took it as the LORD confirming to them that what that woman was saying was true. They were going to act on it but decided to talk to us about it first.

As I heard the story I told them that, in a situation like that, they should not take his dream as a word from the LORD. The pastor became bothered and said that the LORD usually speaks to him in dreams and, therefore, they were taking it as true. I said that I did not doubt that God speaks to him through dreams, but that they had to consider the fact that they had spent a lot of time that night talking about it, and that it was heavy in his mind when he went to sleep. Therefore, they should take that dream with a grain of salt because it could have been influenced by his subconscious. He did not like it but, decided to wait and ask the LORD for more clarity. Soon after, it became clear that the accusations against that man were unfounded.

We also must remember that our morality and principles do not shut off when we sleep and, many times, in dreams they talk to us about things we need to deal with. One time this lady came to me with a strong dream she had about her and this other lady. In the dream they were fighting and not talking to each other and things were getting very difficult, but there was a great urgency in the dream for her to make things right. She told me that she had had this powerful dream from the LORD and that she knew the interpretation but she wanted to hear what I had to say. I knew exactly where the dream was coming from. She and that particular lady in the church had had a fight and were not talking to each other. This had gone on for a bit and people kept telling her that she had to deal with it but she did not want to and was bothered by that. Her subconscious brought it to her attention in the dream and was telling her, "You have to settle this". Then she said, "I knew that you are going to think that, but it is not. It is a spiritual dream about two churches that are going to have a fight." Things continued the same way and eventually she came to accept it, and settled things with her friend.

These dreams are very important, as they show us the things that are in our hearts, which sometimes we do not see or are not willing to acknowledge. They also show us what is important. These dreams are not from God, but they can be stirred by the LORD. The Holy Spirit comes and awakens areas of our heart and soul that are important and our subconscious talks to us as we sleep. These are the second most common dreams we have. These dreams are easy to understand. We do it through symbolism. This is very important and is actually called dream analysis. This is actually a common practice in psychotherapy. That is actually where it comes from. Dream interpretation, as we know from the Bible, is different and cannot be done through symbolism. It is done through revelation. We will talk more about it a bit later. In dream analysis you use symbols to understand the meaning of the dream, and usually the meaning of the symbols is found within the dreamer. It is very personal and different for each person. Here is an example:

A lady had a dream of a cow running away from her house. She was doing all she could to catch her but the cow was slippery and got away at the end.

Question: What does a cow mean to you?
Answer: Provision. When I think of a cow I think of provision.
Question: The cow was in your house, what does that mean to you?
Answer: Provision for our family.
           (Interesting: A cow for me means something else, but since she was the one who had the dream, her meaning is what counts)
Question: Since the cow was running away from your house, are you concerned about provision?
Answer: Yes, my husband may lose his job in a few weeks.
Question: How are you feeling about it?
Answer: I am trying to find a way for him to keep it but it feels that no matter what I think of nothing will work.

Meaning of the dream: As you said, you are very concerned trying to find a way for your husband to keep his job but deep inside you know that he is going to lose it and you just have to accept and let it go. Now, let's pray through this, so the LORD can help you deal with it.

This is an example of a dream interpreted through symbolism. As we can see, it is not a spiritual dream. It came from her heart. In a case like this, once we know what the situation is, we can help the person deal with it. The important thing is not to make a formula about the meaning of symbolism. That does not work. Remember that we are all different and things mean something else to each person. For instance, we love dogs, so, if I see a dog in a dream, to me that represents something wonderful but, if you were bitten by a dog when you were a child and have fear of dogs, then a dog in your dream may represent something bad.

Once upon a time, someone at church tried to interpret a dream I had in which I saw seagulls. The lady hearing my dream immediately said, "Oh, seagulls are wonderful, free, and fly. Birds represent angels and these seagulls represent angels coming". I shook my head in disagreement because I greatly dislike seagulls and there is no way that they would represent angels to me. I have seen many people trying to interpret dreams for others, using formulas like this, and the answers they have given are not at all what those symbols mean.

A friend of mine went to a particular church where there was a team interpreting dreams. She told them her dream which was about her estranged husband. The people in the team said to her, "Oh, a husband represents Jesus, therefore, that dream is about Jesus coming and doing this and that for you". She did not feel right about it. She shared her experience with us. We knew her situation with her husband and, therefore, we fully understood what her dream meant. It had nothing to do with Jesus. It literally had to do with something her husband was doing to control her. This was a dream from her heart, which could have been interpreted through symbolism, but they used a formula to do it and it did not work.

Another friend also went to one of these events and, upon sharing her dream with them, they gave her an interpretation based on symbolism, which did not sit right with her. When she told us the dream, immediately the Holy Spirit gave me revelation of what it meant and I gave her the interpretation. This was not a dream from the heart but from God and dreams from God cannot be interpreted through symbolism. They are interpreted through revelation. Hearing the meaning of her dream led to big changes in her marriage.

Dreams that can be interpreted through symbolism are not prophetic dreams. We know a lot about dream analysis because we have two friends who are psychotherapists and specialize in dream interpretation. Through the years we have shared about this subject, and have heard them analyze many dreams. Other things that come from psychotherapy are numerology and colors (New Age use these a lot too). We often hear people at church saying that the number five means this, therefore, this is the meaning of your dream or vision, or yellow means that, therefore, your dream means that. Again, a formula made by someone, but not a 'one-size-fits-all-rule'. Something that puzzles us a lot is hearing people at church use this to interpret dreams from God. The Bible does not talk about it.

Again, formulas are dangerous. We have a friend who says that, for him, vehicles mean ministries so, every time he heard someone say that they had a dream in which there was a vehicle, he would interpret the whole thing as a dream regarding ministry. Something that I found very interesting was that these same psychotherapist friends told me many times, "We cannot understand what is happening but your dreams are the only ones we cannot interpret". That was correct because those were dreams from God and they could not be interpreted through human reason and symbolism. We must keep in mind Joseph's words when he said, "Do not interpretations belong to God?" (Genesis 40:8) ("Interpreting dreams is God's business". NLT).

DREAMS FROM GOD

Dreams from God, or prophetic dreams are wonderful but actually less frequent than people want to think. God does speak through dreams, but once we learn to discern dreams correctly we find that a lot of the so-called dreams from God are not from Him. How do we recognize these dreams? We do it in the same way we learn to discern His voice. This is simply another way of hearing God's voice. This is a revelatory anointing and, therefore, it carries the pulse of His word and His presence. Remember God's word is alive and beats within us. It also releases the fruit of the Holy Spirit. A rule of thumb is that if you can interpret the dream through symbolism, then it is not a dream from God. Yes, there is symbolism in God's dreams but they are understood through revelation. In dreams from the heart, the dream is interpreted through symbolism, but in dreams from God it is through revelation that we understand the dream and its symbolism. There is no formula for this. The only thing that works is inquiring of the LORD and asking Him for an impartation of the Spirit of revelation. Interpreting dreams (parables/riddles from God) is a spiritual gift and comes from God. It is amazing when a person with the gift of interpretation gives the meaning of a dream from God. We have also noticed that those who receive this gift have a stronger discernment to know if the dream they are hearing is from the heart or from God.

When you interpret a dream through the spirit of revelation, you do not ask the person what it means to them, and do not focus on the symbolism. You inquire of the LORD and He reveals the meaning to you. He may give you the interpretation as whole or may tell you what the symbolism means. The understanding comes from the Holy Spirit through revelation, just like prophecy, tongues, words of knowledge, etc. We have some friends who are pressing in for dream interpretation. One day, they were visiting with us and I shared a dream I had had the night before. It was a dream from God and I knew what it meant. I shared the dream with them and Ivan and asked them to give me interpretation. My friend heard it, thought for a few minutes and then said, "Is there somewhere in your life that you feel like this or that and..." I stopped her and said, "No dear, I do not want you to analyze my dream. I want you to interpret it." When I heard her question I knew that she was going in a completely different direction, because she was looking at the symbolism to understand the dream, but that was a dream from God and by analyzing it that way, she would have given me a different meaning than what God was saying. I then turned to Ivan and he said, "This is what the LORD is saying to you....", and he gave me the exact meaning the LORD had given me, word for word, which has now come to pass. The difference here was simple. While my friend looked at the symbolism, Ivan inquired of the LORD for revelation.

Imagine what would have happened if Joseph would have looked at the symbolism to interpret the dreams of the cup bearer and the baker. A psychotherapist would have given a completely different interpretation than Joseph gave. I am always fascinated with Nebuchadnezzar's dream. He wanted to know its meaning but did not want to tell the dream. His magicians, conjurers, and sorcerers kept asking him to tell them the dream because they needed to hear the symbolism in order to give an interpretation, but Daniel proved that, to interpret a dream from God, he did not even need to hear it because he went to the source of the dream. He inquired of the LORD. Nebuchadnezzar's dream was filled with symbolism but Daniel did not approach it by saying, what does a statute mean? What does a head of gold represent? How about thighs of bronze? What are thighs for and what would they represent? No. He inquired of the LORD who gave him the interpretation and explained what everything meant. Again, through revelation all the symbolism was understood.

Interpreting dreams from God is not something we can teach people to do in workshops. We can teach people to analyze or understand dreams of the heart and that is good, because many of our dreams are from the heart, and we need to understand them. However, these are not the people or the method to interpret dreams from God. Those dreams should be left to people who have the gift of interpretation of dreams like Joseph and Daniel. We know that there are many people who have a calling in this area, and, as we prophesy, we hear the LORD offer this to many. However, there is a cost to it. You must invest into inquiring of the LORD on a regular basis and press in for the Spirit of revelation, wisdom, and of the knowledge of God. Practice and you will see the evidence, people will tell you, "Yes it is right". In time, you will see the dreams come to pass and this evidence will give you confidence to continue. Remember at the beginning you will hit and miss, on and off, but that is normal in all situations.

DREAMS FROM THE DEVIL

These dreams are not so difficult to identify because they carry the character of the devil and leave his fruit behind. We wake up from these dreams with fear and confusion. There is death in them. For many years I was tormented with these kinds of dreams, to the point that I did not want to go to sleep. I received prayer for them and asked the Holy Spirit to watch over my dreams. Then I slept with worship music in the room or listening to the word of God and it changed.

Once I heard someone say that you can identify dreams from the devil because they are in black and white and dreams from God are in color. That unfortunately is not correct. I and others I know have had very colorful dreams from the devil. Again, we cannot make up formulas based on a personal experience.

SECTION TEN

MINDSETS, THE ACCUSER, AND THE COMFORTER

Mindsets are very powerful and deeply influence our ways. They determine what we believe and our reactions in life. They are strong-holds in our lives and can be positive or negative. Most of our mind-sets come from our experiences and our imprinting as we grow up. If we have a mindset of success, everything we do will carry that tone and success will come our way. The same thing will happen if we carry a mindset of failure, negativity, etc. A mindset of unbelief will also taint all we do, so, no matter what God says, it goes through that grid of unbelief and will keep us going through the wilderness in circles. This is a common occurrence when we receive prophecies and it hinders the releasing of our prophetic destiny.

We must be attentive to what the Spirit is saying. What normally hap-pens, when we receive prophetic words from the Father, is that we listen through our grid and hear what we or what the enemy wants us to hear. This is our filter. We have found that when people receive prophecies they focus only on part of what they hear and not on what God is saying. As with all things, it is so easy to take things out of context and misinterpret what God is saying.

I remember once, after a meeting, the pastor of the church where we were ministering told me that there was a problem. A lady complained to him about the prophecy I gave her that night. She was in tears and said that I had told her that she was angry, bitter, and hopeless. She said that the prophecy I gave her was almost abusive and she was deeply hurt. I was very surprised hearing this as I have never given words like that to anyone. I said that to the pastor and asked him to

101

tell the lady to come the next day with her tape. I wanted to listen to the tape together and, by all means, I was more than willing to repent if I had hurt her in any way. The next day this lady came early to meet us. She said that she was very upset when she left the meeting the night before, but, decided to listen to the tape on her way home. She was completely amazed as she listened to it the second time because what she heard was completely different to what she 'heard' when I prophesied over her. This time as she listened to the tape, she realized that there was no criticism, negativity, or accusations on it. She said that all she could hear were words of life, love, hope, and encouragement. She was shocked and could not understand what had happened the night before.

It was clear that she had a strong mindset of rejection, accusation, and criticism which turned everything she heard into something negative. This was her grid. The unfortunate part is that this filter was always active and it manifested in all things in her life, causing her to live in this cave of rejection, hurt, and frustration. I was most grateful that we record all prophecies, as otherwise she would have not been able to hear what the LORD really said and would have continued believing that what she heard the night before was real, and this would have caused her to believe that God had also rejected her and that there was no hope for her. This was the enemy's greatest strategy. He had caused her to believe that the whole world had rejected her and she was in great bondage. The only hope of love and acceptance she had was God, and now the enemy was trying to steal and kill her last hope, by twisting the words of the prophecy and making her believe that even God saw her in the same way. This would have brought ultimate destruction to her as her only hope would have been taken away. We see this often and, as we teach people, God uncovers the plans of the enemy and the mindset that strengthens it, so healing can come to their hearts setting them free, and restoring all that the locusts have eaten in their lives.

This is common with people who are not able to discern the voice of the accuser and the voice of the comforter. The devourer comes to kill, steal, and destroy and he is doing that by deceiving God's children into hearing him and believing what he says. He has many convinced that his voice is the voice of the LORD. The main reason he gets away with it is because we are predisposed to negativity, criticism, and discouragement. That is what we are used to hearing in the world. We are familiar with the voice of the accuser, as that was the only voice most of us ever heard before meeting Jesus. It is familiar but, more than that, it is imprinted within us and that is what we expect to hear. It is subconscious and at the emotional level of our lives.

LIVING UNDER THE SHADOW OF THE ACCUSER

I was eight years old when I was taken to the hospital for what I was told was a routine checkup, only to find out I would have to stay for a few days, or so I thought. The days turned into weeks and the weeks into months. We lived out in the country, an hour away by car. Mom didn't drive at the time, my dad had a full time job at a factory, and I was the third of six kids in our family. Visits from my parents were sparse and I found myself looking for love from anyone.

I remember having to go in for major surgery on my left lung and, unknowingly, watching the nurses draw straws to do a task none of them wanted to do. I soon realized I was that task, and was told I had to go in for an operation right away. I was devastated and quite fearful hearing such news from someone other than my parents, especially people I didn't even know, while wondering in my heart where could my parents be at a time like this? I was already filled with great fear and abandonment and this only heightened the negativity in my heart. I carried this abandonment and an orphan spirit for many years to come.

I was quite dyslexic. The doctors and teachers said I would never accomplish anything in life and expectations should not be put on me. I went to school for ten years and only moved to the next grade because I was getting older. Many times while growing up I would tell people what I dreamed of doing when I got older only to be discouraged and disappointed when I found out it would not be possible. They said that none of those things would ever be possible for me. I was an under achiever in every area of my life. I was quite emotionally disabled and expected to fail. Physically I was uncoordinated and weak.

As I got older, I began to look for comfort and love wherever I could find it. I grew very distant from my family and felt very alone and misunderstood by the world. I was hurting and looking to be loved.

Day after day, I would go to school wondering what life would hold for an inadequate young man, full of rejection, like me. For ten years I had been the smallest kid in my class and was continually picked on. I was an easy target. At the age of sixteen I was 79 pounds soaking wet and about 4'7" tall. I was the smallest and weakest amongst all of my peers. I was lost and wallowing in my abandonment, taking whatever drugs I could get my hands on to ease my emotional pain.

My family sold our farm in 1980 and we moved to an apartment in a city nearby. It was then that I met neighbors who agreed to let me baby sit their 6 kids. They accepted me, just as I was, and I immediately became part of the family. When I was in their home I felt loved, accepted, and encouraged (My parents loved me too but due to my abandonment issues and anger I could not receive the love they had for me). I loved spending time with our neighbors, as they were similar to my own family, and many times being with them made me feel the way it was before going to the hospital.

One Sunday morning, when I was setting off to have breakfast with my new found family, I found them all getting into Roger's car. Roger was the uncle. He had visited many times during that year and told us stories about the Bible. He shared the gospel with us. Finding out that there would not be any breakfast until later, I decided that church could not be so bad after all and I joined them.

We arrived at church which, to my surprise, was not in a church building but rather in a school gym. I sat in the last row, in the chair closest to the door at the back of the gym. Roger sat next to me, which was a little comforting. I could watch him in order to know what I should do. I was quite unsure as to what to do because I was not brought up in a church and had no idea what to expect.

I can still remember this service like it was yesterday, well at least parts of it. It started with this big tall guy (John Arnott) playing an autoharp, which I did not enjoy. A lady standing beside him singing in an octave and key I was unable to reach. I remember hearing the song Lift Jesus Higher and wondering how carrying Jesus would do anything for Him. I did not understand and seeing all those raised hands did not help. If breakfast had not been a carrot hanging before me, I am not sure what would have become of the rest of the service although I was a little fearful of moving from my seat. This whole church experience was quite threatening as it was something new and I was not comfortable with new things.

The singing and the sound of the auto harp ended and John started to preach. "How long can he be?", I thought to myself, not really understanding a thing he was talking about. It was all going over my head and through my ears until, finally, he was finished and the most important words in my life were spoken, "Does anyone want to know Jesus today?" I remember those words as if they have rung through my head a million times. I knew, with everything in me, that I wanted to know Jesus and I wanted to know Him today. Roger turned and asked if I wanted to go and meet Jesus and, shocking myself, I said no. I wanted to go but I was so afraid. At that moment I saw this lady in the front row stand up and walk right across the front and down towards my chair. When she got to me she stopped, turned towards me holding out her hand, as if to take me somewhere. At that moment I was physically pushed from my seat and landed in that lady's arms. She grabbed me and walked me to the pulpit, where John was standing ready to receive me. In front of the whole congregation, with no eyes closed or heads bowed, John prayed out loud with me. He then held me in the most loving embrace I had ever felt.

After asking Jesus into my heart I floated back to my seat. I was filled with a love I could not fathom. I felt whole and supernaturally loved. No one could tell me Jesus was not real because I had just met Him. 1 John 4:16 tells us God is love. He is, and love was manifested all through me. I asked Roger (who has become my best friend) why He had pushed me out of my seat. He assured me that he did not do it. I then realized that it was the LORD who pushed me out of my seat and who had sent that lady to take me to the front.

At this moment John asked if anyone would like to be filled with the Holy Spirit. I asked Roger what is the Holy Spirit? His reply simply was, "Go find out". I went up, with great passion, only to find myself involuntarily falling on the floor. After a while I got up and tried to question what had just hit me but discovered that I could not speak in English. This other language came out of my mouth, which I could not understand. I did not know what had just happened but I liked it. Roger spent that afternoon explaining the gospel and all that had happened to me.

That day I was released from drugs. The things of the world fell off and I no longer had the need to suppress my hurt with them or by other means.

The next day I was in my math class at school and, as usual, no one expected anything from me. My math teacher was also the narcotics officer of the school and I guess he felt that I was taunting him because I had a smile and for the first time ever I was doing work. He came over and, before I knew it, I was flying across a row of desks with him right on top of me screaming, "Stop taunting me. I am tired of you coming to my class stoned". As he was yelling I tried to tell him I had just found Jesus and, for the first time ever, I was not on drugs in his class. He then went to look at my paper and realized that it was answered correctly, and was shocked to find out that I no longer had dyslexia. He later apologized for his actions and we became good friends during my last two years of school. I was changed, instantly healed from dyslexia and, to everyone's surprise, I graduated as an honor student with a 98% average in English.

This was amazing indeed, but my mindsets of rejection, insecurities, and inadequacy did not change right away. I struggled with them for many years. No matter what I saw God do in my life, deep inside I still felt like a failure, a loser, and could not expect great things for my life. I was so used to the voice of the accuser that I shut the door every time the Comforter tried to talk to me.

One day John Arnott asked me, "Ivan, what would you like to do with your life?" That was a new thought, one that was never a possibility for me in the past. I thought about it and said, "I don't know". Then he asked again, "Tell me what would you like to do?" I said, "You know, John, I do not really understand this, but somehow, I want to travel all over, encouraging churches." Now, all these years later, that is exactly what I am doing. My wife and I are encouragers to the church and travel all over the world, building up the Body of Christ. Who would have thought back then the plans that God had made for me? He took me from being a loser in the eyes of men, with no hope and no future, and turned me into a man who today gives life, and speaks hope and future to multitudes. Surely, the foolish things that confound the wise, but make God famous and bring glory to His name.

Yet the journey was not simple. It required much forgiveness, healing, and freedom because, deep inside, there was a part of me that needed to strive in order to prove that I was not a write-off. I went to the other extreme and had no rest. I was trying to earn everything because I thought that it was through performance and achievements that I would please God. It was hard, as I could never measure up to the yardstick in front of me. My mindsets from the past were so ingrained in me that, subconsciously, I reacted accordingly. I kept hearing a voice saying, "It does not matter because you are a failure and will never accomplish anything". I struggled so much to do any and everything.

John and Carol Arnott were amazing to me. They loved me unconditionally and took me in as a son. They believed in me and for me. They believed in God's plans for me and in His calling on my life, pouring life and encouragement into me daily. Carol literally loved me back to healing and restoration. She showed me the fullness of the Father's love as she never gave up, and never looked back no matter what I did. She never got discouraged or, if she did, she did not show it; instead she always made me feel like a conqueror. I felt that I could do anything when I was around her. They invested into me and began to teach and mentor me. They made way for me and created opportunities for me, something no one had ever done for me before. Yet, I was still tormented every time I had to preach. Then, afterwards, discouragement would fill me, as I felt that I had blown it. John and Carol always told me that it was great and encouraged me to no end. However, deep inside, I could not really believe it.

I continued pressing-in and learning. People did not know about my great struggle with inadequacy, inferiority, and rejection. One day a prophet came to minister to us. We were in John and Carol's basement with the leadership of the church. As this man prophesied he said, "In the name of Jesus, I break off the spirit of inadequacy that is on you" and he hit me on the back with all his might. I have a big scar on my back from the surgery when they removed my lung as a child, and that whole area was always very painful. It had healed well, but no one could touch that part of my back, not even gently, because I would feel the most intense pain imaginable, and that was the exact place where this man hit me. Everyone in the room gasped as he hit me, but I did not feel a thing. I listened to the tape of the prophecy later and, sure enough, the smack on my back sounds loud and clear. Yet I did not feel it.

Time went by and nothing seemed to change until, one year later, I was praying by myself in the bedroom when, suddenly, I felt a strong smack on my back, which literally threw me across the bed. It was big and loud. At that moment, I felt the spirit of inadequacy fall away from me and it was as if my eyes had been opened for the first time. Suddenly, I saw it for what it was and I was free from the stronghold. It took a whole year for the breakthrough to manifest but it came. Another amazing thing is that, after that, the pain in my back disappeared and, since then, anyone can touch that side of my back without a problem.

However, even though the stronghold had been broken I still had some of its effects through the mindsets, thinking patterns, and behaviour patterns that had become part of my life. Then when I was 30 I had three major mid-life crisis episodes in one year. It is sad when you experience this at that young age, but it happens. As I was having my third mid-life crisis I was at a temporary job I had taken for a year. I was reading the file of one of our clients. He was a man, my own age, who had succeeded tremendously in the world and had great accomplishments, and was also very wealthy. At that moment this sense of failure came over me as, at the same age, I had nothing to show in the eyes of the world. I was trained as a minister and had served the LORD in many ways, but, suddenly, a great need for identity came over me. I thought of going back to school and doing something else with my life. I thought that this would make me 'somebody'.

As I was going through this, the LORD came and met with me. He said, "Ivan, what have I ever asked you to be, tell me?" I began to tell Him everything I thought He wanted me to do. He said, "No, that is not it. Tell me, what have I ever asked you to be?" I thought harder and again told Him, in detail, everything I thought He wanted me to do. Then a third time He said, "No Ivan, tell me, what have I ever asked you to be?" I felt frustrated and said, "I give up LORD. I don't know what you want. Tell me, what do you want me to be?" He said, "Ivan, I only want one thing from you. I only want you to be my son. That's all I want from you. Just be my son." At that moment everything came together and full revelation of sonship filled my heart. He then said, "Ivan being a son is not a privilege. Being a son is a right. Being a son is something that you are and can never lose. You cannot earn it, buy it, or sell it. Sonship is your right." I heard Him and understood. I am His son, not because of what I do, but because He made me His son and no one can take that away from me. It is His gift to me and being His son is all I ever need and want to be. I received revelation of the full and unconditional acceptance from my Father in heaven. That became my identity and all the striving fell away.

Being His son took away all the inferiority and all the rejection. I no longer needed the approval of men, or of the world, to be whole or to feel good about myself. It is not what I do. It is who I am that matters. I am 'Ivan the son of God'. This is my identity. What peace! For me this was the key to rest. I live and minister out of that place of complete rest. I no longer strive for ministry. I don't need it. Ministry simply is My Father's business and, as His son, I help my Dad in any way He asks. The only reason I do what I do is because my Father says to me, "Son, I need to you to go and do this for me". Because I am His son, I am happy to please Him and do what He wants me to do, but I do it all for Him. I no longer have any personal ambition. Isabel and I travel a lot ministering but we actually do not like to travel. We love to serve the people and are honoured that the Father trusts us to serve them. We do not take that lightly, but there is no personal gain in it for us. We only do it because we will do anything for our Father and the Bride.

Before I understood this, I could not believe that He would ask me to do great things but, after this revelation came, I believe and expect great things from my Father. Before I was always beat up by the voice of the accuser, but now the accuser has been silenced and my ears have been opened to the Comforter. When I hear my Father talk I believe what He says, because today inferiority, rejection, negativity, and inadequacy are simply memories of the past. Now I have a filter of love and acceptance and I enjoy the freedom of being His son.

WHO IS THE ACCUSER?

Satan

He is the accuser of the Brethren	Revelations 12:10-11
The father of lies	John 8:44
The Adversary	Matthew 13:39 &
Your great enemy	1 Peter 5:8
Angel of light	2 Cor 11:14
The thief, the killer, the destroyer	John 10:10
The murderer	John 8:44

He is also described in scripture as the devourer and condemner, the spirit of death, and much more.

As the accuser, he is always pointing out everything that is wrong in our lives, and never mentions anything good or positive. He only focuses on the negative and brings up things from the past, as well as the present, and tells you that the future will be the same. He leaves you feeling discouraged and hopeless. He speaks words that cripple, condemn, kill, and destroy, and will always push you away from God.

As the father of lies Satan will try to destroy you, making you think it is the Father speaking. He pretends to be the Father to deceive you, but unlike the pulse of the word of God that is alive, His voice carries death and leaves you feeling condemned. This leads to a general feeling of despair, makes you believe that there is no way out, which leads to hopelessness, depression, and urges your destruction. Pay attention to the fruit left in you. If it is anything like this, then rebuke and discard it. It is simply the accuser and you have the power to silence him.

WHO IS THE COMFORTER?

The Holy Spirit.

The Comforter (KJV) Helper (NASB)	John 14:16-17
The Spirit of Truth	John 16:13
The Edifier	1 Cor. 14:3
The Exhorter	1 Cor. 14:3
The Teacher	John 16:13
The Convicter	John 16:8

He is the Spirit of Life and the Encourager. The one who reveals God to us. He also fills our hearts with the love of God, and makes His heart and thoughts known to us. He is ever present in our lives and will never leave us nor forsake us. He exhorts us (1 Corinthians 14:3), and corrects us but God's correction is different from the correction of men. In Scripture correction means to take someone aside and encourage a different course of conduct. That is what the Holy Spirit does. His presence always brings comfort and uplifts us. Even when

He corrects us, He does it in such a way that He leaves us feeling life, hope, love, and encouragement. He does not drag up the past as the accuser does because our past is forgotten (Psalm 103:12).

He always shows us the way out, the solution, gives us the keys to freedom, leaves us feeling closer to the Father, and gives us a greater desire to follow Him. It is wonderful to hear the voice of the Encourager and know that, no matter what He has to deal with in our lives, He will love us and protect us. He will lead us into all truth, will show us a different way, and will encourage us to   please the Father.

It is unfortunate to see how many of God's children live without the comfort of the Holy Spirit. This seems to be possibly the biggest problem of all. The Holy Spirit is amazing. He is gentle, yet immensely powerful. He is filled with love and holds us together while we are on our journey to heaven. I cannot imagine one single second of my life without Him. He is also a person with feelings, just like the Father and Jesus. We desperately need Him, yet we mistreat Him regularly and take Him for granted all the time. He is so loyal and faithful and will never leave us nor forsake us, yet we live without experiencing the fullness of the benefits He brings to our lives. He wants to have fellowship with us. Like Paul said, "May the grace of our LORD Jesus Christ, the love of God, and the fellowship of the Holy Spirit be with you all." 2 Corinthians 13:14.

Scripture teaches us clearly how to release His presence, character, heart, and ways in our midst. It is, however, very easy to grieve (or hurt) the Holy Spirit because of things we do. Scripture compares the Holy Spirit to a dove. Doves are very gentle and get spooked very easily. Any strong noise, or rattle, will cause them to fly away. The same thing happens with the Holy Spirit. He is gentle, kind and full of love, but it is very easy to cause Him to withdraw. He will never leave us nor forsake us but when grieved He withdraws. If He withdraws, then all the benefits of His presence cease until He is able to be Himself again.

Here are the things that hurt the Holy Spirit. Ephesians 4:29-32 says, "Don't use foul or abusive language. Let everything you say be good and helpful, so that your words will be an encouragement to those who hear them. And do not bring sorrow (do not grieve) to God's Holy Spirit by the way you live. Remember, He is the one who has identified you as his own, guaranteeing that you will be saved on the day of redemption. Get rid of all bitterness, rage, anger, harsh words, and slander, as well as all types of malicious behaviour.   Instead, be kind to each other, tender-hearted, forgiving one another, just as God, through Christ, has forgiven you" (NLT).

These things: foul and abusive language, bitterness, rage, anger, harsh words, slander, malicious behaviour, hardness of heart, and unforgiveness, hurt the Holy Spirit and, if you have these things in your life, the Holy Spirit cannot comfort you and make you happy. You know how it is when you get hurt. Suddenly you are not yourself anymore and hold back. You are not happy and free to be yourself. The same thing happens to Him. Another thing we have found that hurts and grieves Him is when people find comfort in other places. For instance, if you seek comfort in food, alcohol, drugs, cigarettes, pornography, etc., the Holy Spirit cannot comfort you. Those are false comforts that will not give you life. The Holy Spirit is the Real Comforter who will give you life and will transform you forever. Remember, Paul encourages us to be in fellowship with the Holy Spirit and, for that, we need to create an environment where He will feel comfortable and not be grieved. As we live in fellowship with Him, we will get to know His presence, His voice, His heart, and then the accuser will not be able to deceive us because we will be able to tell them apart.

GOD'S AGENDA

Now there is another side, about mindsets, that we need to address and that is when someone has a strong mindset of pride and arrogance. This is hard because when God speaks to them about the work He needs to do in their hearts, they cannot (or do not want to) receive it because their filter of pride does not let it through. The thing here is that, to receive prophecy, we must have an open mind and an open heart. We must get rid of our agenda and must be open to God's agenda. He is more interested in our lives and destiny than we are. I remember once, that a prophet came to minister to the leadership of our church. I had an agenda and wanted God to speak certain things over me, especially in front of the others. I had obviously the wrong heart motivation. The prophet gave me a powerful word from the LORD, which I rejected at the time because it was not what I expected. I was very angered by what he said and I did not even think he was hearing from God. He spoke about a healing God was going to do in my heart that was going to transform me forever. I was so upset as in my eyes I did not 'need' any healing. I was still filled with pride so I thought I was just fine and the prophet was wrong.

Later on, God began to work in my heart and I remembered that prophecy, which started to make sense. It is amazing how things change as our hearts change. Suddenly, I heard things I did not hear before and began to understand. It is so good that God is so patient and understanding. We have seen this happen often. People assess their prophecies according to their present understanding and most of the time only hear part of what is said. Now, all these years later, I can truly say that that prophecy was correct and God has brought it to fulfillment in my life. He has done a great work of healing in my heart and the result of it is exactly what the prophecy said it would be. I am so grateful that we kept that tape, as it has become part of the road map to our destiny. We must open our hearts and our minds as we are dealing with God's agenda, and His priorities are usually very different from ours.

When I was young I used to go to visit this old man. He was lonely and liked to chat. I used to read the newspapers and watch the news, in order to have things to talk about when I was with him. However, he never wanted to talk about the things I had in mind. He had his own agenda and led the conversation accordingly. God is that way many times. He has His own agenda and sticks to it. The best thing is to be open to whatever He wants to talk about.

I remember another time when someone gave me a prophecy, which was contrary to what I had planned to do. I had made some particular plans according to the desires of my heart and then, when the prophecy came, I immediately said that it was not from God. I talked to the pastor and told her that this fellow had given me a prophecy that was not from God. She then talked to him and, bless his heart, he came and apologized. Over a year later, I decided to ask the LORD about these issues and lo-and-behold, He told me exactly what that fellow had prophesied over me. I was shocked and realized how I had misjudged that prophecy and did not even bother to ask the LORD about it at the time. I had to go and repent to that fellow who prophesied over me. As I repented and accepted God's word, He then began to unfold the details and steps that would lead me to the fulfillment of the promise. We have learned not to reject and throw away prophecies based on the first reaction we get when we hear them even if, at that time, they don't make sense.

Lots of people have come to us and said, "When you prophesied this or that over me I could not quite embrace it because I did not understand it and I could not see what you were saying, however, I decided to listen to it six months later and, suddenly, I heard things I never heard before. Also, when I later listened to it again, I heard more things and it all made sense. Now I can see what God was saying. I understand and embrace it." It is important not to discard it but wait and listen to it again and again, asking the LORD to show us our filters and mindsets so we can process them and not miss anything He has for us.

ACCUSATION

As we are advancing in the Kingdom we see new things arise as God is teaching us a much better way. A big change is in the models that we have seen emerge through the years. One of the models we were used to seeing was prophets who would call out the sins of people and would air everybody's dirty laundry. Everyone used to think that those were the true prophets of God and marveled at them, and as much as we wanted God to speak to us, we were terrified of them. I remember being in many of those meetings. I would sit there repenting of every sin I could think of, and then I would make up sins and repent from them because I wanted to be safe in case he prophesied over me. Then one day, as we were in the fields with Jesus, He said, "Did you know that you do not need to be prophetic at all in order to call out everyone's sins and reveal all their hidden secrets?" That surprised us because we had heard that doing that was one of the marks of great prophetic accuracy. Then He continued saying, "No, you do not need to be prophetic at all to do that, if you want to do that, and do it accurately, all you have to do is listen to the accuser. He will tell you everyone's hidden sins and dirty secrets. He will tell you every wrong thing in the life of everyone around you, and if you want to help the accuser all you have to do is repeat it. He is looking for people who will help him accuse my children".

We were shocked but realized that He was right. As we watched Him minister we saw Him encounter sin in the lives of people and instead of pointing His finger at them, with much love, kindness, mercy, and gentleness He showed them the way out of their sin, and left them with good news, a hope, and a future. He came along and showed them a better course of action. Watching Him we learned that for every temptation there is a way of escape, and prophecy reveals that way of escape. He does not condone sin, but does not accuse us either. He deals with it in a heavenly manner because He came to proclaim good news to the poor, to bind up the brokenhearted, give liberty to the captives, freedom to the prisoners, to give them a garland instead of ashes, and the joy of gladness instead of mourning (Isaiah 61).

When we have this revelation, deep in our hearts, we will approach prophecy in a different manner and receive it differently. We are able to trust Him and believe what He tells us. He speaks according to who He is and what He can do. When we prophesy we see that many people are expecting to get beat up and criticized. They are expecting accusation and cannot understand why it does not come. What a change! Again, God does not condone sin, but He deals with it in a different way than we thought. Scripture tell us clearly in 1 John 4:16 that "God is love". God does not have love. He IS love. Therefore, 1 Corinthians 13 is the perfect description of Him:

"God is patient and kind. God is not jealous, or boastful, or proud or rude. God does not demand His own way. God is not irritable, and He keeps no record of when He has been wronged. He is never glad about injustice but rejoices whenever the truth wins out. God never gives up, never loses faith, is always hopeful, and endures through every circumstance." Scripture also says that His love leads us to repentance, so why are we surprised when we see Him being kind and loving to those who are struggling in the journey. (NLT)

We have seen Him be this way many times. We have watched Him face sin, brokenness, challenges, walls, and much more, and He has always brought life, healing, freedom, joy, restoration, and great hope to everyone He encounters. We have seen many come to meet Him with their heads down, filled with sorrow, hopelessness, depression, and desperation, and leave with a smile on their faces, life in their eyes, with a heart filled with love, joy, and expectation, with a hope and a future. Many of them did not have a future to look forward to but, after meeting Him, everything changed. Remember, He never gives up, no matter what, so you should expect good things to come when you receive prophecies from His heart.

Another fascinating mindset we hear is people saying that they put on the armor of God as if it were clothing (Ephesians 6:13). People ask me sometimes if I am wearing the armor today, if I put it on in the morning. I always answer, "No, because I did not take it off last night". A long time ago, however, I was taught that I had to recite every morning: "I gird my loins with truth, put on the breastplate of righteousness, the helmet of salvation, and take the shield of faith" (Ephesians 6). Supposedly, that was sufficient to keep the enemy away all day. Sometimes if things were not going well people would say, "You probably did not put on the armor of the LORD today and that is why the enemy got through to you." I used to hear that but something inside of me did not quite click. Of course not, because the armor of God is not something we put on like that. Reciting it does not have any power. It is the revelation of those things that has power, and living in them is what keeps us safe and in victory.

SECTION ELEVEN

DEFEATING MINDSETS

As you can see, it is very important to defeat the power of mindsets. A lot of the prisons we live in are the result of unhealthy mindsets. We are spirit, soul, and body, but somehow after we get saved we seem to forget this and think that everything is spiritual. We have seen great breakthrough in our lives, and in the lives of many, since we began to deal with things appropriately, realizing that there is an element to all three parts in every situation we deal with. Many times we see people who go for ministry in a particular area of their lives but somehow the freedom they so long for does not manifest, so they keep going back in circles for more and more prayer, but nothing seems to happen. This used to confuse us because we know the power of the LORD, and of the name of Jesus, so why was it that things did not change? We began to search for the answer because Jesus came to set the captives free. Then the LORD began to show us this key. As we explained before, mindsets are attached to something else, which usually is an experience that has generated a lie in our lives, which, in our perception, has become a truth. Perception is a funny thing. It is neither right, wrong, false nor true. It simply is our reality and, as such, is true to us. We may all see the same thing at the same time, but each of us has a different perception (view, opinion, assessment) of it and to each of us that is the truth. So it is important to understand this and respect other people's perceptions. Many people waste lots of time trying to change the views of others by trying to make them believe their own. That does not work. What we need to do is find where they come from. Once we find that, we can help change it by bringing healing in that area of their lives. When the heart changes, their perception automatically changes too. It is easy. We all go through this, so this understanding will help us relax.

First, we deal with the spiritual stuff (forgiveness, repentance, judgments, vows, releasing, etc., etc.), next we need to find the mindsets and behaviour patterns that have developed as a result of that, and deal with them so they can change. Let's look at some examples, which will help us understand this better.

IMPRINTING

A while ago we were doing a conference in another country and one day the pastors asked our advice about a big problem they had with a lady in their church. She was the kind of person who liked to be the centre of attention. She would constantly do things to cause people to notice her and would, especially, corner visiting speakers to show them how gifted she was. She was now experiencing much rejection because people could not stand her ways. She had come to realize her problem and had been working with her pastors to get healing and freedom. She had gone through different methods of counseling and ministry. However, the results only seemed to last for a short time and then she went back to her old ways.

Her pastors were asking us what other kind of ministry could be available to help her break free for good. She was very beautiful, had been prom queen, and beauty queen at many levels, and was married to a wealthy man as well. As we talked, it became obvious that they had dealt with all the spiritual sides and had prayed through it well. So we told them about the imprinting, mindsets, and structures that had formed in her life. She was the only child of a very wealthy couple and had grown up being the centre of attention and receiving everything she wanted. The world revolved around her. That was normal for her and became a pattern that was registered in her subconscious. They were now dealing with a behaviour problem, an imprinting that had to change.

An imprinting is an experience that is registered in our subconscious (a preprogramming) which, later in life, dictates the way we react in different situations. Our imprinting takes place during the first seven to ten years of our life. It comes from the way the world around us is, the way we are treated, the experiences we have, and the behaviour of our parents, or those we look up to in life. All these things send messages to our subconscious, which get registered there. We are not even aware of them, but they are powerful and will define the way we behave later in life.

For instance, you touch a hot stove once and burn your finger. As a result of that experience, a message is registered in your brain and your subconscious that says, "Never touch the hot stove". From that moment on, every time the stove is on, you do not have to make the conscious decision not to touch it. It becomes a reaction, which comes from deep inside.

That was her case. The experience registered in her subconscious said that when she was with people she should show off, to get them to notice her. There was a great subconscious need in her to be the centre of attention, which was like a craving that she could not help. We explained to them that, now, the next step was to make her aware of her behaviours and develop a strategy to help her break those patterns. For instance, they can help her identify the signals when the reaction comes up, by mentioning it to her. Then she can stop and remind herself, "No, this is no longer necessary. This is the way I used to behave but things are different now, and I no longer need to behave like this. I do not need to be the centre of attention anymore", and then she can walk away and do something else. She will have to do this, probably for a while, because structures and patterns that have been active for years do not come down overnight. But, in time, her ways will change as her patterns change.

For years we used to tell people, after a pastoral counseling or ministry session, "OK now go and walk it out", but they did not know how to walk it out so nothing changed. We did not have the practical steps to walk it out either, but through the years the Father began to show us the practical side and we have seen it work greatly in our lives, and in the lives of many others. Something that is very important is to understand how memories work in our brain.

MEMORIES AND THE BRAIN

Our brain is absolutely amazing. It really shows us the greatness of God. According to Demitri F. Papolos, M.D., an associate professor of psychiatry at the Albert Einstein College of Medicine in New York

City, the human brain is the most complex structure on earth. Packed into three-and-a-half pounds of grey and white matter, compressed into a structure, no larger than a grapefruit, are perhaps 100 billion brain cells, each linked to as many as 10,000 others. It is said that the number of possible interconnections between the cells is greater than the number of stars in the universe.

We truly are wonderfully and fearfully made. Memories are really powerful and affect our lives forever. They have feelings and emotions, which we are supposed to experience. Every memory is registered in our mind and the feeling and emotion of each memory is stored in our brain as a chemical. This is fantastic because that is what allows us to relive memories. For instance, when you were a child you used to go to your Grandma's house on Saturdays. Every time you walked in, you smelled the fragrance of fresh baked cookies. You always had a wonderful time with Grandma, and your times with her became one of the best times of your life. Years go by and Grandma dies, you move far away and life goes on, but every time you smell the fresh baked cookies, immediately you go back to Grandma's kitchen when you were six years old, relive the experience, and the feeling comes back to you. It is a wonderful thing! The smell of cookies is what is called a trigger or an anchor to a memory, and as a response your brain searches for the file where the feeling of that memory is stored as a chemical and releases it allowing you to re-experience the whole thing: memory feeling, and emotion. This happens a lot at Christmas. The sound of carols takes you back to happy memories of the past and you relive them all over again.

Now, the same is true when it comes to negative memories and that is where the problem and the confusion come in. I am sure you know people who have gone through a divorce, or the death of someone very close, and every anniversary of that event they go back to the depression or the grief that they experienced when the incident happened. They get counseling, go for ministry and deal with it, let it go and so on. They get relief for a while but as soon as the anniversary comes, they revert all the way back to where they were before. Then they wonder what happened? Why was it that the ministry did not work? What more can they deal with? We know this one too well. A lady came for help and said to me, "I do not understand what is wrong with me? I pray and give it to the LORD. I really do, but then somehow I take it back and go through it all over again". That is not what is happening. All that is happening is that, when the date of the anniversary comes, she remembers what happened that day, and that triggers the memory, which causes the brain to respond by releasing the feeling and emotion of the memory, and she relives it all over again. That is exactly what is supposed to happen. So it is not that she was still stuck back there. It simply means that she was reliving the memory and that could easily be changed.

I know this because I lived through this process several years ago. I was incredibly busy, burning the candle at both ends, and began to get 'burned-out'. Then, in a period of twelve months, I experienced three very traumatic situations. When the third one happened I went into a deep depression. The day of the third trauma was November 16. It was about 6 p.m. It was cold and dusk outside with snowflakes blowing in the air. The next two years were challenging as I walked through a healing process with the LORD. Finally, it all passed and I recovered completely from the burn-out and the trauma. It was truly wonderful to get back to normal. However, when the next winter came I began to experience, on-and-off, the feeling I had when the depression began that dusk evening of November 16. I was so discouraged because I thought it was over, and I had moved on, and now the feeling was coming back. It was very scary to think that I was not free from it as I thought. I prayed much and began to look for more prayer and more ministry that could heal me and set me free. Then, through much prayer, God began to show us what was happening. These episodes only took place when the weather was exactly the same as it was that evening on November 16. The weather was the trigger that activated the memory and, as a response, the brain released the chemical to give me the feeling of what happened that day, so I could relive it. Once I realized this, things began to change. Having knowledge and understanding brought 50% of the relief. I did get over it, and moved on. It was over. I was now simply dealing with the memory registered in my subconscious.

I prepared myself for the next time the weather was the same and, as soon as the memory and its feelings came back, instead of getting worried, I took a deep breath and said to myself, "It is OK. That is the way it was then but I am not there anymore. That was two years ago not now. It is over. The LORD released me from that and I do not need to experience this anymore. Things are different now and everything is fine". Upon saying that, I chose not to think of the memory anymore and that caused it to stop. Sometimes it would come back again shortly after and I would do the same thing all over again, and so on. Slowly, I noticed that my thinking patterns began to change. By the end of that winter the triggers were gone, my thinking pattern had changed, and the chemical of that feeling and emotion had been flushed out. After that, I noticed that when the dreadful weather came things were fine. I always remember what happened that November 16, but the effect of the memory is completely gone.

As we can see, our brain is very powerful and it commands our whole body. It is the center of operations. It registers everything we hear, see, and do, and brings it back, when it is appropriate. It also regulates our body through signals. I read a medical study about a man who had lost his left arm in an accident and, even though his arm was gone, he could feel it and sometimes he felt it hurt. They tried different things but nothing took the feeling away. It was so real that often he would reach to rub his arm. As they were trying to find the answer they came to the conclusion that the cause was the brain so they decided to trick it. They sat the man in a special desk, with a mirror in front of him, and told him to look in the mirror. As we know, images in the mirror are reversed. The left is right and the right is left, so when he looked in the mirror he saw a left arm and the pain ended. They said that the brain was used to having a left arm and was sending signals to it but the signals were not landing anywhere. The brain was desperately looking for the left arm and kept sending the signals over and over. That was the pain and discomfort he was feeling. So, by doing this experiment, the brain saw a left arm and calmed down completely. I have a friend who is missing most of the fingers of one hand and he says that he can still feel them. Now I understand why.

It is common knowledge that the hardest thing for people who are trying to quit smoking is the habit more than the nicotine. The experts say that the patterns registered in the brain such as the hand-to-mouth motion, the sucking motion, etc., are the most difficult things to overcome. The brain registers every single detail and knows what to do at any given time. That is why you do not have to make a conscious decision to move your hand to take the glass of water to your mouth, or to move the fork up and down to eat. The brain recognizes the scenery and knows that is it time to eat, so it sends the signals to the arm and to the mouth do their job. So, for smokers, one of the best strategies is to change their environment and routine. For instance, every day after dinner you go to the living-room, sit on your favourite chair with the paper and a cigarette. Then, when you are trying to quit smoking you follow the same routine: have your dinner, go to the living-room and sit on the same chair with the paper. Immediately your brain recognizes the environment and sends the signals to the arm and the mouth to do their job because, according to the pattern, you are supposed to smoke. So, in order to help yourself, the best thing to do is to change your routine. After dinner, instead of doing the usual, do something else. Go sit in another room and watch the news instead of reading the newspaper. Slowly you will see that your habits begin to change and the desire to smoke lessens even more.

I remember when we changed cars several years ago. We had had a standard car for about ten years and I got used to changing gears. Then we bought an automatic and I went through a very hard time with it because every time I heard the sound of the engine my foot would automatically reach for the clutch pedal and my hand would reach for the stick to change gears. I did not have to think about it. It was an automatic response because it was a pattern registered in my brain, "When the engine sound changes, I change gears". So there I was, needing to shift gears but there were no gears to shift. I knew that, but the programming of my brain had to change. Oh gosh, every time I heard the engine I felt this urge down my arm to grab the stick and shift and my foot needed to push something.

It was a strong ache and it would not go away so I devised a strategy to pacify my brain. I put my left foot under the seat, where it could not hit the brake pedal, and I got a little ball to squish with my right hand every time I felt the urge to shift gears. As soon as I did that, things got better. This allowed me to make the transition easily. In time, I did not need to squish the little ball anymore.

One day, this young lady came to me with a huge problem. She had been a serious drug addict, and had been in much trouble in the past. She had given her life to the LORD and had been going to church faithfully. She had not taken any drugs now for several months and was making great progress. One day, she fell off the wagon and ended up in the hospital with a drug overdose. She was mortified about it and went to her pastor for help. The two of them tried to figure out what happened and what had triggered it. But they could not come up with an answer. She had not done anything to awaken the desire, and could not understand what had happened.

I asked her to tell me exactly everything that happened that day. She had completely lost all desire for drugs about ten months before and had not even thought of it, which was amazing. Then, that afternoon, her former drug dealer called her to offer her drugs and invited her to come to his place for some. She said no, and told him that she had not taken any drugs for about ten months and had no desire to have any. She put the phone down and, immediately, memories of past times in this man's house, doing drugs, came to her mind. Instantly, a craving for drugs arose in her. She said that it was so overwhelming that she could not contain it and she ended up in that man's house.

As I heard that, I realized what had happened. She was fine because she was out of the environment and away from any triggers. That man's voice was a trigger, which brought back memories and the brain did what it is supposed to do. It released the chemical of the feeling of that memory and the craving came right away. It was simple, just like when you think of chocolate, or your favourite dessert, the craving comes and your mouth waters. We talked about it at length and set up a strategy so she could be prepared, if that man called again. She went for more prayer ministry and, at the same time, we arranged for her to have some safe places to go right away, if that man ever called again. That way she could flee from the temptation like Joseph did. Now she had understanding and a practical safety net that, along with prayer, would help her be one step ahead of the enemy and break free and out of the old structures and habits.

Another fellow was struggling with internet pornography. He was trying very hard to break from it. He continued getting prayer and dealing with it, but kept falling. One day we talked about his routines and patterns and realized that he was doing pretty good, most of the day, but shortly after he sat in front of the screen, memories of watching pornography would come and immediately this great urge, like a craving, would arise and he ended up on those sites. Again, the sight of the computer activated the memory which released the feeling so he could relive it again, so we set up a strategy with him. He was a musician and a worshiper, so that was his way of escape.

First, he put his computer away for a while, so he could get used to being without it and doing other things. Then, when he was ready to have it back, we asked him to get one of the instruments he liked to play and place it nearby, so he could escape the temptation. He did, and every time he was working and the memories came, he would get up and play his instrument. Then, when the urge left, he would go back to the computer and continue. Sometimes he would go back and forth several times but, eventually, things changed and he was able to work, free from all desires to watch pornography. After a while, the computer room was no longer the room where he would watch those sites, but became a worship room as well. For years now he has not had any similar problems. He is completely free.

FAMILIARITIES

One of the functions of our psyche is to keep us safe and give us defense mechanisms. One of them is to look for what is familiar. That is another key to understanding some of our reactions. We always seek for what is recognizable, even if it is not the best for us. There is comfort in familiarity. This includes our feelings and emotions. When Amanda first came home to us she was used to living in and experiencing rejection. This feeling was very familiar to her and gave her comfort. She was not used to love and acceptance and was uncomfortable in that environment. We actually noticed that she would constantly do things to cause people to reject her and then she would cry and go into a pity party, which made her 'feel at home'. It was the only thing familiar in her new environment and life. She had a subconscious need to feel rejection. We prayed much for her and also began to tell her, over and over, that she no longer needed to feel that way, because things were different now, that she was loved and accepted, that she was a beautiful and a good girl, but she could not accept it. Every time we said it, she got really angry and would yell, "No, that is not true! No one loves me. No one cares about me. I am ugly and bad." It was a challenge but slowly she began to believe what we said and her mindsets changed. She became used to being loved and accepted. Eventually that feeling became familiar to her and replaced the old feeling of rejection.

I was at a pastors' conference and the person leading the event told me that, for about four weeks, they had been helping a pastor's wife who was attending. This lady had serious issues of rejection which particularly affected her in groups of people causing her to withdraw and run away. Obviously she was struggling greatly in ministry and in life. They had done all the proper counseling but, for some reason, this lady still could not be in groups. Every time she was in a group she would be OK for a little while but then, suddenly, someone would say or do something, and immediately she would withdraw and run away feeling completely rejected. The thing was that no one was doing anything to reject her. They all loved and liked her. The solution was very simple. They had dealt with all the spiritual side of things but now it was time to identify all mindsets of rejection, that were causing her to misinterpret things that others did and said. Everything was filtered through her powerful grid of rejection.

I told them how to identify her mindsets, the structures, and the familiarity. Her imprinting was rejection and that feeling was familiar to her. Being in a group of people and being accepted by them was very unfamiliar. Subconsciously she needed to find a reason to feel rejection, and she managed to find it constantly. Every time she walked into a group setting, her memory got triggered, the feeling came, and her psyche would tell her, "This is how you must feel and react". Old mindsets spoke to her, and subconsciously she reacted the usual way, which left her feeling very bad because she had failed again. I explained to them that the uncomfortable feeling was normal in this kind of transition, and that they had to set up a strategy, to help her break out of that cycle, so she could become familiar with the new feeling. They were thrilled because, now, they had practical tools to walk her into freedom.

I used this approach with a lady I was counseling a long time ago. She had suffered something very traumatic when she was about 6 years of age. She had been ridiculed in a group setting and, ever since then, she could not be around groups of people. She remembered the horrible feeling and the devastation she experienced when it happened, which caused her to run way in tears. She was now over 50 years old and could not understand why was it that she was comfortable in all other situations but, when she was in a group gathering, she reverted to her 6 year old behaviour. She would start re-living the same emotions, and would run away in tears feeling completely devastated for days and sometimes weeks.

We dealt with all the spiritual stuff: forgiveness, judgments, vows, the fracture, and the lies she had believed. These had become a foundation in her life upon which she had built a huge structure (behaviour pattern). Then we identified and acknowledged the mindsets and behaviours she had developed. Next we set up the strategy to break from them. We agreed that every time we were in a church gathering and her triggers got activated causing her to feel the panic, pain, etc., and the urge to run away, instead of doing it, she would pray and ask the LORD for help, then she would tell herself, "It is OK, that was then, but now is different. I have grown up and do not need to feel this way or run away anymore." Then, instead of running away, she would come to me regardless of where I was, stand by me and gently touch my arm. That was my indicator of what she was going through. I would then stick by her, for however long she needed, until she felt safe. Slowly, she was able to break free from her bondage. Her old ways came to an end, and a new structure of freedom was built. Her brain was reprogrammed with a new message, "It is safe to be in group settings and enjoy myself." Thank you Jesus!!

THE EXAMPLE OF OTHERS

Another source for mindsets and imprinting is the example of others like our parents, siblings, authority figures, etc. We are impacted by the way they treat us, the way they act with each other, the way they react to different circumstances, etc. As little kids we watch them and take it all in. We are open books with empty pages and all the things they say and do get written there and stored away for the right time. Years go by and we go along living our lives, but then something happens and we find ourselves reacting like they did, even though we might have disagreed with their ways. It is a subconscious reaction.

When we became parents, suddenly we would hear ourselves saying the things our parents used to say, and reacting in some of their ways. We were surprised and did not know where it came from. Then we realized that it was the preprogramming (imprinting) of our childhood, which said, "This is how you must react in this or that situation". Years went by, and we never saw it manifest, but it got activated as soon as we became parents. This applied to good things and not-so-good things. For instance, we began to fix things the way we saw Dad do it, cooked the way Mom did, etc. Then, when it came to the not-so-good things, we dealt with them immediately. We dealt with judgments, inner vows, forgiveness, repentance, etc., and chose to walk out of the structures we had inherited.

I remember counseling a young man at church who suffered from panic attacks every time he had to pay his bills at the end of the month. He had gone for ministry several times but somehow still continued having the problem. The funny thing was that he had the money to pay his bills, which made the situation even more confusing. As we talked we discovered that he had a subconscious mindset that said that he should be afraid and panic every time he faced that situation, because his father used to do that. He grew up seeing his father acting in that same manner, and a message was written in the heart of the child that said, "One must panic when bills have to be paid". This did not affect him for years but it got activated as soon as he had his own place and had to pay his own bills. It was a subconscious reaction. Again, that mindset had developed into a behaviour pattern, or structure, that became familiar to him. Therefore, his reaction was involuntary. As soon as the situation arose, his subconscious sent the message to activate the structure, and the reaction came.

We have found that a mindset of strategy keeps people moving forward to freedom. Most people have become accustomed to getting stuck in their problems, but God wants us to be people who find solutions. A proactive attitude of problem solving and freedom will keep us ahead of the enemy. God wants us to be people who know how to work with the Holy Spirit and listen, so we can discern the way of escape the Father provides for us. Understanding how to overcome our mindsets will help us advance tremendously and become all our Father created us to be. We know that if you use this key you will be able to attain the fullness of your Kingdom identity and will take hold of the Kingdom of Heaven on earth.

STRATEGY & PRAYER

A few years ago, the LORD told us that, as leaders in general, we have failed to teach people about strategy. There are many giants in the Promised Land and we must learn to fight for our promises and our destiny correctly. We are in a war and here is where real warfare comes in. The enemy will fight us, with any and every weapon he can find, in order to steal, kill, and destroy all the plans and purposes of God in our lives. Scripture says that "He is like a roaring lion seeking whom he may devour" (1 Peter 5:8).

I was watching the Discovery Channel one day and saw an illustration of this scripture. It was a documentary on Africa. There was a group of buffalo and, suddenly, the lions began to walk in large circles around them roaring, trying to scare them. The buffalo gathered together in a tight circle, with their heads inside (like an American football team). As the lions came close, they would kick them with their back feet. They were safe and protected as long as they kept together like that. However, the lions had a strategy and kept on roaring until one of the buffalo (usually a young one) would get so frightened that he could not take it anymore. The young buffalo then left the group and began to run and, of course, the lions caught him and had lunch. Their strategy worked. They knew that there is always an unwise young buffalo that falls for it.

As I saw this, I realized the importance of church. I have heard through the years people say, "Why do we need to go to church? We can have a relationship with the LORD without having to go to church." Recently a fad has arisen in this regard; more and more people are talking about taking a break from church. This clearly is a strategy from the enemy and is targeted at wounded and disillusioned Christians. Scripture tells us not to stop gathering as some have a habit (Hebrews 10:25).

It also talks about how wonderful and pleasant it is when brothers dwell together in unity (Psalm 133:1). As I saw this documentary I knew the strategy from the enemy. Yes, it is true that one can be saved without going to church, but the purpose of church is the same as with the buffalo. Church is a place where we gather, in unity, to help and encourage each other. It is a place where we can be accountable to others, encouraged when things are down, built up and nurtured by each other. It is a place where faith is built together, and where we can fight together to finish the race. There is safety and protection as we are together in unity but the enemy is roaring like the lion seeking whom he may destroy. As soon as one steps out of the circle, he or she becomes lunch for the lion and, because they are alone, no one can help and rescue them.

We must be aware of the purpose of strategy. Anyone who plays chess knows it is important to be patient and wise. A good game cannot be played in twenty minutes. It takes time, as one must understand and 'play' both sides of the board. One of the rules of chess is that you do not make a move, unless you have at least three other moves behind that move. If you do not have a strategy behind your move your opponent will checkmate you quickly. One of the problems with young and inexperienced players is that they focus on the moves and miss the strategy behind the move. In chess, one must invest in getting to know the mind of the opponent, in order to anticipate his moves and strategy. It is said that the great general Napoleon used chess to teach his young soldiers the strategy of war on the battle field, thus keeping them from going full force against the enemy and being slaughtered in the process. Something that we also need to keep in mind, when playing, is that many times the move is a distraction and, if we do not pay attention, the strategy from the opponent succeeds. It is the same with our enemy. He has plans and strategies and we must be aware of them. Scripture teaches us his ways and his thoughts, so we can be prepared. We are not into focusing on the devil, not at all. We are very busy making God famous and therefore, we do not have time to pay attention to the enemy. However, we have learned strategy and that way, we are able to stay one step ahead of him.

For instance, a common move from the enemy is to cause something to happen or someone to do something to you at church, in order to hurt you and disillusion you. Most people focus on the 'move' (what so-and-so, or the church did to me) instead of looking beyond and discovering the strategy behind it. What is the ultimate goal of the enemy? To steal, kill, and destroy you, your destiny, and inheritance. We remember a time when something happened and we were greatly wounded at church. It was very hard. Immediately the enemy's thoughts came to us, "Forget these people. Get out of here. Take a break, etc." We were wounded and bleeding, but we recognized the strategy from the enemy. He wanted to isolate us so he could bring destruction to us in such a subtle way that, by the time we became aware of it, it would be too late. We knew that walking out forgiveness and healing is harder when you are isolated and we were determined to move forward. We also knew that our destiny is to serve the church (Body of Christ) and that the enemy's plans were to ultimately take away our destiny by creating a wedge between us and the church. So we looked again at the prophecies spoken over us which helped us remain focused, reminded us of God's plans, and brought light to our path.

We dealt with our issues, walked out forgiveness, and got healing all within the church. We did not take one single step back and refused to leave the circle of safety. We knew that the roaring lions were out there and outside that circle we would become prey to unforgiveness, hurt, anger, bitterness, deception, disillusionment, pride, etc. and, in the end, those roaring lions would destroy us. It was not easy because we had to deal with the issues of our hearts daily. We actually chose to stay close to the particular people who hurt us and that forced us to deal with the issues and get healing. It was intense but, this way, our issues could not hide away. It would have been easier to run away justified by what they had done to us but, this way, the result was life, healing, freedom, and restoration for all involved. It was well worth it and at the end we can say that the LORD gave us ultimate victory and we have enjoyed the plunder from that battle.

About a year ago, the LORD spoke clearly to us and said, "An attack of persecution has been released from hell against My people. It is an attack of sickness and financial trouble. The purpose for this attack is accusation against Me. The enemy is going to try and make My children blame Me and accuse Me for the circumstances that will arise. This attack will mainly come to My people in the Western world because they do not understand and do not have a mindset of persecution. Teach them and prepare them for this." We immediately did as the LORD told us. In our church we taught them much about the reality of persecution, how to find the strategy behind the move, and how to respond properly like Job when he said to his wife, "You speak as one of the foolish women speaks. Shall we indeed accept good from God and not accept adversity? In all this Job did not sin with his lips" (Job 2:10). He chose not to blame and accuse God and, therefore, he did not sin with his lips like so many do. Very shortly after teaching this, we began to see a major onslaught of sickness and financial trouble come against many, not just in our midst but all around the world. Because we travel so much, we have the opportunity to see what is happening in many places first hand, and one of the saddest things we have seen is the amount of accusation made against God.

The thing here is that because of the current mentality in many Christians, especially in the western world, this strategy from the enemy has worked. The attacks come and people see the move of the enemy and react according to it, but forget, or don't know, that it is about the heart and the strategy behind it, which is to cause you to blame God for what is happening and accuse him like Job's wife did. May you have ears to hear and a heart to perceive, so you can learn to go beyond and don't partake of this sin. For many years we have heard people teaching about the victorious Christian life and how it is a life without troubles and pain. Many times people in our church would come and say, "Where is the victorious life we are supposed to have? Here I am being faithful to the LORD, coming to church, tithing, doing all He tells me to do and look what is happening? When are things going to get happy because I see no difference between the world and us, so what's the use in all this?" After a while of hearing this I realized that many people have been lied to. Somebody has been giving them a false gospel.

I think that because I came from a country where to become a Christian had a price tag of persecution, I saw things differently. For me, I knew what Scripture actually says about victory and what it means to live a victorious Christian life and it was different. Scripture is very clear, Jesus said, "In this world you will have tribulation, but be of good cheer for I have overcome the world" (John 16:33). How much clearer can this be? Scripture also says, "How blessed is the man whose strength is in you, in whose heart are the highways to Zion! Passing through the valley of Baca (of weeping) they make it a spring (It will become a place of refreshing springs NLT). The early rain also covers it with blessings. They go from strength to strength; every one of them appears before God in Zion" (Psalm. 84: 5-7).

That is what the victorious Christian life is about. It is not that we will not struggle and will not face trials; Jesus said we will, so let's get on with it. However, the victory is found in how we go through those trials. We have the ability to turn them into refreshing springs. We can go through them with peace, the peace that surpasses all understanding (Philippians 4:7) and joy. We can rest in the midst of the storm, knowing that no matter what happens, at the end, it will all work out for good because our Father is so faithful and never sleeps, but guards us and watches over us. That is what sets us apart. We have access to another kingdom and realm at all times. An example of a victorious Christian life is found in Acts 16. There Paul and Silas are serving the LORD, doing everything right and, as a result it seems, they end up in a terrible situation in prison. But the story says that about midnight (the darkest hour of the night), they began to pray, sing, and worship the LORD, which caused the chains to break, the prison doors to open, and all others around witness this, causing the jailer and his family to come to Jesus. Here we see the manifestation of their victorious Christian life. God's power was released because of their response. They turned the valley of weeping into a place of refreshing springs.

Someone was telling us, a while ago how they had been hurt in some churches they had been in and how people had made different decisions that had closed all doors for them and now they were out in the cold and hurting. They were living a defeated Christian life but it was not because of what had been done to them, but because of the way they reacted to it. It would be lovely to blame others for it, but the truth is that no one else is responsible for our reactions, which come from our hearts and are very much ours. Others can hurt us but, they cannot be blamed for our response. However, we too can turn our darkest hour into a place of refreshing springs by choosing how to respond to it. We can grumble and complain, blaming everyone around us, and end up like the children of Israel walking in circles in the wilderness, or like Paul and Silas we can react in a way that causes heaven to open right there and then, giving us ultimate victory. To top it off, all the multitude of witnesses that surround us (relatives, friends, co-workers, etc.) will get to see the glory of our LORD and His Kingdom in our lives so they too can believe, learn, and desire to know the God we have so they too can live a life like ours. The difference rests in how we deal and respond to the situation.

We both have experienced this many times in our journey, so we know exactly what it feels like. It is not easy at the beginning but, in time, our hearts change and the right response becomes a fruit of the heart. I remember a couple of years ago we were teaching a prophetic school when I got word that my sister was dying in a hospital far away. She had been in a tragic car accident. I heard the news, felt the pain, cried, then responded. I said to my LORD, "This is so hard. My sister is dying. She is very far away and there is nothing I can possibly do, but I know You can. You can help her and do a miracle.

I want to ask You to please save her, heal her, and restore her. I know You can do it and I trust You. But I need to make a choice and this is it: I would love for You to do a great powerful miracle to save and restore her completely. However, You are still LORD of Lords and KING of Kings, so I want You to know that if, for some reason, You choose not to do it, I will still love You. I will serve You just the same, and I will make You famous every day for the rest of my life. My decision is that no matter what You do, whether You save her or not, I will continue doing what I do with all my heart and will live every minute of my life to make You famous".

At that moment, I was filled with the greatest peace, rest, and joy I had felt in a long time. I went and taught a full session and then ministered to many people, and no one could tell that I was in midst of the valley of weeping, because it had been transformed into a place of refreshing springs. Later people there heard about the news I received from home, and marveled at what they saw happening in me, and at the spirit that was flowing in and through me. They saw first hand the Kingdom of my Father manifested on earth. Then, to top it off, within about 24 hours I got news that my sister was out of all danger and two days after that she was released from the hospital because, in the doctor's words, "She was the recipient of a miracle and could go home". In two weeks she was released to go back to work. Hallelujah!!!!

We have stories that could fill books and books as we have walked through this endless times, yet each time, we have come out with victory and have a story to tell. Truly there is no God like our God who is alive and responds in our time of need. There is nothing like it on earth!

STRATEGY AND WARFARE

We are in warfare and, as we know, wars are not won on the battle field, but in the strategy room. This is where the apostolic comes in, the generals in the army who help us and direct the troops in the battles. I watched a history movie once, where I saw the general sitting on a high hill watching the battle. He could see both sides fighting and in doing so was able to understand the ways of the enemy's army and got to know the mind of his opponent. He then gathered the leaders of the army and gave them the battle plan. He had complete vision and a perspective of the whole field and could lead them with understanding and wisdom. The important thing was that the leaders of his army followed his instructions and, as long as they did, they never lost a battle. As I saw that, the LORD spoke to me and said, "What you are seeing is symbolic of what the apostolic leaders are to do, the generals of my army. They will sit on the mountain top and get vision, direction, and strategy to help my people advance. The apostolic fathers will lead my people through battles and will bring them to victory. Teach them and prepare them to find strategy for battle." This opened a new dimension of the Kingdom for us, enlarging our vision and giving us tools for the Kingdom to advance.

There is a powerful story that illustrates how strategy works. One time, many years ago, we did a long conference in Europe. We did many meetings and prophesied over close to four hundred people in several places. We are used to large crowds for ministry and do not usually remember the things that we prophesy over anyone in particular. However, there was a couple who came to every meeting and stayed close to us, so we actually remembered them well, and, for some reason, recalled part of the prophecy spoken over them. They were very impacted and encouraged by the LORD. They got vision, direction, and destiny. It was amazing to see the transformation in their lives as they received an impartation of the Father's heart. Time went by and, about five months after we came home, we got an e-mail from one of the leaders of the church over there saying that there was a problem with that particular couple.

The wife was in the hospital because she tried to commit suicide and the husband was trying to divorce her because he said that she was holding him back. They thought that this was backlash from the enemy because of all they had received from the LORD, and the great impartation and vision given to them. At that moment I had this open vision and saw what had happened in the heavenly realm. We know the devil is not omniscient. He only knows what he can see and hear but, unlike God, he does not know everything and for sure he does not know God's plans for us until they are spoken out. He needs to hear them just as we do. Therefore, prophecy is also very important to him. When you are prophesied over, you are not the only one getting the news from heaven. Your enemy does at the same time.

In the vision, I saw us prophesying over people and there were two little demons whose only job was to gather news and take it back to the enemy's camp. I particularly saw us prophesying over that couple in trouble, and saw the listening demons getting the scoop on them as we declared the news from heaven over their lives. Then, as soon as we finished, they took off and rushed back to the strategy room of hell. I saw them enter and report the news they had on this couple. Immediately, they began to strategize how to stop that from happening. It was amazing. I heard them plan, based on the information received and on the knowledge they had of these people. They were figuring out what they could do to spoil the plans of God before they came to pass. That is what happens in war.

At that point, I remembered portions of the prophecy spoken over them. These are just three points from a long 20 minute prophecy:

- God would raise them up to minister together as a team and they would model what real team ministry is all about. They would become a father and a mother in the Kingdom. They would receive an anointing like Abraham and Sarah and would have spiritual children all over the world. God would use them in such a way that they would model what it means to be a father and a mother in the Kingdom, not only in their own town, but also in the region, and surrounding areas. People would learn from them and others would follow.

- They would receive a ministry of healing and restoration and God would use them in counseling, family counseling, and particularly in marriage for all kinds of people but especially to heal and restore the marriages of leaders.

- God would bring healing and restoration to their own children freeing them from addictions and, as a result, they would receive a great anointing to work with young people (they later confirmed that their children were into drugs and alcohol). Street kids would come to their house and would be set them free from bondages of alcohol & drugs.

Then the LORD said to me, "If you were the opponent what would you do to stop this couple from receiving their promises and entering into their destiny?"

Immediately, I thought of strategy. If I were the opponent and my job was to stop them from achieving those three things alone, what would be my best move. I know that in warfare they do not waste attacks but they have purpose in everything they do. So I thought, "What would I bomb that would cause the most damage in the shortest time?" Answer: their marriage. As I looked at the prophecy spoken over them, all those promises were for them as a couple, therefore they hinged on them being together. If I could blow up their marriage, then I would spoil God's plans for them. Just like in chess, it is all about advancing and retreating, which means that my job is to cause my opponent to retreat, so I can advance on the board. As I realized this, the LORD spoke to me and said, "Now tell them this, and also tell them that there is still time. It is not over. Now that they have this information, they (the leaders and pastors) can heal them and restore them. Tell them to strengthen their marriage and invest into them so their promises can come to pass."

When we receive prophecies from God we listen carefully. Again, we do not focus on the enemy and are not paranoid as to what he can or cannot do, but we know we are in a war and want to advance. So we listen and then ask ourselves, "If I were my opponent, what would I do to stop this?" For instance, God has clearly called us to minister as a team, and build the Kingdom together, equally as one. So we know that we have to protect our marriage and invest into strengthening it and keeping it safe. We have a shared destiny, so we plug all the holes as soon as we become aware of them. We cannot afford to leave cracks for the enemy to come in.

When our church receives prophecies we, as a leadership, meet and talk about them. We do two things. First, we respond to the LORD and see what we are required to do and, second, we find the areas that the enemy can attack to get us to retreat. We then plan a strategy to strengthen them so we can advance and are prepared. As a result, we have spoiled the plans of the enemy time after time.

We do the same thing with the people in our church. We listen to their prophecies and then work with them, determining what their response should be and how we, as leaders, can help them align their lives according to the plans of God and their destiny. Secondly, we talk to them about the areas of their lives where the enemy can bombard them, in order to steal their promises. Then, we plan a strategy to plug those holes. We find a way to help them if they need healing, counseling, training, equipping, etc. We want to see them advance and attain all God has offered them. We help them prepare on how to overcome and spoil the plans of the enemy. Many times when people come to see us, because they are under attack, we ask them to bring us their prophecies and, as we read them, we see that nine out of ten times the attacks they are having are because of their prophecies. These attacks are part of the enemy's strategy to cause them to re-treat. We need to learn to think as conquerors and develop a mindset of a strategy so we can keep advancing.

We, as leaders, need to take a more hands-on approach in helping the people walk across the waters and into their promised land. We need to believe in them and in God's promises for them, so we can help them and stand with them as they fight the giants in the land. As leaders, we need to plan a strategy for this. We have seen churches where, as well as the pastors, the cell or kinship leaders, and other leaders take more of a role in this area, and that way the work is distributed among all the leaders. We know many who use their prophecies as a road map to their destiny and they are actively involved in following them each step of the way. As a result, prophecies are being fulfilled in their lives. God seeks stewardship in all things, as it is a key to unlock His promises.

There is also a great Strategy Room in heaven. God is more than will-ing to give us access to it and will send His armies to help us fight well in His battles. He will also give us wisdom from heaven as we need it. We need to learn to be a step ahead of the enemy and spoil his plans. From the moment we began to apply this revelation, we have seen great results in our midst. We have also been teaching this strategy to people and leaders from all over the world and, in the same manner, those who have listened and learned have advanced. These are keys to victory and are available to us all. We must also realize that our Father is almighty and has the greatest army in the world.

Many times we hear people talk about fighting demons and stuff like that. Sometimes it sounds amazing and sensational, especially when they tell how they defeated principalities, etc. However, it is not Scrip-tural. From cover to cover in the Bible we do not see where men or women were sent to fight demons. Scripture shows us clearly that when demons had to be fought, God sent Michael, Gabriel, and the armies of heaven. The warriors of heaven, the mighty angelic armies fight them. That's what they are for. Scripture tells us to imitate Jesus and, "Submit to God, resist the devil and he will flee from us" (James 4:7). It also tells us that, as we draw close to Him, "He sets a table for us in the presence of our enemies" (Psalm 23:5). Many times it tells us that God will fight and defeat our enemies. What rest it brings to know that all I have to do is draw closer and closer to my Father. When the devil looks at me cross-eyed I simply tell my Father, "Look at him. He is bothering me," and my Father, who loves me with passion, immediately steps in and calls His armies to go and deal with that devil. I like this so much better than the other way.

THE POWER OF WORSHIP

I remember, a long time ago, I was being tormented by demons. They used to literally come to visit and torture me, especially through the night. It was getting so bad that I did not want to go to sleep. We used to pray and fight them and did all the warfare we knew how, but it was not changing. Then, one day, I made a decision. I went and bought a tape player that could play worship music day and night non-stop. I put it in the bedroom so it would play as I slept. I had to learn to sleep with soft worship music. It was a challenge, at first, but I had no choice. Then, when I set it all up, I stood in my room and said out loud, "Demons this is how it is going to work from now on. I am going to worship God day and night. Even when I sleep I will worship Him. There will always be praise and worship in my presence, so I am not going to bother with you anymore. I don't want you here, but if you choose to come, you will have to worship the LORD with me". Believe it or not, that was the end of it. They never ever came back.

Worship is, indeed, the greatest weapon of warfare and, from experience, I know that demons do not want to come and worship the LORD with us. Imagine! My sister said that, a while ago, she began to see some dark shadows around the house, and began to feel a not-so-good presence in the house. Of course, fear was trying to get in and then she remembered this story of how worship gave me victory and kept the demons away from my house, so she decided to try it. She filled her house with worship day and night and, as a result, the shadows and the bad presence left forever, and the peace and presence of God completely filled her home. I also know that just as demons are repelled by worship, angels rush to come and worship the LORD with us.

There is nothing that draws angels to our midst like worship. Whenever there is worship happening they come and join in. It is amazing and powerful. They love it. Very often we hear angels singing in our home. People who come to visit have heard them too and some have run into them upstairs. We like to leave worship playing in the house when we are out. We have pets at home (two dogs and two cats) and we can see the difference in them when worship is on. They are clearly less happy, and less peaceful when we forget to leave worship playing.

A long time ago, we had a young man living with us who liked to listen to some particular secular music that was not edifying to say it nicely. He did it when we were out. For a while, we did not know what was happening, but we could tell when we got home that something was not right. The atmosphere was hard and tense. The peace was gone from the house. It just did not feel good in there. Then, after praying much we found out what was happening, so we asked him not to play that music in our house anymore, and began to fill our house with worship once again and everything changed. The peaceful feeling returned and, once again, it felt good to be there. The angels came to sing again. When our young daughter asked us about our rule of only playing worship music in our home, in a child-like manner I simply explained to her, that we like our house to be a place where angels come to sing and laugh with us.

King Jehoshaphat knew the power of worship and that is why he placed worshippers in front of the army which caused God's power to come from heaven bringing complete victory over his enemies (2 Chronicles 20:20).

Worship caused the tormentors of King Saul to leave. I remember once, when I went through a depression that caused my soul and mind to be in turmoil day and night, I felt great relief in worship and listening to the Bible on tape. I even slept with a headset on. These were the only two things that brought peace to my mind and rest to my soul, allowing me to feel the comfort of the Holy Spirit and hear His voice which, in the end, brought me out of that dark valley and into complete freedom and utter victory!

INTIMACY

Another powerful way of knowing and discerning the voice of God is through intimacy. Intimacy is, perhaps, the biggest thing that people struggle with. Most people are filled with guilt and condemnation because of lack of intimacy and their inability to attain it. Recently, someone gave me a paper teaching about intimacy and it was mostly about guidelines to win that battle. It was about six pages long and filled with things to do to overcome. By the time I finished reading it, I was exhausted, just thinking of the long list of steps and guidelines to follow in order to have some intimacy with the LORD. One thing was for sure, if I had to go through all of that to have intimacy with the LORD, it was just not going to happen. It was long and complex and I am not into that 'complicated' anymore. I know that way quite well but, as I said before, when I learned that His yoke is easy and His burden light, I got rid of complicated. We have actually found the easy way to intimacy with the LORD and it works wonderfully. It is a powerful key and we know, for a fact, that it will work for you as it has worked for us and for thousands of other people around the world who have received our teachings in this subject.

As we have looked into this subject, we realized that there is a misconception of what intimacy is. It simply means, "Knowing each other's heart without limitation and sharing each other's heart without reservation". Now, the thing is that in any relationship in life it takes time to get to that point. First, we meet someone, then we become acquaintances then, if we choose to invest into the relationship, we become friends and, as we continue, we become close friends, then best friends and at this point we are close, meaning that we trust each other enough to openly share our hearts with each other without reservation and, as a result, we know each other's hearts fully and truly. This is intimacy.

These things cannot be forced or imposed. The same thing happens with the LORD, but somehow people think it is different. We must understand that the 'key' to intimacy is friendship. Friendship is an amazing thing and a great tool to know the hearts of people and to share your heart with others. It works the same way with the LORD. In our next book, we will share in detail the practical steps to attain these three stages and how to become a friend of God, because prophetic people need to flow out of that place.

Most people think that intimacy is attained through praying and reading the Bible. That is not true. Doing devotions is not the way to intimacy with the LORD. We must pray without ceasing and must read the Bible as much as possible. We want to make it very clear that we are not saying or implying that you must not do devotions. What we are saying is that there is a difference between this and developing intimacy with the LORD. Prayer and intercession are important, but they do not facilitate a venue to get to know God's heart and hear His voice enough. God is very relational and desires to walk with you in the cool of the day, just like He did with Adam. He wants us to know His heart not just His ways.

How often we see this happen with God and His children. It saddens His heart when His children do not invest in getting to know Him as a person and His heart. Things would be so very different if we would only understand and apply this. God is good and can be trusted. That is one thing I know. There are many things in life I do not know, and many things I do not understand. I have much to learn and it is scary to think that I have gotten this far, knowing as little as I know, but there is one thing that I know as I live and breathe. I know my Father. I know Him with everything in me. I know Him. I know His heart and I know His ways. There is much I still need to learn about Him, but what I already know is amazing and I trust Him. I have realized that if this is the only thing I ever know, if I never ever learn anything else in life, I will be just fine, because knowing this has brought me this far and will take me safely home one day. He is the best thing that has ever happened to us and we can trust Him. I promise you that. He is good and can be trusted without reservation.

He is an incredible person, with a great character and heart. He is funny and loves to laugh, sing, and whistle. He is very relaxed, which is amazing, considering the kind of life He lives being the Sovereign LORD and all... He gets hurt, upset, and has problems. Actually He deals with problems constantly but is an amazing problem solver. He is the essence of all good things. He is love, kindness, power, mercy, gentleness, perfection, joy, and much more. He is almighty and He is my father and also my friend. Sometimes, it is hard to believe, that someone like Him is absolutely crazy about us and we are the apple of His eye. Wow!!!

Friendship with God will take away the confusion and will make recognizing His voice very easy. As in the natural, when we become very close friends with someone and spend much time talking to them, we can hear their voice and recognize them immediately. We also know their presence and fragrance. The more we hear them the easier it is, to the point that when they call us on the phone we hear them say, "Hello" and immediately we know it is them, just by the sound of their voice. That is the same with the LORD. Hearing His voice becomes clearer as our friendship with Him grows. As we grew in friendship with the LORD we began to know the sound of His voice, the pulse of His words, His presence, and we can recognize it easily now. This is a powerful key to releasing our prophetic destiny and becoming who God created us to be. The more we know His voice, the easier it is to recognize it anywhere. We can hear the sound of a thousand voices and we recognize His clearly even if it comes as a soft whisper. This is very important when we prophesy and also when we hear prophecy because one thing is for sure; God only fulfills what He says and not what other voices say. This has brought a great freedom as we minister and more confidence as we obey Him.

KNOWING HIS VOICE

We know His voice, simply because we walk and talk with Him and He shares His heart with us. Scripture says that His sheep hear His voice and follow Him (John10:27). I used to raise sheep and goats and learned the difference between them both. Sheep are not the sharpest tool in the shed. They are known for being naive and unwise. A common occurrence was to see one sheep come and touch the electric fence with his wet nose, get a big shock and run away screaming. All the other sheep would stand there watching and wondering, "What happened to him? I have to get myself some of that!" And, sure enough, they would all line-up to try it. We saw this day after day and understood why scripture says that "We are led like sheep to the slaughter". Goats on the other hand are way smarter and learn from the experience of others. We saw one goat come and get a shock from the fence and all the other goats would back off and stay away from the fence. It is interesting that God calls us sheep and the world goats.

The way we used to teach the sheep to know us and follow us was this. When it was time for them to stop nursing from their mothers, we would take a big bucket, make many holes in it; stick a straw in each hole and a nipple at the end. We filled the bucket with milk and came out to feed them. We called the little lambs, placed each of them on a nipple, and taught them to drink from the bucket. From that moment on we became 'mom' and they got to know us well and followed us everywhere. That is what the LORD wants to do with us. He wants us to depend on Him as He feeds us and takes care of us, so that when He calls us we can follow Him everywhere. It is easier said than done because we have become used to hearing and following the voices of others. God's voice is distinctive and alive. One word from Him can change our lives and turn the darkest day into a glorious brightness. It can turn our sorrow into dancing, and fill our hearts with the most inexplicable love and joy we can imagine. There is a reason why the enemy wants to confuse us so much and fights us in this area so much.

I remember, many years ago, I received a letter from a lady to whom we had ministered, in two different conferences, a couple of years apart. In her letter she said that when she came up she was really afraid and was expecting to be corrected and to be told everything that was wrong with her as usually happened. She said that her life was a mess. She was struggling with everything and she knew God would call her on it again. However, to her surprise, there was no correction at all in the prophecy and instead of being reprimanded for all that was wrong with her, for the first time in her life, she heard that she was useful and God had plans for her life. The things that her eyes had not seen, her ears had not heard, and her mind had never imagined about her life. (1 Corinthians 2:9). She heard about God's immense love for her and what He thought of her. For the first time ever in her life, she had a hope and a future, and heard the Father's heart for her. She went home after the meeting and did not know what to do or what to think. This was a voice she had never heard before. She had always heard condemnation, accusation, and discouragement, yet, this time the voice she heard lifted her up, encouraged her, gave her life, made her smile and, most of all, drew her closer to God than ever, which was new to her.

She paced her apartment for hours wondering if I had heard from God or not. She thought that I could not be prophetic because, if I were, I would have seen that she was a mess, and would have told her about it. That was how she knew people were prophetic; they always told her what was wrong with her. However, she could not deny what she felt in her heart and the witness of the Holy Spirit in her. She tried to phone me but could not reach me, so she had to ask the LORD if

I had heard from Him or not when I prophesied over her. The LORD replied in a very clear way and said, "Yes, it was me. It was my voice you heard in that prophecy. It was MY heart you heard." At that moment, everything changed in her and, for the first time, freedom and purpose filled her heart as a future opened up before her. The fruit of it was life and healing. Her life began to change.

She said that the second time we prophesied over, her two years later, God built on the first prophecy and, this time, she was able to believe it because now she knew that God was for her and not against her. She knew He loved her, and had great plans for her. She was drawn closer and closer to the Father and there she found the truth. I remember, when I saw her the first time, I saw the condition she was in. I saw her conflict, her struggles, and the mess her life was in at the time. But I also saw a child of God, coming up the road to meet the most loving, generous, and amazing Father in the whole universe. I saw into her heart and found the Father's hand prints and His heart for her. I saw what He placed in her heart when He created her and felt His love for her. I knew that if I wanted credibility in the eyes of men, all I had to do was call it as it was and everyone around would have been impressed by how prophetic I was, but what would that have done to her? After all she is the precious Bride of our LORD, the most glorious treasure before His eyes and I have no right to hurt her or dishonour her.

She was coming covered with mud and rags and I saw the Father get excited and run to meet her. His love for her covered her multitude of faults, as His mercies were new that day for her. At that moment I forgot what I first saw, looked through the Father's eyes and said what I saw. Then He said to me, "Put this robe on her, wash her feet and place these sandals on them, then put this ring on her finger, and present her to my people as I see her, not in the condition in which she came to see me. Then let's rejoice and celebrate because My daughter has come to meet me".

Scripture teaches us that "His kindness leads us to repentance" (Romans 2:4). Therefore, we know that an encounter with the Father's heart and love changes and transforms us forever. No one can be that close to the Father's heart and His love and remain the same. Prophecy is a way to bring people that close to the Father's heart and one thing is for sure, all sin falls away when that love enters our lives.

His love sets us free and makes us whole. That is what Jesus came to do. He came to give us good news, a great destiny, and to show us that there is a piece of the Promised Land with our name on it. The voice of God is the most beautiful thing we can ever hear. Jeremiah 29:11 says, "For I know the plans that I have for you says the LORD, plans of good and not of evil (plans to bless you and to prosper you), plans to give you a hope and a future". Prophecy from the Father's heart reveals exactly that, and this is what we should expect.

THE IMPOSSIBLE PROMISES OF GOD

Once we have a better understanding of who God is and of what His Kingdom is really all about, we can then understand prophecies in a much better way and know what to do when we receive them. God is completely supernatural and everything about Him is supernatural. He is not limited to your limitations or to the limitations of the kingdom of men. He can do anything He wants, at any time He wants. We have experienced this kind of sovereignty many times. It is very important to remember that, even though He is our perfect and loving Father, He is still the great I AM who met with Moses and parted the waters. The One who performs mighty deeds and miracles and no one can stand in His way. He is the Sovereign LORD (completely independent, supreme ruler, self-governing, absolute, and supreme.) About a year ago the LORD spoke to me and said, "I am about to release power like the world and the church have never seen before, but for this to happen My people need to accept My sovereignty. They must understand that My power and sovereignty come together. Many people seem to have forgotten that I am Sovereign, but I am coming to restore that reality in my people. Tell them that if they want My power they need to accept My sovereignty and they must trust Me till the end."

MEETING THE GREAT "I AM"

Several years ago, I had a powerful experience in which I had an encounter with the Great I AM, and I must say that it was one of the greatest experiences of my life. I was in Brazil on a business trip. (I spent many years in the business world until the LORD took me out of it and fully into the work of His Kingdom). I was down there for two weeks, setting up a program with the government, and had to travel across the country to meet with government and embassy officials in different states. I was in a place in the North by the edge of the Amazon River. I had a Brazilian lawyer with me and a translator, as we had to make deals and negotiate with judges and government people. One morning we went to a particular government building, where the highest judges in the field worked. I had a meeting with the judge who was head of the adoption department. As we were in our meeting there was a knock on the door and this man walked in. He seemed distinguished and was wearing a long coat of many colors. I had never seen anything like it before. As he walked in everyone gasped and stood up. Everyone but me, as I did not know who he was or what was happening.

He introduced himself to me and I realized that he was a very important judge, probably the boss. He was on his way to a big court hearing but wanted to stop to meet me first. He was very kind and courteous to me and was really pleased that I had come to deal with them. As he was about to leave, my lawyer and translator told me to ask him for a meeting. I did not really want to because I did not know who he was or why I should meet with him. They both told me very strongly, "Just do it. Ask him to meet with you. We will explain later. This is a once in a lifetime opportunity and you cannot miss it." They were so insistent that I did it. He said that he had meetings all day long but that he would see me for 15 minutes during his lunch hour. My lawyer, translator, and the other judge could not believe that he granted my request.

As we left they told me that this man was the highest legal authority in the land and that no one surpassed him in authority or power. This man could create a law, at any time he wanted to, and could change laws and make anything happen just by saying the word. His words became law in the land. I did not know that a person with such unlimited power existed on earth.

As we were about to leave, to go and see another judge nearby, I realized that I needed to meet with the head of another department in the building, the director of the department in charge of the orphanages and the protection of children. I tried to get an appointment with him but he politely said that he could not see me as he was too busy. I was very disappointed, because I really needed to talk to him in order to present our case. I needed his help, but there was no way I could see him. I prayed for something to happen so I could meet with him. We went to our meeting and rushed back just in time for my meeting with the high judge. We walked into his office, which was huge and furnished very luxuriously. It had the most exquisite leather furniture and crafted wood tables I had ever seen. He was delighted to see me and we had our meeting. I explained to him why I was there and presented my request. He listened and said, "I understand what you want, and I see that you need the law to change in order for your project to take place. At this moment the law here does not facilitate this, but I will change the law for you, so it can accommodate your request and that way you can accomplish what you want." He asked my lawyer to send him the information needed, in writing, so he could take care of it right away. Then he said to me, "Once I change the law for you, I want you to come so we can have a meeting with all the judges in the land who deal in this field. I will summon them for a day's seminar in which I want you to explain your project to them. Then I will explain the new law to them, and will tell them to give you whatever you want."

Then he looked at me and said, "Come with me. I want you to meet Mr. So-and-so, the director of the department in charge of all the orphanages and the protection of children because you are going to need his help, follow me". I did not tell him that I had tried to meet that man already without success. He walked ahead and I followed him. It was amazing to walk behind such authority and might. As he walked, people literally got out of his way, and because I was with him, and was walking in his train, they stepped aside and made room for me too. We got to the office of the head of the department for orphanages and the protection of children, and the high judge knocked on the door. The fellow inside indicated that he was very busy and asked who it was. The high judge identified himself and there was complete silence for a few seconds and almost immediately the door opened and this fellow was standing there almost bowing down.

The high judge introduced me to him, explained why I was there and what was happening, and then said, "She is going to need your help and I want you to do anything she wants. I want you to help her and make all she wants and needs possible." Then he stepped aside and motioned me to step forward. The other man fully agreed to his request, and shook my hand as he gave me his promise to do all that had been requested and to please me in any way he could. After that, I shook hands and walked away in complete amazement at what had just happened. I had witnessed the earthly version of supreme power and authority.

The LORD then spoke to me and said, "I wanted you to have a demonstration of what this kind of power is like, and to understand what it is like to have the favour of someone this powerful in your life, because I want you to understand who I am, the power that I have, and how My favour is even greater than what you have just seen. I will teach you how to walk with Me in this manner and how I can make a way where there is no way. You will see that there is nothing impossible for Me and, if you walk in that closeness with Me, you too will walk through impossible things and unprecedented power".

Two days later, I was in a hotel room in another part of the country. I was exhausted and could not sleep. It was about midnight when I heard the audible voice of God say, "Deuteronomy 4:7". He said it three times out loud so, by the third time, I figured that I should read it. This is what it said, "For what great nation is there that has a god so near to it as is the LORD our God whenever we call on Him?" I read it and it stayed engraved in my mind and heart. It became very alive, although I did not know really know why I needed to know that.

As my two weeks were coming to an end, I found myself in what seemed to be the most difficult situation of my life. I was facing a series of completely impossible circumstances which, as far as I was concerned, were beyond God's ability to resolve. I was scheduled to fly back home in 48 hours and, because of the nature of my trip, I could not leave the country until it all got accomplished. So, at this point, I was stranded in an impossible situation and there was no way out. I remember sitting in the room where I was staying, feeling complete despair. I was exhausted and could not see how in the world I could make it.

I sat there and wept with the most incredible agony I had ever felt in my life, feeling completely lost and defeated. It was beyond hopelessness. I was experiencing utter despair. At that moment, I heard word for word Deuteronomy 4:7, and I called on Him in my time of great need. As I did, He immediately responded and began to tell me what to do guiding me, step-by-step, through the most supernatural series of miracles I had ever seen or experienced in my life up until then. I literally saw the impossible happen. The waters parted in front of me. I felt like Moses when he faced his impossible experience and God parted the waters and destroyed his enemies. It was absolute power and authority. Twenty-four hours later I was sitting in the same room in complete amazement and awe. Everything was done. The impossible had been accomplished and I could go home the next day. I could hardly believe what had happened. I did not know what to say or think. I was trying to process the incredible revelation of God I had just received. I had seen the Sovereign LORD and had walked in His train. I had seen mountains move, just like it had happened with the high judge earlier that week, except that the power and authority I had just seen was far superior to the judge's. I had met the Great I AM and I was transformed in the process.

After those 24 hours something was written deep into my heart and spirit. I knew, as I live and breathe, that He is close to me and will answer whenever I call on Him. I know I can call Him in my time of need and He will move heaven and earth for me. I now knew Him in a very different way. I had heard stories about Him being that way, but now my eyes had seen Him and it was, and still is, indescribable. I know His power and authority and know I can trust Him, no matter what. Yet, by walking with Him through this experience, I had received a greater impartation of faith and authority for the impossible. As I sat there, pondering on what had happened and being overwhelmed by the freedom and release that I was feeling, and most of all, by God's greatness, He came to meet with me. He sat by my side and said to me, "In the last 24 hours you have seen who I am and the kind of power I have. You have seen that there is nothing impossible for Me and no one can stand in My way. I can do anything I want, at any time I want. You have experienced My greatness and power in a very tangible way. However, I want you to know that I do not display this kind of power for show. I only display it when it is called for." He paused, looked at me and said, "Are you willing for Me to put you in situations that call for this kind of power to be displayed on earth?"

This was a big question. As I heard it, I remembered what I had experienced and I never wanted to go through that again, but then I remembered what I had lived through in the last 24 hours and the revelation of God I now had, and how I had been transformed through it all. It is impossible to meet the great I AM and remain the same. Then I realized that, as hard as it had been, it was all worth it and I would not trade it for anything in the world. So I said, "If as a result the world and the church will know you as I now do, then Yes, I am willing."

A few days later He said, "I will do the same things with other people. I want to invite many to partake of this kind of power and experience, but they have to volunteer. This is very important, they have to volunteer." Psalm 110:3 says that God's people will volunteer freely in the day of His power. He wants us to volunteer for this, so we both volunteered. As a church we volunteered, and ever since then we have lived through incredible situations and have seen God's power be released without measure. We have walked through the impossible promises of God, and have seen mountains move out of the way as He walks ahead and we walk in His train.

IMPOSSIBLE PROPHECIES

One of the things we commonly hear from people, as we prophesy over them, is how incredible some of the things are, and how impossible they seem to be. We know this first hand, as we both have heard the same kind of things spoken over us. Many times we received impossible prophecies and did not know what to do with them because we just could not see how they could ever come to pass. We have come to love hearing the impossible promises of God, as they lead us to supernatural experiences, open heavens, glory, and, at the end, have amazing stories that make our Father famous! We now want to share three keys that will unlock the doors that will take you to your destiny.

FIRST KEY: WEAPONS OF WARFARE

1 Timothy 1:18 says, "This command I entrust to you, Timothy, my son, in accordance with the prophecies previously made concerning you, that by them you fight the good fight" (May they give you the confidence to fight well in the LORD's battles).

Here, Paul is giving Timothy instructions based on the prophecies spoken over him and is charging him to use them as weapons to fight a good fight. This is very important. Prophecies are weapons to fight your fights and to overcome. They are a source of confidence as we face the enemy and "take the Kingdom by force" (Matthew 11:12). We are in warfare against our enemy and need to learn how to fight effectively in those battles. Our prophecies are more than pretty words, or nice tapes, that we collect in a drawer somewhere. This has been a very common thing in God's people. We know of many who simply put the tapes away somewhere and do not use them. What a waste!!!

God's promises are powerful and fulfill His purposes. We need to change our mindsets and realize that we can use our prophecies to challenge our circumstances, instead of letting our circumstances challenge our prophecies. When Jesus was being tempted by the devil in the wilderness, three times the devil challenged what God had said and each time Jesus responded with the Word of God and silenced him. He overcame by using the word of God to fight him off. The same thing is applicable to us.

The enemy will come and challenge your destiny and your promises from God. You can be sure of that. He may not appear physically in front of you, as he did with Jesus, but he will cause circumstances to arise that contradict God's promises and will whisper in your ear, "See it is not true. God never said so. He is not going to do it. If God said so then how come this is happening?" That is when we need to be prepared. We need to know what God has said and remember His promises so that, when the challenges come, we can stand in front of them and simply say, "No, this is what the LORD has said…. This is my promise…. I have a prophecy that says this…. and I believe it". Trust me, it works, because the enemy cannot stand against the LORD Himself and His word is as good as He is.

I remember the story of Moses when he finally got his great breakthrough. Pharaoh let the people go and then the LORD came and hardened Pharaoh's heart and sent him after Moses, while Moses was heading up to a dead end road. They were trapped between Pharaoh and the river. I can only imagine what Moses must have felt as he was standing there facing these circumstances. Everything God had said to him was being tested. The circumstances turned against him. Instead of breakthrough and freedom they were now facing death or going back to slavery in Egypt. As a leader, I can only imagine the pressure from the people against Moses. Scripture tells us in Exodus 14:11-12 that they turned against Moses and complained. Then in verses 15 & 16 the LORD gave Moses a brilliant answer that has always encouraged me greatly, "Why are you crying out to me? Tell the people to get moving! Pick up your staff and raise your hand over the sea. Divide the water so the Israelites can walk through the middle of the sea on dry ground. (NLT).

In other words, the LORD said, "What are you crying to me for – do something about it". Moses had a promise from the LORD to take the people to the other side of the river. God had told him to do it, but when the circumstances arose, Moses stood there with the rest of the people waiting for God to do something, and God simply said: "You do something". A promise from the LORD brings authority to defeat our circumstances and move mountains. The LORD once said to me, "A lot of people are asking me to move their mountains out of the way so they can keep on going. However, I have already told them to move the mountains themselves. I will empower them but they have to stand up and do it". In Matthew 17:20 Jesus said that we only need faith as small as a mustard seed to move mountains. The faith of a mustard seed is a next-to-nothing amount of faith. It is so small that it is not even worth talking about. He wants us to acquire that kind of authority so our journey will be easier and we will move forward. Moses did it. He heard the LORD, lifted the staff and the waters parted. I am convinced that if Moses would have just fixed his eyes on the promise the LORD had given him and would have said to the circumstances, "I have a promise from God that I will take these people to the other side, therefore, we are going to keep on going," the circumstances would have given in because they cannot oppose what the LORD has said. The word of the LORD is incontestable and hell, heaven, and earth know that. We are the ones who doubt it.

We know from experience that this works. Ivan has had a degenerative eye condition since he was a child and, medically, his eyes are expected to get worse regularly. He has a very strong prescription for his glasses and the norm was that each year they would increase it a bit more. However, the LORD has given him a personal promise to heal his eyes, and many times through the years people have prophesied the same thing. Shortly after we got married, I had an amazing dream in which I saw the LORD heal his eyes. So we both believe, with all our hearts, that his eyes will be healed and much glory will come to the LORD as it happens. As the years have gone by, the prognosis in the natural realm continued being discouraging, but we have always faced that circumstance with the promise and the prophecies spoken over him. We constantly speak the promised healing over his eyes. I lay hands on him regularly and bless that healing.

Each day we wake up believing that, "Today is a good day for a miracle" and choose to live that way. Three years ago Ivan went for an eye exam and to the doctor's great amazement instead of deteriorating his eyes had improved, slightly, but, nevertheless, had improved, which is completely impossible. The doctor was in shock as she could not find an explanation for it, and wrote a prescription for a weaker pair of glasses. Then this year he was having trouble reading so he went for another check-up. The eye doctor said, "You probably will need early bifocals because your eyes have probably deteriorated more". She did the examination three times, because she found out that the reason why he was having trouble reading was because his eyes had improved yet a bit more, and his current prescription was a bit too strong. Again, she was utterly shocked and, again, she wrote a prescription for a weaker pair of glasses. Ivan's eyes are slowly receiving their promise. If you have a promise from the Father, then be strong and courageous. Take that promise like a mighty sword and use it to fight the good fight and overcome your enemies.

THE CHURCH BUILDING

We planted our current church in the fall of 2000 based on a word from the LORD. He spoke to both of us, individually, and gave us specific instructions and mandates. Then He spoke, in the same manner, to John and Susan Brown, our associate pastors. As we planted this church, the LORD gave us a vision greater than life. But we believed God and have never looked back. We began the church in John Brown's living-room with just a handful of people. Then the LORD began to speak and to give us more detailed instructions along the way and we began a journey of many stepping stones and transitions. As God enlarged the vision we went from the living-room to a conference room at a hotel. We were so few people that, the first Sunday, there we sat together in a circle in the center of the room feeling overwhelmed, but we had promises from God and shortly after the room was full and then we moved to a school gym.

A few months after the gym was getting full and we needed more space for Sunday school and youth. So the LORD spoke again and we rented a warehouse building. The financial overhead was too much for us but we had a word from the LORD to take it, and He provided miraculously to cover all the expenses for the three years that we were there. Our church and ministry grew tremendously as we were there. People from all over the world began to come and amazing miracles and heavenly visitations have happened and continue increasing in our midst daily.

A year after we moved there, the LORD spoke and said that He was going to give us a building, and then we received specific prophecies giving us encouragement and direction in the matter. One of the prophecies spoken over us said, "I see God has called you to be harvesters and to collect a big harvest for the Kingdom. Great and amazing things God will do with you and through you. I see you both standing together looking at a huge harvester.

The harvest is ready and you know that you need to buy the harvester, in order to do all God wants you to do. There is no other way. But you do not have the money to do it. Then I saw Jesus come up to you both and hand Ivan a briefcase. You opened it and it was full of money for you to buy it. Then I saw you driving the harvester. It was big and a bit stretching at the beginning, but quickly you got the hang of it and started going through the fields collecting the harvest. Then I looked and saw a multitude of gleaners in the field. I saw every person, who is part of this church, as a gleaner in the fields collecting all the grains that are left, making sure not one stays behind. The LORD has called you to be harvesters. He will fill this place with gleaners and you will collect a mighty and powerful harvest for the LORD. Prepare for it".

As time went on, we received other prophecies with more confirmation. God kept reminding us of His promise and His instructions. He does not forget! So, a year ago we had to move out of the warehouse building because it was sold. We rented a room in a community centre in town. This was very hard, as the space was small and some areas of ministry became restricted. However, the vision kept increasing and the call to the harvest kept growing. So we continued pressing in for the harvester. We needed a building of our own, in order to do all God wanted us to do and to raise up the people that come to us, so they would become gleaners and harvesters. At the same time, as we were facing the great need for a building, the finances of the church dropped tremendously and we were barely paying our bills. Our congregation went down in size because people found the rented space we had too restrictive (we were sitting like sardines in a can). So, at different times, discouragement tried to come our way, but we continued fixing our eyes on the promise the LORD had given us and continued praying and looking for the right building to buy.

Many people, even in our church, tried to discourage us because of the circumstances. Some said, "Why would you need to buy a building? Look at the amount of people we now have, and there is no money at all. The offerings are going down by the week. The finances have dried up. You are crazy." Many in our congregation were part of David's army (we still have them but they are becoming a great army of mighty men and women of valour) which meant that they were people in need and debt, people who had no money, many had no jobs and needed our help. So, in the natural, it did not make sense for us to plan on buying a building, but we had a promise from the Father. From time to time, we would stand in front of the church and remind them of the promises God had given us, and about our expectations to receive the briefcase from Jesus, so we could buy the building. Many said that what we were going through was simply warfare and demonic opposition. "Look what the devil is doing", they said. We replied by saying, "No, that is not what is happening. Our Father is greater than that, and He has simply allowed these circumstances to happen in order to position us in the perfect place for a display of His faithfulness and power. We have been strategically positioned to witness a great miracle as only God can make this happen. Do not focus on the devil. Focus on the LORD, and you will see the mighty deliverance that will come from His hand." We declared that we would not retreat because of the circumstances but would go ahead no matter what. We told the mountains to move out of our way because they would not stop us. God had told us to go ahead and do this and, at His bidding, we are doing it! We had weapons and our God is alive!

Time went on and things got more challenging, but we had a promise and expected our miracle to take place each and every day. Each morning we woke up thinking, "Today is a good day for a miracle," and expected it. Then a building was offered to us. Another church in town was closing down and they asked us if we wanted to buy their building. It was a beautiful and traditional church building, with all the room we needed. It also came with a manse (we had been praying for the LORD to give us a house for our students to live in, so this was perfect). We saw it and prayed about it. The LORD encouraged us and we knew this was our harvester, but we had no money, whatsoever, to buy it. Our offerings were at their lowest. They wanted $430,000 for the church and the house, which came as a package, as they are in the same property. That was a very good price but still impossible for our little church. We felt like Gideon's army, knowing that only God could make it happen. It was a perfect set-up for a mighty miracle! We asked the LORD and He said, "Wait for the price to drop". In the meantime, they put the building on the market. All circumstances pointed towards us losing it, but we kept praying because we knew this was the harvester we needed, and we needed that briefcase to come.

After a while the price dropped to $299,000 but the LORD still said, "Wait a bit longer". Other people were very interested in the building and it looked like they were going to buy it, but after a while they decided not to. Then, finally, the LORD said, now go and offer them $200,000 for everything. The real estate lady was very angry with that offer but Ivan stood firm and explained to the members of the board our vision to keep the building as a church and carry the mandate for which it was built over a century ago. That church was built in the mid 1800's because of a revival in town. Ivan delivered a speech like the ones the apostle Paul gave when he spoke being filled with the Holy Spirit. The members of the board were very moved indeed.

The real estate lady asked how much of a down payment we would have if 'for some reason' they considered selling the building to us. At that moment the LORD spoke and, without questioning it, Ivan said what he heard the Father say. He said, "At this moment I have nothing but in two weeks I will have $50,000 cash as a down payment." She asked where the money would come from and he said, "I do not know exactly where it will come from but I guarantee you that in two weeks we will have it. God will provide it." She still was not happy and for two more weeks she tried to sell the building to someone else for more money, but could not. Finally, they accepted our offer.

In the meantime, Ivan and John went to the banks to see about getting a mortgage. In Canada, banks do not like to lend money to churches, so it was a big challenge for us and we prayed for favour. Many of our friends were also praying with us in different places. The banking officer asked them, "How much down payment do you have?" Ivan gave him the exact same answer he gave to the real estate lady. The officer looked at Ivan as if he was crazy and laughed, but Ivan was completely sure of what the LORD had said, regardless of the fact that, in the natural, there was no way for us to come up with that kind of money.

He shared with the church what was happening and we all prayed together for a miracle. God heard us and in a week-and-a-half He provided the $50,000 promised, but it does not end there. He continued providing and, in three weeks, we had $93,000 cash for the purchase of the building. This was a powerful testimony to the real estate lady, to the bank, to our church, and to many others who witnessed and/ or heard of the faithfulness of God. So we got the property for our church (with everything inside from the pulpit to the spoons, forks and salt shakers in the kitchen). We got a beautiful and wonderful building in perfect condition and the manse together for $200,000, less than half the asking price.

There was still the matter of arranging a mortgage for the rest of the money we needed. The bank we were dealing with did not seem too willing to help, so Ivan decided to apply to other banks. One of the banks responded to our request in 24 hours. The banking officer of that bank said, "As you know banks do not like to lend money to Christian churches because no one wants to foreclose on a church. However, I am a Muslim and I would have no problem, whatsoever, foreclosing on a Christian church. Therefore, I will give you the money you need and, just know that if you cannot pay, I will simply take the building from you". Funny how God uses all things for good! So we got the mortgage from the bank for the remaining money. God truly opened up His briefcase and it has not closed

TRUSTING GOD TILL THE END

One of the things we often hear people say is that, if things turn hard, then it was not from God because He is a loving father who would never do that. Yet we see in Scripture that Moses was not the only one God placed in a hard situation. He did it on other occasions with others. He allows things like this to happen in order to do mighty things AT THE END. People say that God always comes at 11:59. That is not always true. Sometimes He arrives at 12:15. We have seen 11:59 come and go, and then, when He arrives at 12:15, the miracle He does is much greater than if He had arrived at 11:59. I must admit that it is easier when He shows up earlier, but it is greater when He comes later. Lazarus can confirm this as, in his case, Jesus arrived at 12:30!

The problem, as we said before, is that many people do not wait till the end and quit before God accomplishes the work He has planned. We both know this one so well. Again, if we are able to marry the revelation of the Father's heart and love with His sovereignty, we will enter into a supernatural realm of miracles and power filled with trust, rest, and peace. When I think that the LORD God, KING of kings and LORD of Lords, who is almighty and sovereign is also my father and loves me more than life, that I am the apple of His eye and everything about me is the most important thing in His life, I am overwhelmed with the greatest sense of peace, knowing that I can trust Him till the end.

Our friend, Paul Morley from England, once told us a story that stuck with me forever. Paul was in the Royal Navy and, for a while, worked for Prince Charles. He used to fly in Prince Charles' helicopter sitting by him at the front. Paul said that one day, while they were taking off, a great fog came. It was so thick that they could not see anything. Prince Charles called the tower for instructions, knowing that they could see what he could not see. Immediately, they began to direct him step by step and he obeyed everything they said. He flew blindly, trusting the instructions of those men and landed the helicopter safely in the right place. He could not see where he was going but the men guiding him did. Paul said that, for him, it was a great lesson to trust God who knows the way even if we don't, and cannot see one step ahead. He is able to get us there safely. This truly is a great lesson to learn. I also marveled that Prince Charles, being the heir to the throne of England, would trust those men in such a way. Then I realized that the reason why he could trust them like that was because he knew that his well-being was the most important thing for those men. They had been trained to protect him and would do anything for him. That was their mandate and they knew it, but, more importantly, Prince Charles knew it too. He did not question, doubt, or argue with what they said. He trusted them implicitly!

We say that we trust God but, when He tells us something, we always question what He says and argue with Him. We need proof before we trust Him. He has to convince us before we step out. Oh, if we could only learn to be like Peter, who fixed his eyes on Jesus and trusted Him enough to step out of the boat. If we ever come to know that our well-being is the most important thing in God's heart, then we would be able to trust Him in reality, not as a concept and, at that point, nothing would stop us. We would enter into the supernatural realm, where the impossible is possible and God's power would always be available to us. That is a powerful key to enter the realm where miracles abound.

We have been in this situation several times and it has always been amazing. Several years ago, the LORD opened a door for us to start a business and He clearly confirmed that He wanted us to do it. We began it and it went well at the beginning but, soon after, due to some circumstances that were out of our control, we had to close it down and were in great debt. It was very discouraging and we could not understand how this could have happened if God had spoken and confirmed it the way He did. Did we miss Him? Did we misunderstand everything? No, we knew God had spoken but could not explain what had happened to the many people who questioned it all because of the circumstances. Shortly after, the LORD spoke and said that we were to step out into more ministry. Then He came and spoke to Ivan audibly and said, "It is time for you to stop building your kingdom and start building mine". He said it twice. This was scary for us, as we owed many thousands of dollars and needed income to pay it and to live. However, we knew He had spoken and decided to trust Him through the fog.

We went through seven horrible years of financial disaster. It was one of those things that we would not wish on anyone. Our finances were getting worse by the day and we had no way of getting out of it. For seven years, we worked really hard to reduce the debt and, as soon as we got it down to about half, something would happen and it would go back up again. This happened several times. It was unreal. We paid thousands and thousands of dollars and continued owing the same amount. We knew it was God who was doing it but could not understand why. One thing we can say is that God was incredibly faithful and never left us. Each and every month He met our needs. We were not sure how sometimes, but He did. However, through the challenges and struggles of those seven years we learned so much.

God taught us to trust Him in a different way, to depend on Him. He broke our pride and independence. We lost so much and many criticized us and doubted our hearing from God. We lost much reputation and trust in the eyes of men. This caused our character to change tremendously. We also broke free from the hold of Mammon (the love of money and riches) in our lives.

During those years we remembered a prophecy we had received a year before the bottom fell out. We have a tape with a prophecy that says, "God is going to give you finances. He is going to give you 'X' amount of dollars, etc." The amount prophesied was the exact amount of our debt. When we got the prophecy we immediately figured that the money would come soon and began to plan what to do with it. Obviously we did not know God's plans.

We prayed much and reminded God of His promise to give us that money. At the end of the seven years, (eight years after receiving the prophecy), God answered and fulfilled His word. In a matter of three months He supernaturally provided every single penny to pay the debt in full. We would have never imagined the journey that would lead to the fulfillment of that exciting prophecy. We saw God redeem absolutely everything. We were shocked to see the miracles that took place, as supernatural finances came to pay everything off. When the debt was paid in full, I went to the bank to update our bank book and the most amazing thing happened. It was eerie really because the amount that was in our bank account was, to the penny, exactly the same amount that was in our account when we started the business seven years before. It was like a full circle. God wiped the debt and it was as if what took place during those seven years had not happened. We experienced full redemption to the penny and it was as if we had never lost anything. Yet we were changed and transformed forever. The Ivan and Isabel who began that journey were not the same ones who finished it. We were literally made better by it all. It was a terrible time, but we would not change it for anything as the fruit of it has brought life to us and glory to our LORD. At the end it all worked out way better than we could have ever imagined.

About two years ago, I spoke at a ladies' meeting about this particular subject, "Trusting God till the end". It was a powerful meeting and afterwards I ministered prophetically for several hours. The presence and power of God were truly present and tangible in the room. I was full of the Holy Spirit and the Father's love when I left. As I got home Ivan was rushing our daughter Amanda to the hospital. She suffers from seizures and, from time to time, she would have big fits that would last for a long time. When that happens we have to rush her to the ER immediately. I went to the hospital with them. Ivan took her in as I parked the car. When I got in, she was hooked to several machines and a team of doctors and nurses was working on her, trying to get the seizures to stop. It was the worst we had ever seen. They did not know what to do as she was not responding to any of the drugs they were giving her. As time went on things looked worse and worse, so they called the doctor, who was the head of the department, to see if he could help her. They asked Ivan to go outside to fill out some forms as I stayed in the room.

At that time, one of the doctors came to ask me for information on Amanda's background. I told him that I did not know because we had adopted her from Guatemala when she was seven years old, and I did not know anything about her past or her birth family. His reply was, "Oh how sad for you to have gone so far away to adopt a child and then end up with this." I told him what a blessing this child is but he just shook his head and went away. A few minutes later, the head doctor came in. He checked her and talked to the other doctors and nurses. He said to me, "It seems that due to the severity and the length of the seizures (two hours seizing non-stop) her brain has been damaged and she is now suffering from cerebral palsy". The seizures had finally stopped but she was unconscious. I looked at her and knew that what the doctor was saying was probably correct. I had a cousin who had cerebral palsy and, therefore, I am very familiar with the condition.

Then he said, "I have just found out also that this is the child who nearly died in a drowning accident in the summer, and was here for hours fighting for her life". As he was talking, I could feel the waves of the Holy Spirit filling me over and over, and smiling said, "Oh yes, doctor, she is the one. You have no idea what this year has been like for us. We had quite a time this summer indeed." He then looked at me very intensely and said, "How can you then be like this? How can you be so peaceful and happy when this is so bad?" I then proceeded to tell him about the goodness of our LORD and at that moment I felt His presence more intensely shining in and through me. The doctor shook his head and walked away.

I went and sat by Amanda's side. Suddenly the doctor's words ran through my mind and I noticed that Amanda looked completely like a child with cerebral palsy. Fear ran through my body at that moment but, immediately, I remembered what I had been teaching that very morning and realized that I had a decision to make. I also remembered God's promises over her life and I said to Him, "Father, we have done all we can for her and the doctors are doing all they can for her. But now it is up to You. I have evidence of Your love for her and of Your faithfulness. I know You love her more than we do. You saved her from destitution and death in Guatemala and You brought her here. Against all odds, You saved her from dying in the swimming accident and, if You want, You can also save her from this. I know You are able to restore her if You so wish but, if for some reason you choose not to, I know that we will get through it somehow and at the end, everything will work out just fine. Therefore, I choose to trust You till the end and, no matter what You do, I will love You and will make You famous for the rest of my life". At that moment, I was filled with the greatest release of the Father's love, and the presence of the Holy Spirit filled me completely. I could feel the glory of God shining in and out of me, even stronger than before. I was completely overwhelmed by the peace and the joy of the LORD and could not stop smiling. It was a smile that came from deep inside and I could not help it.

The doctor kept looking at me and I saw him talking to the nurses and pointing at me. They came and asked me if I was OK and with a smile that came from the depths of my being I said, "Oh yes, I am great. Thank you!" They kept an eye on me the whole time. I knew that they thought I was in shock. Ivan came back to the room and the doctor immediately stopped talking to me and only talked to him, yet the nurses kept watching me closely, the whole time. Later on, when Amanda was more stable, they took her to a room upstairs and as they were hooking her up to the machines there, we went to the cafeteria to get a coffee. One of the nurses was there and said to me with great concern in her voice, "How are you feeling?" Again I smiled with great joy flowing out of me and said, "Wonderful, thank you so much!" She turned to Ivan and said, "How are things really going? How is she?" It is understandable that they would be confused about what was happening to me. Ivan was very peaceful and confident as he always is, but I could not hold the joy and glory that was flowing like a river out of me.

Amanda was unconscious for about 13 hours and, finally, woke up late at night. The next morning was Sunday and Ivan went to see her first thing in the morning. She was up and had a big breakfast with him. He went to church and I came at 10 o'clock to be with her. She was sitting there, watching a movie on the TV, and was back to her regular self. She was happy and chatty as if nothing had happened. I was sitting on the side, reading a book, when the head doctor came to check on her. He saw me and out of politeness said, "How are you?", but kept on going. I smiled again and very joyfully said, "I am fine thanks, and how are you?" He did not reply. He got to Amanda's bed and looked at her with surprise on his face. He said, "Hi, how are you?" She smiled and very joyfully responded, "I am just fine doctor and, tell me, how are you?" (She said it in the same tone of voice I had used). He shook his head and proceeded to examine her and then, with great confusion on his face, said to the nurse, "This child is fine. There is nothing wrong with her at all. There is nothing wrong with her. She can actually go home." He kept looking at her with wonder on his face. Then, as he was walking out of the room, he stopped in front of me, looked at her intensely, then looked at me in the same manner and said, "I don't know what it is that you are doing, but whatever it is, it's good." He looked at her again and said to me, "Keep on doing what you are doing because it is very, very good."

Amanda got dressed and ready to go. It was Sunday so she made it clear that she wanted to go to church to praise the LORD. On her way out of the hospital, she stopped at the nurses' station to thank them for all they had done for her, and then went to the head doctor and said, "Thank you for all you have done for me." He leaped from his chair, grabbed her by the shoulders and looking at her with the same wonder in his eyes said, "Child, there is something about you that is very special and different. I don't know what it is but I need to take your picture." She smiled and posed for three photos for him and then hugged him good-bye. He stood there watching her leave the hospital. When it was all over, I looked back at the whole event and realized that God had placed us in one of those challenging situations that call for His power to be released on earth, like He had told me in Brazil. We did not need to go through that. And Amanda certainly didn't need to experience all that so I said to the LORD, "What happen? What was your purpose in this?" He replied and said that the reason for that was because the doctors and the nurses needed to have an encounter with the undeniable power of God and now, they had it. So, at the end, it was worth it, because the experience and the story made God a bit more famous that day.

We have both lived through this many times and have tasted the great faithfulness of our LORD. Therefore, as we go through this journey on earth, we have decided to trust Him till the end and to use our lives and experiences to give him glory no matter what the circumstances are because, after all, "What other people on earth have a god like our God, who is so close to us and whom we can call on in our time of need?"

SECOND KEY: NEW GIFTS

1 Timothy 4:14 says, "Do not neglect the spiritual gift within you, which was bestowed on you through prophetic utterance with the laying on of hands by the presbytery".

This is a very important scripture and gives us another powerful key to unlock our promises. Do not neglect the gifts released into you through the prophecies spoken over you. Gifts are indeed released into our lives when we receive prophecies. Listen to them with care and pay attention to detail. Many times you receive prophecies that speak of things that are new to you and you simply dismiss them because they do not fit. For instance, you receive a prophecy that says that you will write, but you are not a writer. Up until the moment of the prophecy you did not have it in you but, the gift to write was imparted into you through the prophecy. Now it is up to you. You can neglect it or do something about it like Paul told Timothy.

That is what happened with Ivan when he received the prophecy about prophesying and becoming a prophet. Ivan was not prophetic at all and could not prophesy to save his life. Then, someone came and ministered to us, along with the rest of the leadership of the church. When he came to Ivan he said, "The Spirit of the LORD will come upon you, as it did on Saul, and you will arise as a prophet of the LORD but, unlike Saul, the mantle of the prophet will remain on you forever. You will prophesy to multitudes and will travel all over the world teaching, training, and equipping others to prophesy. Even a seer's anointing will come on you and you will enter into the supernatural realm of God." Everyone in that room knew that Ivan could hardly hear the voice of God, so we all looked at each other and shook our heads. Boy, we were shocked. He had been accurate with all the others in the room but when it came to Ivan he really blew it. However, we decided to give him grace because he was tired. He had just finished two conferences, and therefore, we figured that he was so tired that could not help but make a huge mistake...

Ivan's reaction was different. He heard the prophecy which, of course, did not fit, but he did not question it. He responded to the LORD and said, "Yes, I receive it and will do it", then he did something about it. He signed up for prophetic training right away. We laughed when he told us that he was going for prophetic training. "Why, if you are not prophetic at all?" we said. Ivan replied, "I know, but I have a prophecy that says that I will prophesy, so I should go and learn". He went and, by the second week, the gift that was imparted into him that day through the prophecy spoken over him got activated and he began to prophesy. He continued applying himself to it and God has done everything He promised and Ivan is walking in the fulfillment of that prophecy. He could have said, "Oh well, one day God will do it and I will prophesy" but, bless him, he decided not to neglect the gift.

I remember we were doing a prophetic school and we prophesied over this lady that God was going to use her powerfully in dance, prophetic dance to be precise, which would bring great glory to the LORD and would release His presence. It would be so anointed that people would stand around to watch, but their eyes would look at the LORD not at her. She had never danced in her life. It was news to her, but she believed it and became very excited and willing. The next day, during worship, she decided to do something about it and stepped out to dance. The Holy Spirit came and filled her in such a powerful way that, as she danced, the glory of God filled the room. People stood in a circle around her and were drawn to the Father, just like the prophecy said. About six months later we saw her again in another place and she said to me, "Oh, remember that day when I danced. Wasn't it amazing? Well it has not happened since. I am waiting for the LORD to do it again. I hope He does it soon".

I heard that and realized that she did not understand what was happening. A gift was indeed released into her and got activated the next day, but it was up to her to activate it. God will wait for her to do something about it. He is not going to pick her up and move her feet for her. He will empower the gift in her, when she steps out to dance.

Many, many people are in that place. The LORD has spoken to you and has released new gifts into your lives but you are simply neglecting them, and nothing is coming out of it. Then you wonder why is it that you are not doing the things the prophecies said? God is waiting for you to step up and activate the gift that has been dormant in you since the prophecy was given. Perhaps yesterday you were not artistic but today you received a prophecy that said that you are, or that God will use you in the arts. That means that today a seed was deposited within you and if you wish, you can activate it and God will give it life. Ivan and I received words from the LORD that we would write. Neither one of us were writers but when the prophecies came we knew that the gift for writing had been released into us, so we decided that we would not neglect it and began writing articles, reports, papers, and now we are writing books. Slowly we saw how that seed, deposited in us, became alive and grew. We now love writing. It was not in us, but it was imparted into us.

So, go back and listen to your prophecies again. Pay attention and identify the new gifts that were imparted into you and make choices to be proactive and do something about them. We promise you that God will activate those seeds/impartations that are dormant in you and you will suddenly find yourself doing the things spoken over you, and your prophecies will begin to unfold.

THIRD KEY: KINGDOM IDENTITY

Another thing that prophecy reveals is something we call 'Kingdom Identity'. There is a big difference between our earthly identity and our Kingdom identity. On earth we are raised to do and be one thing, but we were created to do and be something else. Take Moses, for example. He was raised to be the next Pharaoh but he was created to be the deliverer of Israel. God had completely different plans for him. I received a full revelation of Kingdom identity once when I was caught up to heaven. In revelations of the Third Heaven twice I have seen God create people. That is one of the most powerful things I have ever experienced in my life. I have seen God do many things but creating people is what He likes the most. He is very relaxed when He does it and enjoys every minute of it. He laughs, whistles, and sings. He sings a song over each person, a different song over everyone. This reminded me of that scripture in Zephaniah that says that "He will rejoice over us with singing" (3:17).

As I saw this, I received a very powerful revelation about our existence and creation. Many, many people on earth have their identity wrapped around their conception. They base their value and acceptance or lack of it on that fact. There is a huge level of shame if a person was conceived out of wedlock, in sin and immorality. There is great rejection when someone's conception was a mistake or an accident. It can be even worse for someone who was conceived as a result of a rape. However, when I was in heaven, I saw that there is a huge difference between conception and creation. Conception is a completely human act. Two people get together and conceive a child. It can be done in a wholesome situation with God's blessing or in a sinful situation. That is their choice. They can conceive but they cannot create. I saw that as the conception takes place God takes over and creates. He is the One who chooses to create.

God does not have to create. He chooses to create. Therefore, if you were born and exist it is not just because your mom got pregnant. It is because God chose to create you. He wanted you to exist and I know for a fact that He delighted in creating you. He smiled and laughed out loud. He whistled and sang a special song over you as He placed His love in your heart and kissed you on the head when He finished. You may have been conceived in pain and rejection, but you were created with joy and delight, and that is where your identity begins. Make no mistake, He kissed you and loved you since the very beginning. Your identity began with creation not with conception. Conception is human, but creation is completely divine.

Another thing I saw is that in heaven we are not called, or known, by our earthly identity, but by our Kingdom identity. It is amazing. In heaven you are not referred to as "John the driver", or "Anna the angry", or "Martha the bitter", etc., but they refer to you as they know God created you to be. They call you "John the pastor", or "Anna the great missionary", "Martha the teacher", etc. It is a completely different world indeed.

Once we understand this, we can embrace our existence. Then, as we begin to know the Father's love and character, we realize that He only creates good and wonderful things. We are His workmanship and He does not make mistakes. All good things come from Him and from His heart. I saw that, as He created and laughed, He spoke the ways and the destiny He planned for each person. He would say, "You will sing and dance." "You will be strong and be a conqueror." "You will travel and be creative." Etc., etc., etc. He took portions of His character and gave them to each as He spoke a plan and a future for them. It is a completely supernatural and divine event. Everything is perfect up until then. The problem comes when we are born because we are born into the Kingdom of men. The Kingdom of men is ruled by the devil and carries his character and fingerprints. In the Kingdom of men there is death, pain, hurt, rejection, and brokenness. These things get us right away. As soon as we are born the labels start. We all get them. We are either too fat, too thin, too dumb, too poor, too short, and so on. Many of those labels are inherited from our family lines and others are added on. No one wins in the kingdom of men. Even those who do well are filled with pride and arrogance and carry their own labels.

We take those labels without realizing it, and embrace them as our identity. That is the way my family is, we say. That is the way I am. We become our labels and they become our identity and shape our destiny. We all have experienced this. The unfortunate thing is that this is a false identity, because that is not who God created us to be. Our real identity is found deep in our hearts and in our DNA. When God created us He placed our identity and who we really are in our DNA, but it gets hidden behind all those walls and labels. We don't even know it and no one else around us cares to find out because they all are living under the same yoke. That is where prophesying from the Father's heart is so powerful, because it reveals those hidden things. The plans that God has made for us – plans to bless us and to prosper us. Plans to give us a hope and a future.

Those plans can only be found in the Father's heart and the gift alone cannot find them (In our next book we will give you the keys to effectively prophesy from the Father's heart, not from the gift). The gift gives us access to the realm of the obvious, but God goes beyond the obvious. Prophecy from the Father's heart reveals the things that the eye has not seen, the ears have not heard, and the mind has not yet imagined, which God has prepared for us (1 Corinthians 2:9). That is what the heart of prophecy is all about. Prophecy reveals who God created us to be, and the identity He planned for us when He created us. Prophecy reveals our "KINGDOM IDENTITY".

Kingdom identity is absolutely amazing and discovering it changes our lives forever. There is nothing like realizing that there is another life we can live. However, we must have Kingdom mentality to understand these things because our earthly mentality cannot process it. Let's illustrate what Kingdom identity is like and how it takes us in a different direction. There was a young man called Gideon who in the eyes of men was not much to talk about (Judges 6). There was war in the land and everyone who was anyone and who could fight was fighting in the battle. However Gideon was at home with the women and children. Obviously he was not much to brag about. He probably had a label of being a 'wimp' or perhaps a 'loser'. This one night, Gideon had gone out to thresh wheat and hide it away when the angel of the LORD appeared to him and prophesied. He said, "You mighty man of valour (mighty hero), the LORD is with you." And then he proceeded to tell him God's plans for him, which seemed unreal and impossible for Gideon to accomplish. Gideon's reply was, "How can I rescue Israel? My clan is the weakest in Israel and I am the smallest [most insignificant] in my whole family" (v. 15). The LORD replied, "I will be with you and you will be able to do it". Gideon received an impossible promise but, most of all, he discovered what he was created to do. He discovered his destiny and his Kingdom identity. As we know, he responded and God did it. Little Gideon became the deliverer of Israel and walked through the impossible promises of God. He went from being the most insignificant one in his entire house to being the mighty hero of the whole nation. Who would have imagined the plans that God had made for him?

Then there is the young boy called David. He was a young shepherd boy and no one expected anything big from him; not even his father had a clue of young David's Kingdom identity. We see the prophet Samuel being sent to Jesse's house to anoint one of his sons to be the king of Israel. All of Jesse's sons were there but David. He was the youngest and was not even considered as a candidate to meet the prophet. God did not choose any of the other boys and Jesse had to send for David who was the one chosen to be king. David had been discarded because of his appearance. He was not like his brothers, but the LORD was very clear to Samuel about Jesse's oldest son. He said, "Don't judge by his appearance or height, for I have rejected him. For I don't see things the way you see them. People judge by outward appearance, but I look at the heart." (v. 7). David received that day a prophecy that changed his life and gave him a new identity – Kingdom identity. Who would have thought that that young shepherd boy had been created to be the greatest king Israel ever had and a close friend of God. The things that no one had imagined.

Then there is the young man called Saul of Tarsus, a persecutor of the church and a murderer. He was raised to do and to be one thing, but no one could have ever imagined what he had been created to be. Then one day he ran into Jesus and found out his destiny and his Kingdom identity. The one who killed the Christians would become a father of the church for endless generations. He was transformed and fulfilled a destiny no one would have ever imagined.

Now, let's talk about people of today. How prophecy has transformed people as they have discovered their Kingdom identity and are now fulfilling their destiny.

JONATHAN'S STORY

Jonathan was a young man living in a third world nation. He was severely dyslexic and had been labeled as a loser since he was little. He could never learn anything in school and could hardly read and write. He could write his name and, perhaps, read a few words but that was it. People began to speak negatively about him and rejection quickly filled his life. Other kids teased him and made fun of him. No one believed in him and no one expected anything from him. He heard over and over that he would never accomplish anything in life. Jonathan believed all he heard and embraced his labels as his identity. He did not even finish grade four and soon started living up to everyone's expectations.

Jonathan's parents were devout Christians and raised him in the church. However, things were no different there. Everyone thought the same way about him and treated him in the same way. His labels followed him there too. Therefore, as a teenager Jonathan decided to leave the church and walk away from the LORD. What difference did it make anyway?

We had met this family and had become friends with them years before so, when we came back to their country to do a conference, we stopped over to see them. That is when we found out that Jonathan had left the LORD and was fully into the world. He had given himself to alcohol, addictions, and sin. His life was a mess and he had become a castaway. No one in the church wanted anything to do with him. All the families whose children had grown up with him did not want their children to talk to Jonathan because he was bad news and would contaminate them. Jonathan was truly and fully living the life of a loser and his labels became his full identity on earth. He had no hope and no future to look forward to. We were terribly sad to find out this news and invited Jonathan to come with us to the conference and help us mind the tapes.

He was not sure that he wanted to be in our team but he knew that there were pretty girls in the church where we were going and he wanted to see them, so he came. Officially he was coming to help us and had to be around us, so the girls were safe.

We got to the church where we were doing the conference for a whole week with Jonathan by our side. The pastors knew Jonathan and were fully aware of his reputation. They were not happy that we had brought him and did not want him there. However, he was part of our team and they had to accept him. Jonathan was pretty good and helped us with the tapes every night. On the last day of the conference, as we finished ministering to the last person, we decided to prophesy over Jonathan. As I looked at him through the eyes of Jesus, I saw his heart and was moved to compassion for him. Then, because I know my Father and His heart, and I know that He does not create a loser or a failure, I turned to Him and asked, "Father, I know You love this young man and I know that You made a plan for him. Please tell me, "What is Jonathan's Kingdom identity? Who did You create him to be? Tell me what song did You sing when You created him? What things did You speak into his heart and placed in his DNA the day of his creation? Tell me what are the things that no one has seen, heard or imagined about this young man? What are the plans You have for him to give him a hope and a future? Show me Your heart for Him and what is hidden behind all those walls of pain, frustration, fear, anger, etc.? Tell me, who is this young man?

At that moment, the LORD began to speak and I began to prophesy. I spoke long and it was powerful. However, as I was prophesying I saw the pastor looking at his wife and then at me, and he had a very angry look on his face. I knew that he completely disagreed with the things that I was saying and I could not really blame him because, among many things, the prophecy said that God was going to raise him up to be a mighty leader and he would lead the young people in the ways of the LORD. That was a problem for the pastor because they did not want Jonathan talking to their kids and I was telling him that he would lead them. I also told Jonathan that he would become a man of honour before his family and others, and that people would look at him with respect. I also said that he would not live in poverty forever, but that he would succeed because God would open doors for him to have a good job and, as a result, he would make more money than anyone else in his whole household and even his family would respect and honour him.

There was a lot more to the prophecy but these are a few of the things I remember. By the look on the pastor's face I knew that if I had prophesied over Jonathan the first night of the conference he would have canceled it. He would have said that I was not prophetic and did not hear from God at all, because he was seeing the appearance and the ways of the man, but God was seeing his heart. However, I disregarded it as we were leaving the country the next morning. I knew God had greater plans for this young man than anyone could possibly imagine.

As I prophesied, Jonathan fell on the floor weeping. When it was all over I hugged him and he wept on my shoulder for a long time. Then he began crying and laughing and could not walk. We literally had to carry him to the car and then home and to his bed. His parents did not know what to think when we brought him home like that. We tried to explain but they had never seen anyone in that condition and could not understand. We put him on his bed and left. We did not hear anything else until two to two-and-a-half-years later when we came back to do another conference in the same place. As usual, we stopped over to see Jonathan's parents and his mother told us that the night we brought Jonathan home he laughed and cried all night long. Then the next morning he got up and bought himself a tape player so he could hear his prophecy. He listened to his tape twice a day every single day. It was the first thing he heard as soon as he woke up in the morning and the last thing he heard when he went to bed at night.

Shortly after, Jonathan began to make choices because he liked what the prophecy said. No one in life had ever said anything good or nice about him. No one had ever believed in him until he heard God speak, and God believed in him. God had plans for him that gave him a hope and a future and he wanted it. He had nothing else to hold onto so he chose to believe God and said "YES" to Him.

He continued listening to the prophecy and, as he believed, faith arose in his heart. Faith comes by hearing the word of God and he was hearing it twice a day. Then he began to make the decisions that aligned his life according to God's plans for him. He gave his life back to the LORD, gave up his worldly friends, the sin, received healing and ministry. He attended every single meeting and service available. He gave himself to it wholeheartedly and God began to work and do the impossible. When we returned, Jonathan was the youth leader of the church and, as the prophecy said, he was leading the young people in the ways of the LORD. Jonathan was also working in a job he was not qualified for. God opened a door for him that no one could open and he was earning more money than his father, and more than anyone in his household.

Soon after, Jonathan bought a car. He was the first person in his household to own a car, and in a third world nation that is huge prosperity. Suddenly, Jonathan was respected by his family, by people in the church, and even in the world. Then, Jonathan, found a beautiful young woman, built a house and got married. Last year Jonathan became a father and has a precious family who love him. He and his family are active in the church and love the LORD with all their hearts. He has the best marriage of all his siblings and is happy. That young man who was lost without hope and future stopped being a loser and became the man God created him to be. Today Jonathan is living his Kingdom identity and fulfilling his destiny.

As we shared before, Ivan is someone who went from being a write-off to becoming a man whose life brings great glory to the LORD. He too found his Kingdom identity and is fulfilling his destiny today.

ISABEL'S IMPOSSIBLE PROMISES

Like Gideon, I was born in a very insignificant third world country, in a very insignificant village, to a very insignificant family, and was a very insignificant child. In a third world country life is hard and people live to survive. No one thinks big or expects big because there is nothing to expect. People live day by day and their greatest goals are to feed, clothe, and house the family. That is all there is and this mindset is passed down through the generations. You work and survive and that's it. There is nothing else to look forward to. No one dreams or expects breakthroughs. So my life and expectations were pretty much the same thing I saw my parents and everyone around me do: work and survive. My family was extremely poor. I know what it is like to lack everything and not know how we would make it. I know what is like to be alone with my mother after my dad died and be on the verge of being homeless not having anyone to help us. There is a huge realm of limitations when you live in these circumstances and you just learn to live within it.

Then one day when I was six years old, I came home from school for lunch and had an experience that changed my life. My mother was serving me at the kitchen table. She went to get me a tortilla and as I looked at her walking towards the stove a vision opened up in front of me. In this vision I saw things I had never seen or heard about before. I saw what later I learned were airplanes. I saw nations, multitudes of people, and many other mighty things. As I was seeing it, the LORD spoke to me loud and clear and said, "Though you were born in this land you will not live here. You will not live the same life that your parents and your ancestors lived. You were born here but you will not die in this land. I am taking you to the nations. You will live in another land and from there you will travel to the nations of the world and accomplish great and mighty things." He said many other extraordinary things as well. I was literally seeing things that did not make sense to me. I had never seen an airplane and had never heard about other nations. I did not know there were other nations.

No one I knew traveled anywhere except to a place called "The Capital". Going there was a big deal and people got a new outfit for it. It was a two day affair and when they came back we gathered to hear the news about this place. Therefore, seeing airplanes in the vision was like when Daniel had his vision of the end times where he saw things he could not explain, but we now understand are aircraft carriers, etc.

When it was over, I told my mother what I had seen and heard, and her reply was, "That's OK dear. It was just your imagination. Those things are impossible you know. Forget about it and just don't tell anyone." I heard that but somehow I could not believe her. I could not forget what I had seen. I knew that it was 'real' somehow.

Years went by and I never forgot what happened that day. Then, when I was 18 years old, I got saved and began to attend church. One day, in another vision, the LORD showed me with more detail the fullness of the calling and destiny He had for me. The people in the church where I attended prophesied over me but they spoke of the things that were possible in their eyes. They prophesied within their realm of limitations. Their prophecies said that God would bless me, provide for me, feed me, clothe me, heal me, and keep me safe. That was all we knew our God could do, and we only prophesy and receive according to our realm of limitations. Then American missionaries began to come to our church and they had a much bigger God than our God. Their God could do amazing things and had resources we had never heard of. We could not fathom that kind of power and greatness. They had a different realm of limitations than us and, for some reason, they would prophesy over me. Their prophecies were very different. They spoke of great things. My pastors and the leaders would talk to me and 'debrief' me after they left. They would tell me, "You know that those things are not possible. You know Americans; they are sensational and sometimes say things to show off. They mean well, but you cannot believe them because all that stuff is just impossible".

I heard that, but in my heart I could not agree with them because the Americans prophesied according to the visions that first occurred when I was six years old and then again shortly after I got saved. Some of the things prophesied over me were that God would take me to the nations of the world to build His Kingdom; that I would walk in and out of embassies and government offices around the world; that I would dine with people in high governmental positions in many nations; that I would shake hands with many diplomats who would bend over backwards to grant my requests; that I would minister to leaders around the world; that the wealthy would seek my favour, that royalty in the world would seek me out for the word of the LORD and that He would give me His word for them, and much, much more. It was a great frustration for my leaders. I would constantly see them shaking their heads saying, "As if she needed that. She dreams already so much and believes things that are completely impossible." But I did not let that discourage me. I believed it all. I believed alone and against the advice of everyone around me. I did not know how it could possibly come to pass and often thought, "I wonder what things God will do to make this happen. It will be so exciting to live through all this". Instead of questioning it, I pondered in my heart and that released faith.

There is a big difference between pondering and reasoning what God says. Pondering is like thinking about it as fact that is coming. And this releases faith and expectation in the heart. A pregnant mother ponders about her baby; will it be a boy or a girl? Will he or she look like me or my husband? Will he or she sing, or dance? The more she ponders about her baby, the more real her baby becomes and she can't wait for the birth.

Reasoning is when we question things and seek understanding. When we reason something we try to figure it out. When we reason God's promises, doubt and unbelief raise in our hearts. That is how we can tell if we are reasoning or pondering what God says. If faith and expectation are growing in our hearts then we are pondering but if the fruit is doubt and unbelief then we are reasoning it. I chose to ponder in my heart the promises God had given me because the flip side of it was not that good. I had no other options really because otherwise I was stuck living the life I was raised to live and not the life that I was created to live.

Against everyone's advice, I aligned my life accordingly and positioned myself in the place of availability, and now I can truly say that every single one of those promises has already been fulfilled. God took me out of the land where I was born. He has taken me to the nations to build His Kingdom, to teach His children, to minister to, teach and help pastors and leaders around the world. I have walked in and out of embassies in many nations. I have been received in embassies with gifts and honour. I have shaken hands with many, many diplomats and have seen many of them bend over backwards to grant my request. I have been sent, with letters of endorsement from the government of Canada, to other nations and have been received with great respect, and all my requests have always been granted. I have dined with high government officials around the world and have stayed in diplomatic hotels surrounded by them. I have been sought out by the wealthy of the land and people of royalty in Europe have also sought me for the word of the LORD. Just as the prophecies said, the LORD has given me His word for them.

Some years ago, when I was in Costa Rica visiting my family, I went to my former church and, as I was sitting there at the back of the church, memories of my years there came to me. Then the LORD said to me, "Do you realize that every single promise I gave you, when you were here, has already come to pass? Now you have walked through the impossible promises I gave you. You have proof that it is possible. Now you are on the other side and nothing has been left undone. Now that you know that the impossible is true and possible, are you willing to speak my impossible promises to others, so they can have the same opportunity that you have had?" I said, "Yes, I am. I will speak Your impossible promises to others and will help them walk into their fulfillment." Many people hear these promises and say, "But this is too big to be true, how can it be?" And my reply is that the more impossible, the better it is.

The greater the better. I get very excited when I hear God speak like that to others, because there is no one on earth that can tell me that God's promises over your lives cannot come to pass, and there is no demon that can stand in front of me and tell me that your impossible promises from God are not possible. I know as I live and breathe that they are very much possible and real because we are living them and if it can happen for us, it can happen to anyone else. We promise you that. Therefore, my challenge to you is this: are you willing to take hold of your impossible promises and see them come to pass? Are you willing to be brave enough and 'silly' enough to believe the impossible and see the great I AM open for you the doors that no one can open? Scripture says that, "From the days of John the Baptist until now the kingdom of heaven suffers violence, and violent men take it by force" (Matthew 11:12). Are you willing to arise, become violent, and take your inheritance and the Kingdom today?

Ivan and I are living a life we were not raised to live. Our families and everyone who knew us and knows where we come from are in awe of what the LORD has done and is doing. We have seen the impossible come to pass, and the thing is that we know who we are. We are still our parents' kids and I know where I come from. We have not acquired pedigree or position to cause these things to happen. We are regular people who discovered their Kingdom identity and who have an extraordinary God, without limitations, who is all-powerful and has made it all possible. We have also been 'silly' enough to believe His impossible promises, and today we live to make Him famous.

I am always amazed when I read in Luke 1, the responses of Zacharias and Mary to the prophecies spoken over them by the angel. These two people received impossible promises from God. Zacharias' reply was, "How will I know this for certain for I am an old man and my wife is advanced in years?" (v. 18) How can I know what you are saying is true...wow! Based on the circumstances, he questioned the authenticity of the prophecy. Oh LORD!

Then there is Mary. She received a prophecy more impossible than Zacharias' promise. What she was told was completely unprecedented and out of the box. She, bless her heart, asked in verse 34, ""How can this be, since I am a virgin?" She was not questioning the authenticity of the word but asking, "How will this happen?" Then the angel gave her instruction and in verse 38 she said, "Behold, the bond slave of the LORD may it be done to me according to your word. (I am the LORD'S servant, and I am willing to accept whatever he wants. May everything you have said come true NLT)" Wow, what heart and inspiration! Then, in verse 45, Elisabeth says to her, "You are blessed, because you believed that the LORD would do what He said." (NLT).

May you become people who are blessed because you believe that the LORD will do what He said.

FOR PASTORS AND LEADERS

Pastors and leaders have a pivotal role in the fulfillment of people's prophetic destinies. We have a huge responsibility in this area because a very important part of our job or responsibility is to help and facilitate the way for people to enter into their promised land. A while ago the LORD said to us, "Why do you think that the people of Israel were willing to follow Joshua to fight mighty giants on the other side of the waters?" I gave Him my answer and He said, "No, that is not why. The reason why they were willing to do that was because there was a piece of land with their name on it and Joshua could help them get hold of it. There was something in it for each of them". That is why they were willing to follow Joshua. They did not follow him so he would make it. They followed him because they all wanted their destiny and knew that this guy, Joshua, could help them get it. Joshua and Caleb also had a piece of land waiting for them, but their mandate was to take the rest of the people into the land and help them take possession of it.

For years we have heard people talk about the destiny of the church and how they are going there no matter what, and that people need to follow them or simply stay behind. As I had that talk with the LORD I realized that we had it backwards. The corporate destiny of the church is made up of the individual destiny of each person the LORD brings to it, and as each person enters their individual destiny the church by default will enter into her destiny. So, as leaders, we need to pay attention to the individual destiny of the people we are called to serve. God will bring those who carry the same spiritual DNA and mandate together and, therefore, we will all share the same vision and will carry the same goal. However, people are tired of doing church maintenance (simply warming pews on Sunday mornings). There is nothing that causes more destruction in a church than this. Church maintenance causes people to become discontented, jealous, disgruntled, critical, negative, etc. As we said before, there is something deep in the heart of every man and woman that calls for more. Deep calls unto deep for that destiny God wrote in our DNA when He created us. People want and need to know that there is more for them than to come to church to make the pastor's dream happen. Well, that would be fine if the pastor's dreams were to help them posses their promised land, but that is not always the case.

MEMBERS OF ONE BODY

Scripture says that we are all members of one body (Ephesians 3:6) and, therefore, we all have a job to do. There is enough for everyone in the Body of Christ. However, the great majority of Christians are not even aware of what their place is in the Body. Many years ago I was very frustrated about this scripture because I did not know what I was or where I fitted in, and no one around me could tell me or help me find out. I know most people feel the same way and are trying to find the same answer. It is very frustrating to do church maintenance when there is a Kingdom waiting to be discovered and attained. Throughout the years, we have found a simple way of solving this great mystery and helping people find their right place in the Body.

The best way of discovering what you are and where you fit in is by simply being you and doing the things that you like to do. Just do what comes naturally to you. What things make you happy? What makes you tick? What is in your heart that makes you feel great and satisfied when you do it? Perhaps you simply like to have coffees with people and listen to them. If that is what you enjoy, then do it, go for it. That simply means that you probably have a gift of counseling and a pastoral gifting and, who knows, today you may just have coffees with people but tomorrow you may end up leading a small group, and in time perhaps a church. The thing is that you do not need to have a church to be a pastor. Pastoring can be done at your kitchen table, at the coffee shop, or at work.

We have noticed that most people spend their lives trying to find out what they were created to do, and that is the wrong way of doing it. Instead of wasting your time doing that, invest in finding out who God created you to be. Because if you become who you were created to be, then you will naturally do what you were created to do. It is simple. That is why healing of the heart is so important. Most people live their lives without being who they were created to be. What a shame! Please do not let that happen to you. Learn to be you and allow God to change you. Learn to do what you enjoy and you will see it grow and grow.

We literally prophesy over thousands of people each year and, up until now, we have never found a person who simply was created to work and pay bills. Not one. Everyone has a piece of land waiting for them and it is time to discover which one is yours.

A common syndrome in the church today is jealousy, envy, and com-petition. There is nothing that gets people going like seeing someone else arise and be used by God. It is sad, really sad. The reason is that people are very frustrated because they also want to participate. They want to be active and build with the rest. We, as leaders, need to invest in helping them discover their destiny, prepare them for it, making a way for them to walk to the other side, and fight the giants with them. We must believe for them and with them. They need us to cheer them on all the way. We see pastoring as parenting. As parents we do the same for our kids. In our church we love our people. We absolutely love being with them and walking with them. We love to believe with them and for them and they know it. We have also taken the risk of making room for everyone to participate and to be an 'all hands on deck' kind of church. We know we do not have it all. We are a body and together we make a whole. What a relief that is! We have been telling this to our people since the beginning and encourage them to step out at the risk of making mistakes. Mistakes are part of the journey. What we have seen is that since they know that there is room for everyone and that they all can participate equally, there is no striving or competition. When God uses someone everyone else is happy and encouraged for them, because they know that tomorrow will be their turn. We don't really deal with jealousy and envy in our midst, but we see the most beautiful heart of unity and love among the people.

BELIEVING FOR OTHERS

Something that has helped us greatly as leaders is knowing the Kingdom identity of the people. We do listen to prophecies and believe what the LORD says. We do not take it lightly because we know our role in it. Many times, when people who look like trouble, or who look hopeless and discouraged, join a church it is easy for the pastors and the leaders to form an idea about them based on their earthly identity. Many, many times those people get labeled, placed into boxes, and hardly ever come out of them. We get this situation in our church but, instead of labeling them, we prophesy over them. We do this mostly for ourselves as we need to know their Kingdom identity. We need hope and faith for them, and also need to know how to invest into their lives. Once we prophesy over them we know what God thinks about them and how He feels about them. Feeling His heart and knowing His plans for them, changes our hearts, and we cannot help but love them and believe for them.

From that moment on, we deal with them according to their Kingdom identity and not their current condition. We do deal with their issues as well, and confront situations but we treat them according to who we know God created them to be. We treat them as God sees them, and remind them, constantly, of God's plans for them and also of their Kingdom identity because we believe it and we are willing to fight for it. It is amazing what happens when they know that it is not simply words but that we really believe it. That makes all the difference.

Some years ago, a fellow came to join our church. He was very hurting, broken, and rejected. He had a very serious bondage to pornography, immorality, rejection, a broken relationship and walls with his parents, particularly his mother, and other deep issues. He was considered a 'write-off' in the sight of others, including pastors and leaders. He met with us and told us what was going on in his life very openly. He told us how there was no hope for him. He had gone to the best for ministry and counseling and no one could help him. He then told us that he wanted to come to our church because we had prophesied over him twice before and the prophecies spoke of a destiny for him, and said things that gave him a hope and a future. He remembered that, but there was something else that he remembered. He said that when we prophesied over him, he looked at us and knew that we believed what we were saying and, therefore, he could come and ask us for help. When we saw him we remembered what the LORD had said and felt His heart and His love for him. We knew his Kingdom identity and that was all that mattered.

This fellow worked closely with his pastor and leaders and they knew he was coming to join us. Everyone was desperate. One day his former pastor contacted us and told us that he knew this fellow had come to us and that we wanted to help him but, he wanted us to know that this guy had gone to the 'best of the best' for help and they had not been able to help him and, therefore, as well-intentioned as we were, he knew we would not be able to help him either.

Time went by and we began to invest into this man's life. He was really willing to do anything in order to deal with his problems and to be set free. Bless him! But there was so much that had to change in his life. He got more ministry and counseling and began to deal with some issues of his heart. At the same time, we began to identify his mindsets and structures and worked on them. We set up a strategy to help him with the practical side of walking out of his bondages, and to find the way of escape. The journey was not easy and there were many bumps, challenging situations, and tests. We went through it all together. There were times when he tested us and, yes, we dealt with the issue, reminding him constantly of his Kingdom identity and never gave up on him. We knew that, one day as healing and freedom came to him, his ways would change and the man we knew inside would be revealed. It took time, but slowly it happened. Healing came into his heart, freedom into his life, and his ways began to change. Then everything around him changed too. The relationship with his parents was completely restored. He loves his mother and greatly enjoys her company. His eyes light up when he speaks of her and he is truly proud of being her son. He has also developed a great friendship with his father and honours him. He is growing in his giftings and ministry. His earthly identity has disappeared and he has started to live his Kingdom identity. He is daily becoming more and more the man God created him to be and is taking the Kingdom by force. He is truly an inspiration to us all.

A long time ago, I went through a season in which I was hurting and 'burned out' and was not sure I would step into the fullness of ministry again. However, the pastors we had at that time believed in me and for me. They made it known by words and actions. I know that this was pivotal in helping me through that transition. We have experienced this on both sides and know that it works. People hear their prophecies and all God has planned for them, but lose sight of them easily because of the trials and difficulties of life. We, as leaders, need to do the Caleb task and keep them alive, remind them what the LORD has said about them and don't give up. They are used to the world giving up on them, and we must be the place where there is security and consistency. We know from 1 Corinthians 13 that love never gives up, and never loses hope. We are the ones that give up but our Father never does and, as Kingdom leaders, we need to reflect this kind of character. When people know that you trust them and believe in them no matter what, there is something deep inside that believes too. I know people's Kingdom identity and invest into it.

The interesting thing is that people know that and trust me. I can talk to people about difficult things in their lives and they receive it from me. Others have actually commented on it. And the reason is that they know I see something in them that they cannot see themselves and I believe in it. I don't just say it. I really do and I am willing to fight for it and see them become all God created them to be. That makes all the difference.

I remember this one time, I was having coffee with a dear friend of mine, who had gone through a powerful transformation in her life. When we first met she was what many call a mess. I had first been her counselor at church and in time we became great friends. Through the years the LORD did great things in her life. He set her free and made her into a woman of valor. So that day she was remembering what the LORD had done in her life and said to me, "Back then my life was a mess and it felt like there was no way out of it. The pastors and leaders of the church did not know what to do with me and constantly got very frustrated. I remember there were times when I would react in a bad way and they would call me on it. I used to tell them, 'You don't understand, that is not really me. I do not know why I reacted that way, but all I can tell you is that this is not who I really am.' They would get very upset every time and said to me, 'Well if that is not you, then who are you really?' I heard that but could not give them an answer. I did not know who I was. I just knew that, in my heart of hearts, that was not who I really was and I wanted to change."

"Also, I was so intimidated by them that I could not open up all the way. It did not feel safe. Then I met you, and you were different. You treated me differently. You never, ever, once treated me as a mess even though I was one. But, no matter what I did, you always treated me with respect, honor, love, and favour. You made me feel that I was more than what you saw and I knew that you believed me and also believed in me. That caused me to trust you and let you in behind my walls so you could help me. As years have gone by and God has healed me, the real me has been found. However, I have noticed something amazing. You treat me exactly the same way as you did then. There is no difference. I can understand you treating me this way now, but why back then when no one else did? "

I said, "Back then when I first met you God showed me your King-dom identity. I knew who you really were, who God created you to be, and heard His heart about you. Also, I heard closely the prophecies spoken over you and believed them. Once I knew all that, I began to treat you and relate to you that way. Yes we have dealt with much junk as healing and freedom came to you, but I never moved my eyes away from what I heard and saw. Today you have become the woman I saw back there."

These are the supernatural things that only God can do. I am pretty sure that after Samuel anointed young David to be king, he treated him differently. He knew that even though in the eyes of man he was only a shepherd boy, that young man carried a great Kingdom identity. He actually was the next King of Israel. What a difference it makes to know that!

We feel very discouraged when we see pastors and leaders who are simply stuck in the way their people are and cannot see beyond that. There was this particular time when our hearts sank completely. We were in Europe doing a conference and one day gave a full teaching on this subject and explained clearly how prophecy and Kingdom identity work. We then explained to the pastors and leaders present about their role in this. Many left feeling that they had weapons and strategy to help their people and to walk with them into their promised land. They were so happy. Then we went to this one church, right after, to minister prophetically to the people there. The senior and the associate pastor had been at the conference and heard the teachings but, one evening as we prophesied over people, one of the pastors kept saying, "Oh, I can't see that in them. I just can't see that happening. Not at all". He said this a lot. We tried to remind them about what we had shared with them earlier but they were so stuck in what they could see, that could not believe for the people. We left that place knowing that all that investment would simply be lost, because the pastors and leaders were not willing to go outside the box and believe for the people. They were caught up in their mindsets and the people were stuck there with them. Needless to say that church did not advance.

At the same time, we have been greatly blessed and encouraged by many courageous leaders, who dared to believe and chose to invest in the lives and destinies of their people. We have seen their churches completely transformed and they are advancing powerfully and making a difference in the world. As with everything in the Kingdom, God seeks stewardship in order to release more. As leaders, we must remember that men see the appearance but God sees the heart, and He wants us to become leaders who see through His eyes, so we can believe and make opportunity for the people we serve, just as He did for David and Gideon. Just like with our children at home, they know if we believe or not, and they can be inspired or discouraged by us. Let's be leaders who can give life and the kind of encouragement to our people that causes them to believe in the impossible, so they can reach the fullness of their destiny. It is not easy, but it is possible.

THE CALEB GENERATION

We have been greatly inspired by Caleb. He and Joshua were part of the team of twelve men who were sent to spy out the Promised Land. As we read the account in Numbers 13, we see that they all went into the land and all confirmed that, indeed, milk and honey were flowing and they brought some of the fruit back. They all also reported that there were giants and the cities were fortified. All twelve saw the same things and gave the same report about the land, but ten of them were afraid of the giants. They liked the milk and honey, but could not see how they could possibly conquer them and take over the land. The circumstances were impossible and ten of them were stuck in that. But Joshua and Caleb had a different reaction. They were not afraid and believed God. That was the difference. Exactly the same circumstances, exactly the same report but two completely different approaches. Joshua and Caleb were different. Verse 30 says, "Then Caleb quieted the people before Moses and said, 'We should by all means go up and take possession of it, for we will surely overcome it'". He did not deny that there were giants and fortified cities, but he did something the others did not do. He believed God and was willing to act on it. He did not focus on the circumstances but on God's power to give them victory and the land.

However, the others were afraid and continued giving the reasons why it was impossible. It got so bad that the people became afraid, cried all night and grumbled against Moses and Aaron (Numbers 14). Next we see that, as a response, Joshua and Caleb spoke to the congregation saying that the land they had spied out was good and that the LORD would give it to them if He was pleased with them. Then, in verse 24, God says that He would take Caleb and his descendants into the promised land because he (Caleb) had a different spirit in him (a different attitude) and followed Him fully (wholeheartedly). God was so pleased with Caleb's attitude and response that He, personally, promised to take him and his family into the land.

We see this scenario repeat itself daily. God gives promises to His people personally and through prophecies and people acknowledge that they are good (the land indeed flows with milk and honey), but immediately they see the giants and fortified cities (all the hindrances and circumstances that oppose the promise). Ah, the famous circumstances. They are so powerful aren't they? The difference between Caleb, Joshua, and the other ten is the way they reacted to the circumstances. Ten spies saw the promise but focused on the circumstances, but the other two focused on God's promise despite the circumstances. Prophecies are glimpses into our promised land. They show us the milk, the honey, and the fruit of it. We like them and want them, but we have to make a decision. Will we believe the circumstances and retreat in fear, or believe God and become conquerors like Caleb. If you read about his journey you see that he never lost sight of the promise and trusted God and, at the end, God gave him the biggest and best portion of the land.

Last year the LORD told us that a change of mantles was coming from heaven. He said that the season of the Moses generation is coming to an end and the season of the Caleb generation will begin. He said that the Moses generation consists of those who have heard the promises of God and believed but their mindset is, "One day this will come to pass"; "One day when things change....". They are waiting for 'one day'. Then there is the Caleb generation which consists of those willing to believe, stand-up, and take possession of it. The LORD said that He will release the same anointing He gave to Caleb to those who choose to let go of the Moses mentality. He will release the spirit of a conqueror to those who respond to this calling. Joshua was also a conqueror. He grew up with, and was mentored by, Moses but he was commissioned by God to fulfill the mandate, so he stopped hoping for, 'one day we will get there', and took the people there. He became aggressive and took the Kingdom by force. You have to be strong and very courageous indeed, but God will empower you and will make you a conqueror.

Look at your prophecies again and focus on the milk, the honey, and those big grapes in the Promised Land (your destiny), and fight the good fight that will give you possession of it, because if the LORD is pleased with you, then He will take you into that land and give it to you.

"Only do not rebel against the LORD; and do not fear the people of the land, for they will be your prey. Their protection has been removed from them, and the LORD is with us; do not fear them." (Numbers 14:9). You have a promise!!!

SUMMARY

Here we are giving a summary of what we recommend pastors and leaders to do. We are doing it in point form so you can use it as a reference as you help the people you serve.

GUIDELINES FOR CHURCH LEADERS:
Following-up prophetic words

- Be willing to change your mindsets regarding the people: Prophecies from the heart of God will speak of Kingdom identity and destiny. They will speak of the heart of man and the heart of God for them. These prophecies have the power to transform their lives and change their destiny. Remember always the word of the LORD to Samuel the prophet: "Do not look at his appearance or at the height of his stature, because I have rejected him; for God sees not as man sees, for man looks at the outward appearance, but the LORD looks at the heart."(1 Samuel 16:7).

- Be willing to believe for them and their promises. Most of the time, they will not have faith to believe for them because they are greater than anything they have ever imagined. "No eye has seen, no ear has heard and no mind has imagined what God has prepared for those who love Him." (1 Corinthians 2:9). Remember that they are like kids and look up to you as parents to tell them that it is possible and that you believe.

- Speak life into their promises. Keep the vision alive and remind yourself of them when the people's ways drive you crazy. Remember that their heart is not their ways and their ways are not their heart. Find the heart and deal with the ways appropriately, always remembering their Kingdom identity and honoring it. They will need to be reminded a million times a day, but it will pay off at the end. Mindsets will fall away.

- Encourage them to listen to their prophecies constantly so they will not forget them. They must let them become part of them (their mind and subconscious). The word of God is powerful. Encourage them to use them as weapons to fight the good fight and overcome their circumstances (1 Timothy 1:18).

- Help them not to neglect the gifts imparted into them. Encourage them to find the gifts released into them through prophecy and teach them not to neglect those gifts but to do something about it (1 Timothy 4:14). You will have to help them and make room for it. Be creative!

• Set up an accountability system for them regarding their prophecies and destiny. Remember to stay away from controlling them.

• Become a strategist. People need strategy to be able to walk out their prophetic destiny. Remember that the enemy is not omniscient but he hears the plans of God when they are spoken. However, the enemy's camp is very well set-up and as soon as the prophecies are spoken the enemy begins to plan a way to spoil them. Therefore, we must right away set-up an individual strategy for each person so they can overcome. As you hear their prophecies, ask yourself, "What would the enemy do to spoil this?" That is his job. He needs to cause them to retreat so he can advance. Find the areas that the enemy can bombard in order to blow it apart. Once you identify the weak areas strengthen them. They may need healing, deliverance, etc. Then, set up the structure for training and preparation. Set them on their way. If you have the means to provide it that's great, but if not, then find where and who can help them and point them in that direction.

• Prepare provision: Be willing to go the extra mile and plan for the next step after they are prepared. They need to know there will be something at the end. Develop a network that will allow vision, (places where those who are called to church plant can go and plant a church. Those called to missions can go out. Places where the ones called to pastor can have a group to pastor like a bible study, cell group, etc.). Trust the LORD for resources. He is looking for people who will believe Him. Remember, "If you build it they will come." We as leaders need to be very proactive in the fulfillment of the destinies of the people God has entrusted to us. He will make it happen if you are willing.

• Become part of the Joshua and Caleb generation of leaders. We must be willing to become leaders like them. People are longing for us to take them into their piece of the Promised Land. The corporate destiny of the church consists of the individual destinies of the people. If we as leaders facilitate the way for people to enter into their individual destiny, the church as a whole will enter into her corporate destiny and we will take on the land. It is time for the inheritance to be released and for the people to eat of the goodness of the land. People's hearts are longing for this and will rise up and if you are willing to answer this call, you will have a mighty army fighting the giants alongside you.

SECTION THIRTEEN

BLESSINGS, IMPARTATIONS AND MANDATES

Now we want to address some very important matters that the LORD has been speaking about to us, quite insistently, as these are also powerful keys that will unlock God's Kingdom and your destiny here today. Scripture says that we perish for lack of knowledge (vision, revelation), and this portion will help you attain your 'impossible promises'. May you have ears to hear what the Spirit of the LORD is saying today.

We first heard these things spoken in heaven, and then we began to walk them out. As we saw the results, we began to teach and impart them to others and have seen God open powerful doors for those who believe and understand. These are things for which we must be heavenly-minded and must really take on Kingdom mentality. We have seen that it is possible for us, on earth, to be people who can open up the heavens, move the Spirit, and live in power. We are different and carry a different spiritual DNA than the world, but we do not seem to understand the reality of this. The enemy has surely blinded us, so we do not discover the potential of the nature that is in us.

We carry Jesus the Son of God in us and He is SUPERNATURAL. Therefore, we should live a supernatural everyday life. We have learned to open that door and, for the last ten years at least, we have been living a very supernatural life seeing power, signs, and miracles be part of our daily life in a natural everyday way, and this is something God wants us all to attain. Scripture says that creation is longing and waiting eagerly for the revealing of the children of God and heaven is shouting for the same thing. Soon we will write a book completely on the supernatural, as we have experienced it, which will give you more details and teaching, but in this portion we want to talk about how the prophetic, in itself, opens portions of that realm and how easy it is to open the door for miracles.

Heaven is waiting for us to understand that we have the ability to cause heaven to open, so miracles can take place on earth. We have had this mentality that miracles are a completely sovereign thing that takes place only when heaven chooses. However, here we will show you how God wants us to cooperate with heaven to cause that kind of power to be released on earth. God wants us to be 'miracle makers' just as Jesus was and still is, in us, and, through us.

As I was with the LORD one day He told me that there are three heavenly things that are greatly wasted on earth, and He was sad about it. These three things are blessings, impartations, and mandates. These are heavenly investments and God said that He wants dividends from them. He is not interested in wasting investments anymore. We have seen God bring change in these areas and He is seeking more accountability. A while ago, we were booked to go to a particular church, out of the country, to do a conference. We had been booked for over a year, to be there and as, time came closer, the LORD said to us, "You cannot go there anymore. I will not let you go because the leaders of that church have just made a decision that has altered the destiny of the church. If you go, they will not invest the impartation that you will bring, and I am not going to waste my impartations anymore. You must cancel that conference and prepare to go to Australia. I have found a group of people there who are hungry and willing to invest anything I give them. I will open a door for you there. Go and take the impartation to them."

We obeyed the LORD and canceled the conference. We did not know anyone in Australia but prepared for when God called us to go there. Within three days we received an e-mail from a pastor we did not know in Australia. Somehow he had heard about us, and the LORD told him to invite us to come to do a conference there because we would bring an impartation that He wanted to give them. To our amazement, the dates for the conference there were exactly the same dates. In the meantime, we heard from one of the pastors of the other church and he told us that, at the time when God told us to cancel the conference there, the board of elders made a decision to pull out of the river and, as a result, he resigned his position.

We went to Australia as God instructed us and what the LORD told us was true. We met a very hungry group of people who were ready and willing to invest the impartation. God opened up the heavens for them and satisfied their hunger. We are in a time when God is coming to collect the dividends on His investments. The problem is that most people have put their talents away and have nothing to give back.

Not too long ago, the LORD also said to us that there is a great redistribution of 'talents' taking place (Matthew 25:14). He is gathering the talents that some have buried and will give them to those who do not take things for granted and who are diligent in investing everything, even if it is small or insignificant in the eyes of men. Remember that God loves small beginnings, let's be like Him and invest in them.

BLESSINGS

A blessing is one of those things that are greatly wasted on earth today. One of the reasons for this is that in our time, age, and culture we do not understand the meaning of a blessing. Blessings are as valuable today as they were in the days of the Old Testament because God does not change. In those days and culture they understood the authority of a father and the word of a father was powerful. Remember the story of Jacob and Esau (Genesis 27) and how they both wanted that blessing from their father Isaac. The reason was that the blessing from the father determined the lot they got in life. It determined their life and future, and established them. The moment it was given everything aligned accordingly in heaven and on earth to make it happen. It was extremely powerful and had ultimate authority. Jacob, then called Israel, called all his children and blessed them individually and they became what he said. Joseph also blessed each of his children before he died.

Blessings are very powerful and I understand this because I grew up in a country where we believed in this principle. Since we were little we would hear people say that whatever your parents said over you would come to pass. They said that parents had a special authority over their children. Therefore, it was very important that they said good things and blessings over us. One of the worst things that could happen to anyone was to be cursed by their parents, particularly their father. I remember once when I was 9 or 10 years old that my mother spoke a very strong curse over me. She was angry and when she got angry she often said things without thinking. This was one of those occasions. She yelled at me, "You will be a prostitute when you grow up". I heard that and it scared me. I remember how fear ran through me. Immediately I went to my bedroom and prayed as I had never prayed before. I called on the LORD and begged with all my heart that He would break those words my mother had just spoken over me, because I did not want to become a prostitute. Needless to say, God heard me and did accordingly. Bless Him!!!

In the Bible we see both sides of blessings and curses. The thing is, that for a blessing to take effect, the recipient has to accept it, take ownership of it. Jacob received Isaac's blessing, took ownership of it, and it became effective. Most people have not been taught how to receive blessings and how to activate them. That is why they are being wasted. The LORD said to me, "I am sending blessings to My children daily and look what they do." I looked over in the direction He was pointing on earth and saw His blessings being sent down like blankets over people and, just as they were going to land on them, they said, "Oh isn't that nice" and walked away, without giving it a second thought. Then I saw people walking over them. The streets were covered with fallen blessings and multitudes are trampling over them. I saw blessings that could change their lives – the things that many had been longing for were already there, laying on the ground and wasting away. There was sadness in the Father's eyes as He looked down on the wasted blessings and the power that people rejected daily. I knew that people were not rejecting them intentionally. They just did not know what was happening. It was as if they were blinded to the rain from heaven that was falling over their heads.

One great wasted blessing today is the blessing of Abraham. That blessing is ours. We know that in theory and concept, but most people do not have its manifestation in their lives, simply because they do not have the revelation of what it really means and how to activate it.

Let's see what it says, "Now the LORD said to Abram, 'Go forth from your country, and from your relatives And from your father's house, to the land which I will show you; and I will make you a great nation, and I will bless you, and make your name great; and so you shall be a blessing; and I will bless those who bless you, and the one who curses you I will curse. And in you all the families of the earth will be blessed"'. (Genesis 12:1-3). This is so powerful and is our inheritance as well. This, alone, should bring security instead of the fear the world gives us. God has promised to make us a head and not a tail. As His children we should reflect our Father and His Kingdom, so His blessings and favour should be a sign in our midst that causes the world to see that we are a different nation. Yet, we accept what the world offers and brings our way without challenging it, as if it were our lot in life. This blessing is a powerful weapon to fight and change our circumstances, and to open doors that only God can open.

We have been paying attention and noticed the great amount of blessings the Father is showering over us daily. Prophecies are a great source of blessings and, if we have ears to hear, we will hear them and possess them. There is a lot more to prophecies than we realize and we want to encourage you to take out all those tapes that you have collected, and re-listen to them with a careful ear, so you can identify each blessing and then take ownership of them. Listen when people pray for you and identify the blessings spoken by the Father. A blessing from the Father has the power to change your day, your circumstances, and turn things around completely. Blessings carry His favour.

Remember, Jesus defeated the enemy when he came to tempt Him simply by quoting what His Father had said. If you have a blessing from the Father, you have a treasure without measure that can make the impossible possible for you and can open doors that no one else can open. We are fully aware of this revelation and have taken hold of it and we have seen it in action in our lives. Because of this, we do not take it lightly when the Father tells us to bless His children. As prophetic people, He has given us authority to speak on His behalf and we listen closely when He speaks and release His blessings over His children, understanding the power that is being released from heaven. However, it is up to you to count your blessings, receive them, and take ownership of them. They belong to you!

IMPARTATIONS

Impartations can change your life and are another powerful thing wasted on earth. Impartation means to 'pass something on'. Through gifts and anointings God imparts who He is into us. He gives us portions of Himself, so we can do His work on earth and His ministry can continue. It is all about Him, for Him and by Him. No one owns any gift or anointing. Scripture says that it is by grace that we do what we do and these gifts are simply tools to do the work we have been entrusted with. One of the characteristics of the ministry of Jesus is impartation. He is a reproducer and makes disciples. He makes us like Him. Today Jesus continues imparting Himself into us and He does it in two ways. One way is through prophecy. Prophecies, as we saw in 1 Timothy 4:14, release gifts and anointings into our lives. They give us impartations of things we did not have before. Thus, we have to listen to our prophecies carefully to find each impartation given to us, as we are accountable for that to the LORD.

Another way is through the laying on of hands. This is when someone who carries a deposit of a particular anointing lays hands on us to transfer a deposit of that anointing into us. All His gifts and anointings are transferable and since they belong to Him, He decides who to give them to, and when. Therefore, we only give impartations of what He has given us when He specifically tells us to. I remember once, someone came and asked me for an impartation of the prophetic anointing God has given us and I graciously laid my hand on her and released it. As soon as I finished, the LORD rebuked me and said, "Why did you do that? It is not yours to give as you wish. It belongs to Me and I give it to whom I choose. I never told you to give an impartation to that lady. She is not someone I will trust with it because she will use it incorrectly. You have made a big mistake." The problem is, once the impartation is given, it goes out and cannot be taken back. I repented greatly but could not change what had taken place. To my great regret I later heard how that lady was indeed using the prophetic impartation she received that day for her advantage and not for the LORD'S glory.

Impartations are powerful and the LORD is very generous to give them. He is very willing to share His Kingdom with us and freely gives but He wants dividends. The thing is, that just like with blessings, impartations must be received and owned. It is important to understand that for impartations to become effective you have to act on them. God will empower them but you have to step out and use them first. That is where the problem is. Many people are carrying impartations that are dormant within and will continue dormant forever. God will not waste His power and will only empower them when you start to invest. Just like in the natural, you do not collect dividends until you take the step and risk to invest your money in the market. Dividends are the result of the investment, not the other way around. There are Kingdom investments for those willing to be strong and courageous. Many of you have lined up in front of people like Benny Hinn, John & Carol Arnott, Rodney Howard-Browne, and many others, whose names may not be as known but whose anointings and impartations are just as strong, real, and powerful. They pass on to you what God has given them. You receive the impartations, go home and bury the talent just received. Then you wonder why it is that God is not releasing those anointings in your lives. We know the stories of men like Benny Hinn and Bill Prankard, who received an impartation from Kathryn Kulmann and invested it right away. God empowered those impartations and continues investing into them.

The question to you is, "What are you going to do with the impartations you have received?"

MANDATES

Now this one is wonderful because it causes heaven to open and miracles to take place. Mandates are commands or orders given to us by God and they carry His authority and power. For instance, if at work your boss, Mr. Smith, tells you "Go to the accounting office and get me the financial records", it is now up to you to do as he has told you. Because he is the boss you will go and do it. So you go to the accounting office and say, "Mr. Smith asked me to take him the financial records." If you were to ask for them yourself it is possible that they would not be given to you but, because Mr. Smith wants them and he sent you for them (you are doing it for him), you carry his full authority behind you. They will not say 'no' to him because he is the boss and the boss always gets his way. An order from the boss is respected and obeyed because he is the ultimate authority. This illustration helps us understand what mandates from God are like. God is the boss of all bosses. He carries ultimate authority and His word is incontestable. In a revelation of heaven, I saw this in action. I heard God speak and heaven and the Holy Spirit began to act immediately upon what He said. No one argued with Him, no one contradicted Him, no one questioned what He said. It was a shock to me to see such obedience and understanding of authority. I honestly did not know that God could actually be in charge in such a manner. In heaven, God is truly the boss and His word is 100% incontestable.

I saw how heaven believes Him and prepares to produce all that is needed to do what God said (to please Him), and the Spirit prepares to empower all that is needed to do the same thing. Heaven and the Spirit want to please the Father and give Him what He wants, but I also saw that, when the mandate came down to earth, people did not receive it in the same manner. That is when the problem starts. People do not have the same understanding. The word of God is incontestable in heaven but, unfortunately, it is very contestable on earth. We must develop Kingdom mentality in order to hear His commands and cooperate with heaven and the Spirit. We need to develop an attitude to always please God. A while ago, the LORD spoke to us and said that He is looking for helpers for the Holy Spirit. He said that things are now changing and He wants people who will be willing to facilitate the work of the Holy Spirit on earth. This really surprised me because I thought we all did that already, but the LORD said, "No, up until now it has been the other way around. People make their own plans and programs and expect the Holy Spirit to come and empower them. So the Holy Spirit has actually been the one helping them. But now I am looking for people without personal agendas who will be happy to be His helpers and who will facilitate His work on earth".

I remember when I had my first encounter with the person of the Holy Spirit. I knew Him and knew much about Him, as most of us do. I had been filled with the Holy Spirit the day after I gave my life to Jesus and spoke in tongues the second time. In church I learned more about Him, yet I knew Him more through concepts than from the reality of Him. I had heard about Him being a 'person' but never gave it much thought. I also knew about not grieving the Holy Spirit (Ephesians 4:30), but somehow I was missing so much more of Him. So, one day a few years ago, we were in a prayer meeting. I was telling the LORD how we wanted people in our church to be free to be themselves, and express themselves as they are without having to behave according the ideas of others but to develop their own identities, and be free to be themselves no matter what that may look like. Suddenly, the LORD spoke and said, "The Holy Spirit is sad". I was surprised hearing that and replied, "Why? What happened to Him?" He said, "He is sad because people do not let Him be Himself. Everyone tells Him what to do and when to do it. He is given permission, or not given permission, to be or do. But He cannot be free to be or do. He is restricted to what people want and/or allow Him to do."

I heard that and felt mortified. I had no idea. It never occurred to me that the Holy Spirit would feel that way. That is the way we learned to treat Him. I apologized to the LORD with all my heart and repented on behalf of myself, our church, and the entire Body of Christ. I explained to Him that we just had no idea. Then the LORD said, "Don't tell me. Tell Him." So I did. I spoke to the Holy Spirit and told Him how very sorry I was that He had been hurt. I repented greatly and explained to Him as well that we just did not know. Then I told Him that, as for our church, we wanted Him to be free to be Himself. I told Him that, from then on, He would no longer need permission to do anything but that He could just do anything He wanted at any time; that we wanted Him to be happy and enjoy being with us; that we did not want Him to be with us just because He is so faithful that will never leave nor forsake us, but that we wanted Him to want to be with us and to look forward to our meetings, so He could have fun with us. I said to Him, "Please be free. Please really and truly be who You are with no reservations or conditions. Whatever you see the Father do in heaven feel free to do it in our midst and, whatever You hear Him say, please go ahead and say it here. I want You to be happy with us. I want You to laugh, dance, jump, and have fun." I meant it with all my heart and I knew that our entire leadership team felt the same way.

At that moment, something amazing happened. All the time I was speaking I could feel His presence standing in front of me and He was listening. But, when I finished speaking, He came over and hugged me. It was the most amazing feeling because it was a personal hug from the Holy Spirit. I have experienced the infilling of the Holy Spirit many times, but this was different. It was a hug on the outside. He hugged me and said, "Thank you!" He was happy and I felt His love and His gratitude in such a real way. His embrace was so strong that He threw me back. He hugged me for a while really tight. It was overwhelming. I cannot explain what this experience was like, but it was powerful. I then told the rest of the leadership what had happened and everyone, of course, agreed because that was their hearts' desire as well. We then decided to give greater freedom to the Holy Spirit and get out of the way more, so that He could truly be in charge. We already had much freedom and were not a regular church at all. However, things now took a greater turn for the unknown.

The Holy Spirit really took charge of the meetings and power began to fall. Healings began to take place during worship, and we began to have an open heaven and corporate Third Heaven experiences. Signs and wonders began to happen and true freedom came to us and has continued. We are having powerful times together. The second Sunday after this began, I heard the Holy Spirit laugh out loud during worship. It was such a beautiful sound. He was happy, so very happy. Other times, I also feel Him dance and leap among the people with joy and excitement. Every time this happens, I know He is having fun in our midst and is being who He really is. We realized one very important thing, if the Holy Spirit is happy we get very blessed. He is truly amazing and loves to be personal and fellowship with us. We must be careful no to take Him for granted and only use Him to bless us and give us. He wants to be close and personal and share who He is with us.

Many years ago, I read a statement that Smith Wigglesworth made, which puzzled me deeply and caused me to search the heart of God for the answer. Someone asked Smith, "Why is it that every time you go anywhere something happens and power is always manifested?" Smith's answer was: "It is very simple. If the Spirit doesn't move, I move the Spirit." I had never heard anyone say anything like that before but I figured that if he could do it then we can do it too, but how? There was no one teaching on this so we had to turn again to the LORD, so He could teach us. Jesus moved the Spirit, so we knew that there had to be a way and we began a search for the key to such a great mystery. God finally spoke and said, "Mandates are the keys to open that door." It sounded so simple and yet so complicated to do at the same time. However, as with all things in the Kingdom, there is an easy way, because His yoke is easy and His burden light (Matthew 11:30).

The LORD said, "Smith Wigglesworth received a mandate from Me to do what he did. He was not doing it out of presumption, or on his own initiative. I gave him a mandate to do it. He believed me and acted on it. I wanted him to do it for me and he became a manifestation of My ministry on earth. Because of his mandate, he had My unlimited authority to do what he did and, as a response, heaven opened up to produce all he needed and the Spirit moved to empower what he did. I told him to do it. He was obedient and became a great investment." Smith Wigglesworth had a personal mandate (commissioning – orders) from the Father to do what he did, and because of that, no one could stand in his way or stop him. God, heaven, and the Holy Spirit stood by him and backed him up all the way till the end. Therefore, understanding the power and importance of mandates makes a big difference but, it is up to us to respond. The Holy Spirit also wants to please the Father and make Him happy and, therefore, He would love to come and help us if we too step up to make the Father happy. God speaks mandates to us personally and through prophecies. So again, we must change the way in which we have viewed and/or received prophecies and pay attention, identify the mandates God gives us, and then obey them.

One of the problems with this is that people are waiting to see the manifestation (result/provision) before they step out to do what God told them to do. Many people, who have received a mandate to pray for the sick, are waiting for God to release healing power before they start praying. It does not work that way. We are not responsible for results as we cannot produce them. Our job is to obey and do what the Father says. One day, when we stand before the Father, He is not going to hold us accountable for the results, not at all, because results are His responsibility. Our goal is that, on that day, we will be found faithful before Him because we believed Him and did as He wished. He is not going to ask you, "How many miracles did you perform? How many people did you heal, or how many people did you save, etc.?" Instead He will ask, "Did you pray for the sick so I could heal them? Did you preach the gospel so I could save the people?" Many will say, "Well, LORD I was waiting for You to release healing in order to do it, but You did not release healing, so I could not pray for them. Or, I was waiting for revival to come in order to go and bring the people in, but . . ." No, results are His business, our job is to be obedient and open the doors for the results to manifest, just like Smith Wigglesworth and Kathryn Kuhlman.

We all have mandates, and heaven and the Holy Spirit are waiting for us to open those doors, to invest in the Kingdom, and bring in the dividends to the Father. As individuals, we have received many mandates from the Father, which we take seriously, and we act on them. Our church has also received mandates and has been obedient. Because of that, we have entered a great supernatural realm and are surrounded by miracles in our daily life. Angels have also become part of our life, as they come to help us do what the Father wants done. This is how miracles are created, heaven opens up and the Spirit comes to release power.

One of the mandates the LORD has given us is to receive His children into our home. He said, "I will send My children to you from all over the world. I want you to receive them, love them, feed them, and take care of them for Me." We knew that this mandate went beyond the gift of hospitality. We said, "Yes" to the LORD and have taken it seriously. Almost immediately God began to send His children to us and we literally have 'the nations' in our home. Some come for short times, others pass by, and others stay for longer periods of time. It has been amazing and truly a great Kingdom experience for us. We receive whoever God sends, even people we do not know, but if God says, "I am sending them", we receive them. We have a mandate from God. Because of this, we have experienced an open heaven in our lives and home. Here are some of the many experiences we have had.

ANGEL IN THE SUPERMARKET

A long time ago, we were having a financial challenge as happens sometimes, and the LORD was sending someone to spend a week with us. That particular week we only had $15 to buy groceries, which was nothing compared to what we needed especially having company to feed. At first, we wondered if we should tell this fellow not to come, but decided that it was not an option because God had given us a mandate and we would not back down. God had asked us to do that for Him and we would do it no matter what. We decided to go ahead, regardless of the circumstances. We went to the grocery store, by our house, where we shopped all the time carrying our $15. As we walked in we prayed and asked the LORD to do a miracle so we could buy all we needed for the week. In the natural it was impossible, but not in heaven because we had a mandate from God behind us, which meant that heaven and the Holy Spirit were also standing with us.

We decided to go first to the meat counter to see the price of meat. Meat was not on sale, so we figured it was good to check that section first. As we were walking towards the meat counter a young man suddenly came out of one of the aisles. He almost bumped into us as he appeared. He turned around in front of us and walked one step in front of us. I literally was walking on his heels. He was about 19

– 21 years old, tall, slim, blond, very handsome, and was wearing the white coat the employees of the store wore. We had never seen him before, so we figured that he was new. We knew all the employees as we shopped there often. He was carrying a pricing gun and walked straight to the meat counter. He stood in front of the roast beef section, chose a roast and marked it down to only 40 cents! He stepped over to the next section making room for me come over. I stepped up and picked up the roast beef. He then looked at the ground beef packages lifted his pricing gun and without changing the numbers (to change the price on those guns the numbers have to be changed manually) he marked a big package of ground beef down to 70 cents and stepped over to the next section. I followed and took the package of ground beef. The next section was the stewing beef packages. Again, without changing the numbers in the pricing gun, he marked a package of stewing beef down to 25 cents. He stepped aside and waited for me to take the meat. I took the package of stewing beef and we both stood there watching that young man walk away and disappear as he turned towards the same aisle he came out of. We then looked at each other holding all that meat for under $2.00 and wondered if the cashier would let us through with it.

We went and got a cart because now we could buy vegetables and anything else we needed. Before leaving, we walked all through the store looking for that young man and could not find him anywhere. We had never seen him before and never saw him again. We bought all we needed and when we checked out, the cashier only charged us the reduced prices for the meat, which, all together, was exactly $1.35. We paid for everything and had 15 cents left over. We walked out of that store knowing that we had just had a powerful supernatural third heaven experience. Heaven opened up to produce what we needed to please the Father and, as a result, an angel came to mark down the meat, so we could do what the Father told us to do. We defied the circumstances with a mandate from God, which altered the natural realm. There is no power on earth that can stand up to God's word. He is the ultimate authority and the buck surely stops there.

THE MULTIPLICATION OF FOOD

One day, we had invited some people to come over for dinner. There were eight of us in total. We had two small roasted chickens cut in

4 pieces each, a bowl of potatoes, a bowl of vegetables, and a salad, which was enough for the eight of us. Just as we were sitting down for supper the door bell rang. Outside were six students from the School of Ministry at TACF, who were passing by on their way to the US. They arrived at our door because they were hungry but had no money. As they were passing by Stratford the LORD said to them, "Go to Ivan and Isabel's house. They will feed you there." We welcomed them in knowing that we did not have enough food for everyone and, suddenly, our little chickens and vegetables looked really sad in the middle of the table. However, we have a mandate from the LORD to house and feed His children, so we very gladly put more plates on the table. Silently both of us came by the table and asked the Father to do a miracle and multiply the food so everyone could eat. We asked them to take food but we decided to wait till the end. They all took a full plate of food. Some came for second servings and, at the end, we had leftovers for three days. John, our associate pastor, was there and noticed the amount of chicken remaining and asked us if we had gone to buy more.

Then, another time, we had cooked food for ten and the LORD sent another group of people, without previous warning to us. This was a larger group. Once again, we prayed and told people to eat. The same thing happened. They all ate to their satisfaction, some had seconds and at the end we had leftovers for three days again.

The next time after that was even more powerful. This time we had cooked dinner for 14 people and, just as we were going to start eating, a family with seven people showed up at our door for lunch. They were going through a difficult time and the LORD told them to come to our house. Now we had 21 people for lunch and not enough food. Again we prayed and asked the LORD to do it again. People came to the table to take food and one of our interns, who had heard about the miracles that were happening at our house, stood by the table to watch the food. Suddenly, she got really excited as she noticed that the food did not go down. This time, only a third of the food went down in the dishes. It seemed that the more people we had to feed the greater was the multiplication from heaven. Anyway, this time, people had seconds, some had third servings and, at the end, we had leftovers for four days. However, it does not end there, the leftovers continued multiplying in the fridge to the point that, on the fourth day, our daughter said, "Dad, are we going to have to eat this food forever? Do you think God will ever let us eat something else?" At that point, we realized that we had to do something, because we were beginning to wonder the same thing. So Ivan took a big pot, put all the leftovers together, made a big curry casserole, laid hands on the pot and prayed for the food to stop multiplying. We invited some friends from church to eat the casserole with us and we sent the leftovers home with someone else, as we did not want anything left in our house. We were afraid it would continue multiplying.

Because of God's mandate we have made a rule that we will not allow anyone in our church to go hungry and we have told people that anyone who is struggling in that area has a place at our table, for as long as it takes until the situation changes. We also give lots of food away to people and have seen the food in our pantry and the meat in the freezer multiply as well. We had a small freezer for meat and then God said, "Prepare because more people are coming." So we bought a freezer twice the size, thinking that we would have lots of room in it. Well, I cannot tell you how, but it filled up in two weeks. One day, I took a lot of meat out of there for a family in need and, in no time, the amount in the freezer was back to the way it was. The LORD has also continued doing mighty miracles at the grocery stores and we can buy more for the same amount of money than is naturally possible. Paul said that to those who give, God will give them more so they can give more, and we have seen that be true (2 Corinthians 9:10-11).

MONEY IN THE WALLET

One day, a girl who was at our house had a miracle happen in her purse. She had some money in her wallet and that was all the money she had in the world, but she needed a lot more. Shortly after she arrived in our house the LORD told her to check her wallet and sure enough, the money had doubled supernaturally. She was completely blown away seeing the heavens open up for her like that.

THE CAR IN THE DRIVEWAY

About a year ago a family came to visit us for a couple of days. They had a minivan which was having some problems and they had a very hard time opening the door. They did not have the money to take it to the shop to be fixed and had prayed for God to help them. They stayed overnight in our house and, through the night, the LORD supernaturally fixed their van. They were amazed the next morning when they went out and realized that their vehicle had received a great miracle from heaven.

NORWAY

Two winters ago we were booked to go to Norway to do a school of prophecy. The day we were leaving for the airport there was a major snow storm here. We live in the Ontario Snow Belt and, therefore, our snow storms are stronger than normal. That day, the storm was so bad that some of the roads in and out of town were closed. Ivan had to go to the church in the morning and, because of the storm, he was delayed coming home. With normal weather it takes us two hours to get to the airport and in that kind of weather it would take us much longer because the roads are bad and traffic is slow. However, by the time Ivan got home to pick me up we only had 50 minutes to get to the airport and catch the plane. Even in normal weather this is not possible but in this weather we knew that only a miracle could get us there. As Ivan walked into the house, he said, "Honey, I don't think we can make it. The weather is so bad and we are so late". I knew he was right but, at the same time, we had a mandate from the Father to go to Norway. For us, ministry is the Father's business and therefore we only go where the Father sends us. We never contact places because our view is that if the Father is not sending us, why would we want to go?

We know that if the Father sends us then He will move, and He had said "I want you to go to Norway". So we said, "Well, we know the circumstances are against us going but the Father told us to go and, therefore, it is up to Him. If He still wants us there He will do a miracle and will get us there in time. He can stop the time for us to catch the plane, (like He did for Joshua) but for that to happen we have to get on the road". So we did.

We left the house and prayed for a miracle. We drove without looking at the clock because the roads were bad. We drove and prayed. Then, to our amazement, when we got the airport, the time was three minutes before the scheduled time for us to be there. God stopped the time and we made it to the airport in exactly 47 minutes from the time we left the house. That was a completely supernatural experience. We had a mandate from the Father to go there and used it to defy the circumstances. As a result, heaven opened up and the Holy Spirit released power to make it happen and together we walked through a miracle. This miracle has been happening more and more since them.

KINGDOM FINANCES

Something we are seeing God release, more and more, is Kingdom finances. Kingdom finances are completely different from earthly finances and church finances. Kingdom finances are God's finances and, therefore, are supernatural and have no limit. However, God is very careful in choosing who He entrusts them to. This is a difficult area as many people do not know what this is all about. As the years have gone by we have come to the conclusion that the key to releasing Kingdom finances is stewardship. Paul clearly explains it when He talks about giving and how God wants us to give just to help and bless others. Remember, God does not need our money. He owns the cattle on a thousand hills, and He is a faithful father who will not turn His back on us. Some people give just to make sure God will take care of them (to secure His provision). How sad to have that attitude. He has promised never to leave nor forsake us. He is not like our earthly parents. He is perfect and we cannot buy or manipulate His faithfulness. He is good!

Once, as we were learning about this, the LORD told us, "Make sure you tell My people who I am and how I am because you cannot change my character out of convenience. I am who I am and I do not change". Wow!! All through the years, we have heard so many wrong teachings on finances that misrepresent God and His character. We cannot buy His faithfulness or secure His blessings with money. He IS faithful, and it is completely impossible for Him to be unfaithful. He cannot do it. It is 100% against His character. A very powerful key is found when we do not give to receive but, simply, to bless. That is who God is. He is perfect love and gives to bless us. It is His very good pleasure to give us His Kingdom and all it contains (Luke 12:32). So God is looking for people who understand His heart and want to be and do like Him. These people will be entrusted with His finances so they can manage and distribute them for Him on earth. The thing we deal with here is the god of mammon, who wants us to worship him instead of trusting God (Matthew 6:24). We have learned and have seen that giving is the key to defeating the god of mammon and opens the heavens over our lives and finances. It is the attitude of our hearts that we need to look at, as that is what determines the outcome. The god of mammon is the love of riches and wealth. There is nothing wrong with having money and riches, the problem is the love of money, which, as we see in Scripture, is a root of all kinds of evil (1 Timothy 6:10).

Scripture shows us that God wants to bless us. The blessing of Abraham makes it clear. He is our father and we must not be afraid of receiving His abundance. Most of God's children are stuck in a mindset of poverty, which does not allow God to pour His financial blessings into them. As we said before, we receive and expect according to the realm of limitations we have and what our parents and family were like. If they struggled in poverty and debt, then we are pre-programmed to do the same thing (imprinting and mindsets) and, without realizing it, we follow their footsteps and our children will do the same. You will never pursue jobs or opportunities above your expectations and will always fix your eye on the perimeter around you. On the other hand, if your parents were prosperous and succeeded, you learn to think like them and to expect accordingly. You will push the limits and reach beyond your abilities. Your eyes will be set upwards and your expectations too. You will pursue better jobs and promotions and will attain them. It is all internal but it can be changed.

I saw my parents struggle greatly and never get anywhere. The mindsets of poverty are a strong prison in themselves. Most of the people we knew were in the same situation and their children were all living the same lives. Then my oldest sister, who is 21 years older than me, decided to come out of the box and change her circumstances. She made up her mind that she did not want to live her life in the same condition and raise children in that cycle. She was brave and courageous and pushed the limits, breaking the mindsets of poverty. She worked and studied very hard and became a professional. She decided to continue pressing in for more change and did everything with excellence because she was determined to break from the mould. By doing that, she showed me that there was a much better way to live. As I grew up, I kept an eye on my parents and an eye on my sister. I had a choice to make. I could settle for the mindset of poverty, and just scrape by in life like my parents, or I could also be courageous and break out of the box. I was 17 when I finished high school and immediately took a full-time job. I took the lowest position in a clothing factory and gave myself to work with excellence.

At 18 I began to walk with the LORD so I started to pray for God's favour and blessings over me. I also started learning Scripture and prayed through judgments, curses, and inner vows of poverty. I chose to speak life and not death and bless my life, finances, work, and future. I enrolled myself in college full-time and I worked full-time. It was very hard. Besides paying for my education, I had to help support my family financially, and gave as much as I could to the church and to people around me, who had less than I did. I did what scripture says. I worked for my bosses as for God and did more than expected, to bless them. I chose to honour them and serve them the best I could because, as a Christian, the bar was higher for me. In less than a year I began to be promoted.

As this was happening my mindsets began to change and so did my expectations. Then something amazing happened. By the time I was 21 years of age I became the second in command in the company, second only to the owner and I had the second highest salary too. That was indeed the hand of God! In my next job where I worked for 16 years the same thing happened. I started in the lowest position available (God loves small beginnings and so do I), but again within a year promotions and raises began to come and, by the end, I was the Director of the agency and was offered the CEO's position. That is when God called me out of that field to work for Him. In the natural I was given a mindset of poverty and hopelessness but, with God's help, healing and freedom came and my mindsets changed. God wants us to choose life and not death, blessings instead of curses, expectations instead of limitations.

God wants to bless us and make us the head and not the tail (Deuteronomy 28:13) but we have to be careful not to make money and prosperity our identity and satisfaction. If we do, then we begin to worship mammon. Mammon has several ways of getting our worship. Some horde money and become greedy, but others become so afraid of lacking that they hold tight to what they have and never get to partake of the abundance of the Kingdom. I used to be like that. I was afraid that there would not be enough for tomorrow and, therefore, I would hold tight to everything I had. Sharing was not part of my life then as I found security in what I had. Where does your satisfaction and comfort come from? If your financial condition gives you satisfaction; if carrying money in your wallet is what gives you confidence; if your countenance changes according to your bank balance, then there is a problem and Mammon is pulling the strings, because those things should be found in Jesus. In Him we should find our identity, satisfaction, security, confidence, and joy because He is the lifter of our heads! Like Paul said, "I have learned to be satisfied with having much and having nothing, in abundance and in need" (Philippians 4:12). Money is a means to an end. It is a resource we need in the world, a tool to build the Kingdom, to bless others, and to honour our Father. He does not need it, but He wants to occupy the altar money has in our heart. We must love the LORD with all our hearts and our neighbor as ourselves, and be careful not to place our affections on material things that are here today and gone tomorrow. Having a good and balanced approach to money is pivotal to understanding and receiving Kingdom finances.

God's Kingdom finances are part of the power that He is releasing on earth. Remember, wealth was one of the three things that the devil offered Jesus in the wilderness (Matthew 4). However, the wealth of the world does not compare to the Kingdom of our Father. God displayed great power as He released financial blessings on Abraham, David, Solomon, Jehoshaphat and others. It was a manifestation of His power and presence. However, He is seeking for those He can trust. There is much to do and much to distribute. We heard from a reliable source that statistics show that about 90% of the wealth of the world is in the hands of professing Christians and most of them are simply holding on to it. There are many whom God has blessed tremendously, some millionaires who are afraid of giving and blessing others and, therefore, their money is not growing as it could. They are burying their talents, yet there are others, who have less and share what they have with others, and they are prospering more and more. Remember, if we keep it we lose it, but if we lose it then we gain it. Kingdom givers receive Kingdom finances. However, to become a Kingdom financier, we first must learn to share what we have like the widow who caught the eye of Jesus (Mark 12:41-44). Many were giving but that woman caught the eye of Jesus because she gave all she had not what was left over. It was the attitude of her heart that pleased Jesus not the amount she gave.

Today, the same thing is happening. Many are giving but only a few are catching the eye of Jesus in their giving. To become a Kingdom investment first we must become Kingdom investors. A long time ago we were going through a very bad financial season and our worship of mammon was being broken. One day I woke up at 7:00 a.m., hearing the audible voice of God in the bedroom. The LORD said to me, "All those $5.00 & $10.00 investments you have made are going to carry you through this season." I shook my head and said, "What? What investments? We do not have any investments." We used to have investments but had cashed them all and invested them into ministry and also financed some ministry trips to poor countries; therefore, we did not have any investments left. The LORD graciously repeated it audibly again, "All those $5.00 & $10.00 investments you have made will carry you through this season." I did not understand what He was talking about. We had been givers and, in the past we both had had great paying jobs making more money than we could spend. We always gave to the church and then gave gifts and offerings to many others. Then, when God called us out of that place, and our finances changed drastically, we could not give in the same manner but continued giving as much as we could. Sometimes, all we could afford to give, aside from our tithes, was gifts and offerings of $5.00 & $10.00. We knew it was not much but it was all we had. That is when we really developed true giving hearts. Anyway, as I was there pondering what the LORD had said, He spoke again and said, "Yes, those are the investments I am talking about. Those $5.00 & $10.00 gifts and offerings you have invested have collected dividends in the Kingdom, which now will come to you." We had never imagined anything like that but those were Kingdom investments and now dividends were coming to us.

The LORD was faithful to His word and finances came to us supernaturally. We could not really tell where the monies were coming from but each week and each month we paid all our bills, bought all we needed, and gave again to others. That is Kingdom in action and God wants us to become people who live and work in His realm. The language of heaven is love, giving, and sharing and we bring heaven to earth when we learn to speak that language. Last year, the LORD spoke to us and said, "There are more people I want to bring to your home." So we figured that we were going to need a bigger house as the house we had was actually small for the amounts of people coming. With that in mind we bought a bigger house so we could fit all the people the LORD would be sending to us. We moved house just over a year ago and even though it is much bigger, shortly after we realized that it was still not big enough as more people began to come right away. So we prayed and decided to expand and build another room in the attic. That was a big project because the house was old, but we wanted to have more beds for God's children so we began that project a few months later.

As we were in the midst of it, the LORD began to speak to us about His ideas. He told us, "There are two people I want to send on a ministry trip to Europe and I want you to pay for the whole thing, including passports". For us that was a big request as by then we both were working full-time for the LORD and living by faith, but God was insistent that He wanted us to do that for Him. So we said, "Yes LORD, for you we will do anything". A few days later He said, "There is this minister who is in need of a computer and I want to give him a very good one, right away. He needs it for ministry." We said, "Yes". Then He said, "Oh by the way, there is this family who is going to have financial problems because of lack of work. I want to give them some money to help them get through it. Please give them 'X' amount of money in the next two weeks for me". We said "Yes" and wrote it down. Then He said, "There is this pastor, who has a debt for this much money and I want to pay for it. Can you please give him the money for that?" We said, "Yes". Then the next request came, God said, "I want you to finance another trip overseas for this fellow by the fall." We added it to the list and, the next day, He told us a few other things He wanted to pay for.

We were getting concerned because, at the same time, we found out that the cost of all the work for the attic, from construction to carpeting and painting, was going to cost double the original estimate. So we prayed some more as we were enlarging the house for the LORD and His people. We also had just changed all the windows of the house, which was a huge expense and we were still paying for it. However, none of that seemed to be a problem to God, who was in a very generous mood. We began to add all the things He wanted to do and it was in the thousands and thousands of dollars, so we had a decision to make. God was asking us to do that for Him. He gave us a mandate to do something beyond our natural means, an invitation to partake in a miracle, to open up the heavens and cooperate with the Spirit. So we said, "Yes LORD. For You we will do anything." We were not sure how it would all come together but God had spoken. Obedience is our responsibility, and the results are up to Him. We chose to believe God and acted on it.

We contacted each person on the list and told them what the LORD was doing. As we did, we found out that each of them had been asking the Father for those particular things and He was answering them. We made sure to tell them that it was not coming out of our pocket, and that it was not our generosity, but their Father was giving it to them. It was all coming from HIS pocket, not ours. We simply were the messengers delivering it for the Father. As we stepped out and passed on the news, we knew that we had crossed the point of no return. There was no turning back. As this happened, our finances threatened to get bad, really bad, so we talked and decided that no matter what the circumstances were we would not back down but would do what the Father requested. It was for Him and we will do anything for Him. Pleasing Him is our delight.

As we made the decision to believe God, heaven began to move, the supernatural realm of God opened up and the Holy Spirit released faith in our hearts and we received the assurance of the things we could not see. We knew God would finance what He wanted done on earth. Within three days we received a call from the bank. Someone in another part of the world had made a deposit in our bank account for $30,000. A miracle had taken place. God moved and Kingdom finances got released to build God's Kingdom. The Spirit moved and contacted some people who had some of God's money and told them to transfer some of it to us, so that the will of God could be done on earth as it is in heaven. Heaven opened up because we had a mandate from the Father to do what we were doing. The money provided was enough to cover all God's ideas, the room in our attic, and it paid for the rest of our windows. I remember thinking, "It would have been much easier if God would have released the money first", and the LORD replied and said, "I wanted to make sure that you would be willing to do what I wanted you do with my money before I gave it to you. I wanted your hearts revealed before entrusting you. I wanted your obedience first".

For us, the most exciting part was to look people in the eye as we delivered God's provision and say, "It is not from us. It truly and really did not come out of our pocket but from your Father. It is not our generosity but His, for He is good!" Kingdom economy is powerful and a great testimony to the world of who God is, of His love, and faithfulness. We have developed a life of giving just to bless others and to share of our Father's goodness.

One day, about a year ago, the LORD said, "I have noticed that you share all you have with others. I have seen that if you have money others around you get money. If you have clothing or shoes others around you receive clothing and shoes. If you have jewelry or perfumes others around you get jewelry and perfumes. If you have vehicles others get vehicles. If you have food others get food. If you have room others have shelter and a place to stay. I have seen that there is nothing you will not share with others and, therefore, I have decided to give you much more so that you can give to many more people." A while ago the LORD spoke to us and said, "Today you are giving small things to others, but the time will come not far from now when you will be giving cars, diamonds, money in the thousands of dollars, and houses to others."

For us, giving was not part of our lives as we both grew up in poverty. We were not givers by nature, but through healing and love God has begun, bit by bit, to make us like Him. We were selfish and self-centered but He is a giver. In the last five years we have seen that word start to unfold. Last year alone we gave more money away than we had ever given away in all our lives, literally in the thousands and thousands of dollars and look forward to more giving this year, next year and for the rest of our lives. We would be thrilled to live the rest of our lives simply being managers of God's provision, delivering His blessings to His children and then to the world. We have given lots of things including cars, and expensive jewelry, all from the Father to His children. I remember the first time I gave diamonds away. We have given diamonds away several times for the LORD but, for me, the first time was quite an experience...

When you grow-up up in a third world nation with utter poverty, the thought of diamonds and precious stones is something that only queens and kings could have and having them was unthinkable for people like us. Then as time went on and I came to Canada God began to bless me with them. At first I could not believe such 'wealth'... real diamonds, sapphires, rubies, emeralds, wow.

Then slowly the Father began to say, "That sapphire ring you have, it is not really yours. I gave it to you so you can pass it on to so-and-so. Give it to her from me." And, slowly, I began to partake of God's generosity on earth and of His displays of love for His daughters. Then one day, I went on a ministry trip, wearing a beautiful diamond ring on my right hand, which had come to me through amazing circumstances. I remember a brief thought passing through my mind before leaving that said, "What if God gives that ring away?" I heard that and thought, "He would never do that. This is mine. He will not take it away." I had come a long way and for Him I had given away all others, but diamonds were different and I could not give those away, at least, not yet.

So I was wearing this lovely diamond ring and our last day there the LORD did it! He said, "Isabel, that ring on your finger is for this young woman there. Please give it to her from ME". I heard that and hesitated for about 2-3 seconds but, along with the request, the Father showed me His heart for her and at that moment His love for her filled my heart. Suddenly, it was my desire to be the hands of her Father as He placed that ring on her finger. How amazing! I did as the Father requested and I saw this beautiful young woman receive a great impartation of the Father's love. As a result she had a powerful encounter with the Father, and received a deep healing in a particular area of her life. I witnessed great freedom come into her life. It was a life changing experience for her and for me. God took us both to a higher level in Him and His Kingdom. But the most important thing for me was that I was truly happy about passing that diamond ring to one of God's daughters, like that servant who placed the Father's ring on the son's finger . Imagine!

So life went on and, less than a year later, I received a gift certificate for a particular store in town and then God gave me some money as a personal gift for me. One day, a week later I went to that particular store and felt a desire to go by the jewelry section as I was passing by. On the bottom shelf there was a section with rings at 70% off. Then, to my great surprise, I saw a diamond ring identical to the one I had given away, and next to it was another diamond ring with the same size of stone on sale for a ridiculously low price. At that moment the Father said to me, "Those two diamond rings are for you. I am giving you back the one you gave away for me, and another just to say thank you. Buy them both because you have enough to pay for them." Sure enough I found out that the price for both rings was exactly the combined amount of the gift certificate and the money gift God had given me. So I walked out of the store with two rings and double the size of diamonds. However, as I walked out of the store, I knew in my heart that, one day, the Father may ask for them to be placed on someone else's finger, and I will be delighted to do so for Him. There is nothing like administering Kingdom treasures for our Father on earth.

Last year, through a series of amazing circumstances, the LORD gave me a lovely brand new Chanel perfume. One day, this lady came to our house and the LORD told me, "That perfume you have is for her. Please give it to her for me". I gave it to her and told her that her Father wanted her to have it. She began to cry and said that Chanel was her favourite perfume but she had not been able to buy it for a long time because she did not have work. Just the week before she had asked the LORD if He would give her some. She kept thanking me for it and I said to her, "Dear, don't thank me. I am not this generous, believe me, but your Father is, and He is the one who sent it my way so I could deliver it to you, but it is from Him".

In this realm we are aware that nothing belongs to us not even our lives. It is all for Him and by Him, and He can do anything He wants with it. One day, I was walking in a nice store and saw something I liked on sale. It was something expensive but had been reduced a lot. As I went over to see it I heard this voice talk to me in the right ear. It said, "Why are you going to bother if God will probably take it from you and give it someone else? What is the use if you do not get to keep it and enjoy it?" Yet, immediately, I heard this other very gentle voice say to me, "Yes, that may happen, but remember you were able to give the diamonds away, and remember what God did". Immediately, this impartation of love and peace came into my heart and I knew that there is nothing I would not give for Him. Ivan is the same way. He loves to give and takes his coat and gives it away, at the drop of a hat if the Father says "Give". I have seen him do it many times.

We hear His mandates, obey them and, in doing so, we have learned to cooperate with heaven and the Holy Spirit so that, for years now, we have been living a very supernatural life in a very natural and simple way.

Sometimes we give just because we like it now. Many times God does not have to say, "Give". We just know He would do it and, since we want to be like Him, we do exactly what we know He would do. Just two days ago we were visiting some friends and I was wearing a brand new pair of shoes for the first time. Suddenly, I said to my friend, "Would you like these shoes? Take them, they are for you." She tried them on and they fitted. She stood there holding them and finally said, "Just this week I prayed for a new pair of shoes. I needed new shoes, but had no money to buy them, and God just gave them to me" Wow!! This is kingdom and this is huge. These small things are not small at all, because they reveal the heart of the Father, release His love and make Him famous.

KINGDOM TRANSACTIONS

Let's now talk about the simplicity of Kingdom economy and Kingdom transactions. We love to see this in action because that is how God moves His provision around on earth. Let's share a few stories to illustrate, in a practical way, how transactions of Kingdom economy happen on earth.

THE PAINTING

A few years ago, we were doing a conference at a church and there was someone there selling wonderful prophetic paintings. I was really moved by a particular painting and told the LORD in my heart that I would like it, which was surprising because I am not a picture or painting person. We taught our session and began to minister to the people and I forgot all about the painting. A while later, I saw the fellow selling them and asked him for the price of that particular painting. He said $200 and without thinking I said, "I will buy it". He smiled big and said, "Really?" I said, "Absolutely" and then I thought I should let Ivan know that we had bought that painting. Bless his heart, he said, "I knew that painting would come home with us." It is good to have a prophetic husband! I went to write the cheque to pay for it and I could not write the amount on it. I felt this resistance on my hand every time I tried to write, so I said to the LORD, "Father I know how much he asked for, but tell me how much You want to give him?" Immediately, He said, "I want to give him $300, my son has need of that amount. He asked me for it". I was amazed that the Father allowed me to witness what He was doing and immediately wrote the cheque.

As we left, I told Ivan what we had actually paid. I apologized because we actually did not have $300 to spend on something like that, plus I never buy stuff like that, and I did it without thinking it over, which was very unlike me. However, Ivan said, "That is not how I see it. We did not just spend money on a painting. Not at all. We just invested $300 in that man's ministry and that I am very happy to do". Wow, what a reply! Then he said, "Oh, as we got into the church this morning, so-and-so gave me this card". We opened the card and found $200 cash inside. Immediately the LORD said to me, "That is $200 to cover the asking price of the painting". The thing is that the card was given to Ivan before we saw the painting. At that moment, I felt the Father's smile because we had done what He wanted us to do. Four days later we were teaching a prophetic school somewhere else and this lady came and gave us an envelope from the LORD. Inside we found another $200 and the LORD spoke again and said, "Here is the other $100 you gave that man, and an extra $100 for you, for your investment". I was utterly amazed. We had just been part of a Kingdom transaction and saw it happen step by step.

That fellow needed a certain amount of money. Two people had the funds for him but were not in a position to give it to him directly, so God arranged a way to get it to him. He used us as the channel to get His money to His son and, at the end because of obedience, we ended up with a beautiful painting and $100. It is amazing the things we get to partake in when we listen to our Father and are willing to invest into His Kingdom.

THE MULTIPLICATION OF CARS

About three years ago we needed a new car. Our car was fine and worked well but we needed a better vehicle for long ministry trips, so we prayed and the LORD said, "Buy a car but do not spend more than $10,000". We did not have $10,000 to buy a car so it was stretching as we did not want to go back into debt. But the LORD said that He would provide. We found the right car and, all included, it cost us $9,998. We could have sold our other car to help pay for the new car but the LORD said, "No, I want to give that car to this family at church who need another car". So we immediately passed the car to that family. We began to make payments on our new car as we waited for the LORD'S provision. We made four car payments and one day the LORD said, "Today I will pay for the car". Sure enough, when the mailman came we received an envelope with a cheque for $10,000. There was a note with the cheque from the people who sent it saying that God told them to send that to us. Bless them for their obedience and investment! We paid for the car less the four payments we had already made. The LORD said, "I want to use the money you have left from the four payments to buy a car for so-and-so from church. In a month he is going to need a car for work and I want to give it to him before that".

We agreed, of course, and the LORD gave us direct instructions of where and when to go to buy a car for this other fellow. The money we had was sufficient to put the car on the road. God is amazing! One car turned into three cars for three families and He paid for all three. What a powerful Kingdom transaction.

Last year the LORD spoke to us and said, "That truck you have (Ivan's car) is for this fellow at church. I want to give it to him because the car he is driving is going to die soon, and he has been asking me for a new vehicle". We were not planning on that at the time, but we were not surprised. By now we know and expect Him to say things like that. So, when we knew those were God's plans, we said, "Yes LORD, we will do it". However, we live in the country and, therefore, we need two vehicles, so we had to trust God to replace the truck. Within 24 hours we supernaturally received a cheque for enough money to buy another car. The fellow who received the truck was blown away at how his Father answered his prayer and displayed His love for him. God bless the people who answered His request to bless us with the funds to replace our car. They did not know of our need, but simply obeyed the LORD and in doing so, became an answer to our prayer and indirectly to the prayer of the other fellow who needed a car too.

Last winter a friend of ours was going on a ministry trip overseas and the LORD said to us, "I want to pay for her ticket. Please give her a cheque for me for the full amount". We did not question it and wrote the cheque right away. She was overwhelmed by her Father's love and care for her. Something unexpected had happened and she had just lost a lot of money, but she felt that the LORD told her to go as planned, so she was stepping out in faith. The next morning we received a cheque in the mail for the full amount. The LORD told someone from the US to send us that money. This fellow answered the LORD'S request but had no idea that he was partaking in an international Kingdom transaction. That lady went on her ministry trip, in which God did great and powerful things. You see, this dear lady who needed the money was here in a small town in Canada and the fellow who had the money was somewhere far away in the US. They have never met each other, but together they caused the Kingdom to advance. Our part on it was to simply be the link between the two.

So our question to you is: Are you willing to become a partaker of Kingdom transactions? God is seeking for people through whom He can distribute His provision on earth. Scripture says in 2 Cor. 9:10-13 "For God is the one who gives seed to the farmer and then bread to eat. In the same way, He will give you many opportunities to do good, and He will produce a great harvest of generosity in you. Yes, you will be enriched so that you can give even more generously. And when we take your gifts to those who need them, they will break out in thanksgiving to God. So two good things will happen-the needs of the Christians in Jerusalem will be met, and they will joyfully express their thanksgiving to God. You will be glorifying God through your generous gifts. For your generosity to them will prove that you are obedient to the Good News of Christ".

This is the best part of all, when we learn to give like this, our joy and reward comes as they break out in thanksgiving to God, for His goodness and faithfulness in answering their prayers and meeting their needs. What glorious experience! Heaven opens and touches earth and, we get to be eye witnesses of such events

SECTION FOURTEEN

THE PRICE OF YOUR DESTINY

Recently, the LORD spoke to us and said that as the time of releasing for many is coming there will also be a strategy from hell coming to stop people from getting their inheritance, our portion of the Promised Land here today. There is always a great pressure from hell, just before breakthrough comes, as the enemy does not want you to become who God created you to be. As we said earlier, your destiny is the most expensive thing you will ever attain. We want to share with you one of the greatest strategies the enemy has been using to keep many from this breakthrough. May you have ears to hear.

THE SIN OF ESAU

The LORD gave us a warning and said, "Tell the people not to commit the sin of Esau" (Genesis 25:29-34). As we know, Jacob was cooking and Esau came home very hungry from hunting. He was famished and asked his brother for a bowl of stew. Jacob took advantage of the situation and offered to trade it for Esau's birthright. Esau was so consumed with his present need, that he sold his destiny and inheritance for a bowl of stew. He did it simply to satisfy a present and temporary need. His regret was great when he realized what he had done but, it was too late and he lost it all. There are many in the Kingdom who are doing that very thing today. The sin of Esau is very common and the consequences of it are detrimental. Many are losing their destiny and inheritance because of fixing their eyes on temporary needs and desires. Esau had very short vision and forgot what was ahead and the price of the decision he was making. Scripture says that by doing that Esau despised his birthright (Genesis 25:34 NAS), and spiritually that opened the door for his brother to steal his blessing. The blessing that belonged to the firstborn.

This is very dangerous because the sin of Esau can manifest in different areas of our lives. We all can have different 'bowls of stew' as we are all different and our circumstances are different too. For some it can be money, reputation, identity, a spouse, a job, pride, etc. Now we are not talking about desires of the heart that God places there. That is different. We are talking about things that become so important to you, that you are willing to walk away from your inheritance for that. We have some friends who were offended in church and the offense was such that they walked out of ministry and of church altogether. They could not let go. They had such a great need for their pride to be satisfied that they did not count the long term cost of their choice. That was their bowl of stew. How sad!

We have experienced this on different levels and, each time, God has been faithful and we want to share some of our experiences to illustrate this. We are going to touch on three of the most common things that cause people to 'sell their inheritance', love, power, and money. We hope this will encourage you to keep your trust in God and be faithful till the end. From personal experience we can promise you that if you make the right choices, the price you pay today will be worth it for the rest of your lives.

WALKING INTO THE UNKNOWN

Dreams are amazing and one dream from God can change your plans and life forever. That is what happened to me. A long time ago, I had taken a sabbatical from full-time ministry for a little while and found a fantastic job, where I was paid more money than I had ever made in life. Everything was going great and I was prospering tremendously. Then, the company had a hard time and I was temporarily laid-off.

One day I had a dream and in it I was in a sick bed and very ill. My boss from work called me, unexpectedly, and asked me to come back to work. He said that they really wanted me back and would do anything to get me back. I told him to give me twenty minutes and I would call him back. I then called my wife and told her that my boss really wanted me back, but that I felt that the LORD was also calling me and that as great as the job was and as generous as the offer was, I had to give it all up to follow the LORD. In my dream, I then called my boss and quit my job. He was surprised because he really wanted me back. Then the most amazing thing happened, as soon as I quit my job I was instantly healed and got up from my sick bed.

The next morning, I told Isabel my dream and told her that I knew God was asking me to give up everything to follow His calling on my life. At the time, I had been out of full-time ministry for a while but I believed God wanted me to walk out like Abraham not knowing where I would end up. We talked about it and decided that I would quit. Lo and behold, an hour later the phone rang and it was my boss asking me to go back to work and saying how much he wanted me back. The dream came to pass, step by step. Without thinking, my response to him was, "Give me twenty minutes and I will call you back". I called Isabel and said, "It is happening, my boss just called and said everything I heard in the dream. I am going to call him back and quit". She agreed and I did it. We stepped out and, shortly after, the way to destiny opened wider than before. God began to direct us to where we are today. It would have been nice if doors had opened first but, sometimes, God wants us to walk into the unknown, trusting that He will open or create the doors we need as we are obedient and courageous to follow Him. Remember, we must trust Him through the fog and, at the end, He we will guide us to land safely.

SECURITY AND PROTECTION

I worked in the business world for over 20 years and climbed the corporate ladder to the top twice. I saw the favour of God come time and time again. One of the things that happen with the favour of God is that He makes us look good at what we do but it is all Him. He greatly blessed everything I did and made me look like a brilliant business woman. Things were really good. I had a full career and great possibilities ahead of me. However, I knew all along that I would, one day, have to leave it all to follow the destiny God had for me.

Then one night, about three years ago, the LORD came to visit me. It was really late and Ivan was already asleep. God's presence filled the room and at that moment, my spirit arose within me and responded to the LORD. I did not know why I said what I said, but I knew it was coming from my Spirit. This is what I said, "Tonight I make a promise to You. I promise You that, no matter what happens, I will not commit the sin of Esau. I choose You and my destiny and inheritance above all else and I promise you that no matter what happens I will not sell my inheritance for money. I will keep my destiny. This is my true and personal commitment to you." At the time I had no idea of what would come in the future.

Then, a year later, I had a dream, probably one of the most important dreams of my life. I was at the place where I worked. My desk was facing the office of my boss. Suddenly, this huge eagle flew in and stood on my desk. It was not one of those majestic bold eagles, but it was the goofiest looking thing I had ever seen. It was brown with huge legs and was completely friendly, happy, and very approachable. It liked to mingle with people and be around them. It was actually funny and had a very simple appearance. The eagle was with me and followed me everywhere I went. Then, at one point, we saw her walk out of the building because she was going to fly. My bosses and I went out to see her because we could not imagine she could actually fly. We could not even see her wings. She walked out and suddenly, these huge wings came out and she caught a strong wind and began to soar. It was the most beautiful and majestic thing ever. We saw her catch higher and higher thermals and something very strange happened. The higher she flew the bigger she became. Normally the higher something is the smaller it becomes but, in her case, it was the opposite and her wings grew bigger and wider with altitude. We were all in awe, as we would have never imagined, by looking at her, that she could do that when she was in the air. After a long flight, she came back down and walked into my office as usual. She was back to her old goofy and friendly self. What we had just seen her do didn't change her ways. She would go and come as she pleased and was happy.

One day I came in and saw that my boss had put a tag of ownership on her leg. I was shocked to see what had happened and told my boss that she could not do that. No one could own that eagle. She had to be free to go and fly any time she wanted and it was very important that no one owned her. My boss said that she understood that, and that she was not trying to own her but that the only reason why she had put the tag on was for security and protection. She said, "I am doing this just in case something ever happens to her when she is out flying and she is not able to come back. I want to make sure whoever finds her knows where to return her. I do not want her to get lost. I just want to protect her and give her security". I heard that and was not sure what to do because I also wanted her to be safe. It was completely up to me to take the tag off or to leave it. I did not really want her to have the tag on, but because of 'security and protection' I decided to leave it on. I trusted my boss and believed what she said.

Then I noticed that after being tagged the eagle stopped going out as much. She seemed to have lost her freedom and her countenance also changed. She looked sad but did not complain. Eventually she stopped flying all together. Then, one morning, I came into the office and could not see her anywhere. I was looking for her all over the place. In my search I walked into the boss' office and on the desk was a wooden box. I looked inside and the eagle was in there. She had been shoved in a cage that was much too small for her. Her wings had been stretched out and tied on the sides with wooden bars to make sure she could not get out. I looked in and it was so small that she could not move at all. She could only move her eyes. She looked at me with the deepest look of pain in her eyes. Things were over for her. She was trapped and I had allowed it to happen. I realized that I had been tricked by my boss. She wanted to trap the eagle, all along, and 'security and protection' was simply a hook to catch her.

I woke up from the dream immediately and I was shaking so strongly that my body was literally jumping up and down on the bed. As I woke up I felt the presence of the LORD in the room. It was very strong and He said to me, "There is a big choice you have to make that will determine your destiny. Tonight I have shown you two 'futures' available for you. That eagle is what I have placed within you and what I have created you to be. I plan to release a greater anointing on you and will use you in ways you cannot even imagine, but be very careful that you do not get trapped in your job because, if you do, then the eagle will die. The choice is yours."

After this, some time went by and an angel came and told me it was time to leave my job and said that God would provide the finances to take care of me. So, after that visitation, I knew I had to step out. However, when I made the decision and told my bosses that I was going to leave, they called me into a meeting and offered to give me the business and all the profits up to date, as a gift, if I stayed. They said that they had planned to give it to me, as my inheritance, when they retired as they thought that I would be there forever. After all, I had built the company and it was 'my baby' but, since I was talking about leaving, they would give it to me now as my inheritance from them. They also said that they knew that it would provide financially for me greatly (as it had provided greatly for them), and would give me 'security and protection' for the rest of my life, making sure that Ivan and I would be financially secure in our old age. They said, over and over, that their main concern was to give me security and protection. They wanted me to consider it for a day and get back to them. They were sure that I would take it as I had invested my life into the business. When this happened I remembered immediately the events that had taken place, the promise of that night two years before, "I will not sell my inheritance for money", the dream in which I saw myself trapped in the boss' office, and the visitation from the angel saying that God had finances to take care of me. The decision was clear, I knew what I was created to be and to do, and why I exist. I have Kingdom inheritance and I know my Kingdom identity. So, I turned down their offer and chose my Kingdom inheritance over this earthly inheritance.

I left the company in May of 2006, knowing that my Father was happy. Just weeks after leaving the security of the job and turning down the offer of the company, we discovered a major problem with the septic system in our house (the house we bought in order to have more room for people to come), and found out that it is going to cost us between $40,000 to $50,000 to fix it. That was an unexpected shock. Two days later, as if knowing what was happening, my former bosses called me to say that the company was doing better than when I left a few weeks before, and that they wanted me to reconsider and take the business, as a gift, because they wanted me to be financially secure. I could not believe the timing of the phone call. Once again, I thanked them for their great offer, generosity, and concern for me. I knew, with everything in me, that I could not walk away from my destiny, no matter how big and pressing the present need was and, therefore, I chose to trust my Father till the end because I know that at the end, He will do something amazing to help us, and we will have another great story to tell that will make Him even more famous in the land of men. Besides, we have a prophecy in which God said that He will pay our house off, so we know that at the end everything will be fine.

As this happened, God spoke to us and said, "This is what is going to happen with My children. This is the temptation and the sin of Esau that is coming to them. Warn them and prepare them for it." He said that all of us, individually and corporately, have a 'bowl of stew' that we have to deal with. We each have one thing that could cause us to sell our inheritance, and that is the very thing that the enemy is coming to offer us in exchange for our destiny. For some it can be a spouse, a job, recognition, fame, etc., etc. In my case, because of my background, my bowl of stew was financial security and protection. That is the one thing I never had and always longed for, and when the time of my destiny came, that was exactly what was offered to me in exchange. It was not easy to say, "No" to the bowl of stew, but it sure is worth it, and we are seeing the faithfulness of God in our lives. The LORD said, "Tell My people to prepare and examine their hearts so they can be ready and not commit the sin of Esau. They must be strong, courageous, and choose carefully." When we share this, many people do not know what their bowl of stew is, but God makes them aware of it and gives them what they need, in order to overcome this temptation, and see beyond their present need. Whether or not you know what your bowl of stew is, the main thing God wants is for you to make the decision that, no matter what, you will not sell your inheritance for anything regardless of the price you have to pay. Just like Elisha who kept his eyes fixed on Elijah in order to receive his promise, "The double portion of Elijah" (2 Kings 2:9).

Esther also had to make a decision and count the cost of her destiny. She was made queen for a higher purpose, and was chosen for such a time, however, fulfilling that destiny had a very high price tag. She could die. She considered the circumstances but when she knew that it was her destiny she stepped up to the plate and chose it. We all know the rest of the story. Heaven moved and released the favour and provision she needed to accomplish it. (Esther 4). We know the price that has to be paid and could not ask you to pay it if we had not done it ourselves. God is good and faithful. He is true and His words are true. He is the God of the impossible and His impossible promises are very possible for us. Regardless of the circumstances, choose your Kingdom inheritance, do not listen to your soul and do not sell your inheritance for a 'bowl of stew' which, in the long run, is a much higher price to pay.

LOVE OR DESTINY

Ron was a young man who came to Costa Rica with the Peace Corps. He was very talented and handsome. He was also a 'Don Juan' and all the girls in town were after him. Ron had known the LORD but was now a backslider. I met Ron through some friends of mine at church. Soon we became friends and quickly developed a crush on each other. Ron was my ideal man and so it was not hard for me to fall-in-love with him but, there was a big problem: he was not walking with the LORD. We carried on a friendship for a while but I knew that it would only be a matter of time before things began to move forward into a relationship as we both were well aware of the attraction of the other. For me, it was very flattering that he would be interested in me when he could choose any girl in town. Yet there was the issue of faith and obedience. Scripture is clear about being unequally yoked. I knew I had a destiny to fulfill and marrying the wrong man would cost me this. I had seen others do that and was not interested in following their example but I was in love with this man. Now I could understand what others had faced. I knew, in my heart, that I would not deliberately compromise my obedience to the LORD and my destiny.

That was a choice I had already made, but the enemy kept telling me that, with me, Ron would go back to the LORD and everything would be fine. That is another trap that many fall into, and I did not want to take that risk. Once, a long time ago, I had a talk with the LORD and I told Him that I had a request I wanted Him to grant me more than anything else. No matter what the price was, I would pay it. I told Him that my heart's desire was that on my last day on earth, the day He takes me home or the day of His return, whichever one came first, I wanted to look back at my life and be able to say two things. I wanted to say, "I married the man God chose for me. I did not make a mistake", and, "I fulfilled the destiny God created me for. God's plans for my life have been fulfilled and my work on earth is done. I have no regrets and can now go home." I pleaded with the LORD to please do anything He had to do, no matter how hard it would be to make this possible and grant me that request. I really meant it with all my heart and I have been mindful of that request ever since.

I knew that marrying the right man was pivotal for my destiny. I also knew that, because of my emotions, I could not trust myself when the time of decision came and I was honest with the LORD about it. I began to call on the LORD, with all my heart, many times a day. My constant prayer was, "LORD, I am weak and you are strong. I need your strength. Ron is my weakness and I need you to be strong in my weakness because I know that on my own I cannot say, 'No' to him. I know that I will be weak and fail therefore, I beg you, please help me and take over when the time comes. Please be strong in my weakness so I can say, 'No' to him." We were not dating, but spent time doing things together with our friends. Time passed and then, one day, it happened. Ron walked me home one night and it was a perfect night for romance. The stars were out, the moon was full, there was a refreshing breeze blowing, and we were in love. I could feel my heart beating fast and my knees going weak. We reached my house and talked outside for a bit. Then Ron leaned over and, looking at me very romantically, asked if he could kiss me. To my great amazement, at that moment, my emotions disappeared and I simply said, "No, you can't, because we cannot be anything more than just friends". He was completely and utterly shocked because he knew that I was in love with him. He was clearly confused, but behaved as a gentleman and left. As I stood there, watching him walk away, I was completely filled with the greatest peace and rest in my heart. God had done it. He came through and took over in my moment of weakness. I did not have to fight it. There was no struggle at all but instead there was peace and confidence that came from somewhere deep inside. He had indeed been strong in my weakness.

A day or two later, I went to visit our mutual friends and Ron was there. He had gone there to tell them what had happened. Unknown to me, Ron had been talking to them about his feelings towards me and had told them that he wanted to start dating me. Our friends had told him that that would never happen. They said that they knew my walk and commitment to the LORD were very strong and that no matter what happened, I would not compromise. They were very confident. Before leaving, Ron apologized to me and said, "I should have known that your relationship with the LORD is real and that you would not waiver. I want you to know that you have earned my full respect and admiration as a woman of God and I honor your walk with Him. You have shown me what a true commitment to Him is." We shook hands and he walked out of my life forever. At that moment I felt the Father smile over me and His presence filled my heart.

Then my friends came and told me how they had vouched with confidence about the decision that I would make and how they had told Ron what to expect. They said that they were sure because, through the years, they had been eyewitnesses of my walk with the LORD and did not expect anything less. I was shocked hearing them speak like that about me and had a new revelation of how important our journey with the LORD is and how it affects those who watch us run the race.

I knew that I had paid a high price letting Ron go but I knew that, even though it hurt at the time, it would be worth it and I would be very grateful for it in the future. Today I can say that it was. I am so grateful that I did not sell my destiny and inheritance for a man. God has given me a man far superior to Ron to be my husband, with whom I am fulfilling my destiny and living my dream. Today, I can truly say that I married the right man. I did not make a mistake and have no regrets, and that is a wonderful feeling. I also realized that God is more interested in our destiny than we are and He will do anything we need to help us make the right decisions that will get us there. Trust me, I know it from personal experience.

UPDATE ON THE STORY TITLED: SECURITY AND PROTECTION
(added for the second printing)
One month after the first printing of this book, the LORD did the miracle and resolved the problem with our house. It was amazing to witness the series of miracles that took place. He opened impossible doors to obtain permits that had been denied, and released Kingdom finances.

Once again, He demonstrated without doubt that, He is the Great I Am. Today we have the ending of another story that is making our Father famous. He has established the fact that He is our security and protection in all circumstances, and we will continue selling all we have for the pearl of great value, regardless of the cost or challenges that come our way. Because after all, what other nation on earth has a god like our God, who is close to us, and answers when we call on Him in our time of need?

SECTION FIFTEEN

GOD'S FAITHFULNESS

The great faithfulness of God is something we often forget and God has to continue reminding us of it. Constantly He tells us, "I am faithful", but we look at the circumstances and forget. Scripture is full of examples about His great faithfulness and the lengths He goes through to show it to us. It is incredible really. There is no one on earth that would do that. That is probably why we have such a hard time grasping the fullness of this concept. Our experiential truth tells us that it is not possible because no one has ever been or will be that faithful. But God is more than willing to show us His reality. A long time ago He said to us, "Look at the evidence of My faithfulness yesterday and today and, based on that, know that I will be faithful again tomorrow." Evidence is something we do not think of often and yet it is everywhere. In legal terms evidence is the undeniable proof of something. It is a reality and a fact. Another great truth is that evidence does not lie and is not biased. It simply is what it is, and it can be trusted completely. David understood this when he said, "The LORD, who delivered me from the paw of the lion and from the paw of the bear, He will deliver me from the hand of this Philistine." (1 Samuel 17:37). He confidently confronted Goliath because he had the evidence and, based on that, he knew that he could trust Him for the giant, and God surely came through.

We have seen this, time and time again, in our lives and have found great rest and peace knowing that He does not change. Our trust in Him has increased tremendously since we began to look at the evidence of His love and faithfulness in all the different areas of our lives. We have overcome great giants, have seen great walls come down, have witnessed and partaken of God's power and miracles, have seen breakthrough and victory become part of our daily lives, and we look at tomorrow with anticipation of what He will do next. Every time challenges arise and fear tries to come into our lives, we simply stop and look back at the evidence of God's faithfulness and love, and immediately the fear leaves and is replaced by peace, as we know that He will come through again. We now have a great confidence when He speaks and know that we can trust Him for that too. Scripture shows us that God takes His promises very seriously. As we see in Hebrews 6:16-18, God bound Himself to His promise by an oath. He wanted to show us the unchangeableness of His purpose, and that it is impossible for Him to lie because, "He is not a man that He should lie nor a son of man that He would change His mind" (1 Samuel 15:29). He never forgets His promises and is always willing to fulfill them.

I have a powerful story that confirms this. One of my sisters is married to a man who has been very abusive and controlling. He actually suffers from psychotic episodes and no one knows what will set it off. They lived together for 24 years before getting married. The abuse began shortly after they got together. My other sister, Lucy, and I began to pray that they would break-up but he told my sister that he would kill her if she left him, and we all knew it was true because he had guns in his house. My niece was born shortly after and he began to hit and mistreat the child too. Sometimes the beatings were so bad that they would end up in the hospital. We did not know what to do. My sister was very afraid of him and, at that time, in our country the police did not help women in this sort of situation. We lived in a 'macho' culture where men ruled and women were beneath them. My sister had accepted Jesus as her Saviour but this man was not in favour of it. We prayed much for his salvation but that seemed impossible. We literally lost all hope of him ever getting saved. In our eyes he was 'beyond hope for salvation'. Things continued getting worse and came to the point that we expected him to kill one or both of them.

Years passed and my sister announced that they were getting married. We were shocked but it was her choice so we respected it and wished her the best. One day, about three months after their wedding, there was an evangelistic crusade in town. My sister insisted on going because she was very sick and they were going to pray for healing. Her husband drove her and was going to leave right away but decided to stay a bit longer in order to keep an eye on her. However, due to a series of circumstances he ended up staying for the whole meeting and, at the end, stood up and gave his life to the LORD. That was a real shock to us as no one expected that to ever happen. We honestly did not have faith for his salvation. When I heard the news I asked the LORD, "What happened? How come, after all those years with no answer, they get married and suddenly he gets saved?" The LORD said, "It is very simple. The moment he married your sister he became part of your household and came under the promise I gave you that night many years ago. I promised you that night when your mother tried to kill you that if you stuck with me, I would save your household and I am doing it. He is now your household". I was speechless. God stood by the promise He made me, all those years back, and did not forget. He and His faithfulness have surpassed our expectations.

Another experience happened when several years ago I got a phone call saying that my oldest sister and her husband had been in a tragic car accident and were in critical condition. This brother-in-law is very special to me as later in life, he became an important father figure to me and is like a father to Ivan. They were going to be operated on right away. I heard the news, cried for a while, then said to the LORD, "Many, many years ago you gave me a promise. You said that if I hung in there and paid the price You would save my family. I believed You and did as You requested, now I need You to do what you promised. They cannot die because they do not know You yet. I need You to do a miracle and heal them so they can know You and be saved. You promised me, and I will not let them go until I know they are going to heaven".

The next day I got another phone call. They had survived the surgery. My sister would be fine but they had removed dozens of blood clots from her husband's brain and he was expected to live but be a vegetable. They said, "The man you used to know does not exist anymore". My brother-in-law is a brilliant man, very funny and witty. I could not imagine seeing him as vegetable on a bed. I put the phone down, and then said to the LORD "I am indeed very grateful that they are fine and that my brother-in-law survived the surgery. Thank You for all You have done so far. However, the news I just received is not good enough. If he remains a vegetable I will never know if he is going to heaven or not, and I need to know that, when the time comes, he will go to heaven. Therefore, I need You to heal him completely so that he can truly come to know You, and I can see the fulfillment of Your promise in his life".

Within 24 hours I got another phone call. My sister and my nephew were going in to see my brother-in-law and the doctor stopped them before they walked into the room. He said to them, "I need to warn you that something very unexpected has taken place and I do not want you be shocked when you go in. He is in a different condition today; something has taken place that we cannot explain at all. It is impossible, yet real, and you have to see for yourselves." They opened the door and he was sitting up telling jokes to the nurse, just like he always did and has recovered completely. Shortly after, they both started watching Benny Hinn twice a day and God began to move in their lives. Isn't God faithful? Nothing can change His character because He cannot deny Himself.

Part of the promise the LORD gave me, back then, was that He would not only save my family but He would restore my household. We were all very broken as our lives had been horrible. All four sisters had suffered so much and my two oldest sisters stopped speaking to each other when I was ten years old. There were too many walls between everyone. There was always tension in the family and someone would always criticize another one. There was never joy and harmony in our family. For many years we would try different things to get my sisters to talk to each other but nothing worked. I used to carry this weight on my shoulders for my family's salvation and reconciliation, but all my efforts were useless. About a year after I got saved, I had to stop preaching at them because that was causing more walls to arise between us. One day, I was in the kitchen, very upset, feeling that I was failing the LORD because my family was not responding and, therefore, I thought I had to try harder.

The LORD then spoke to me and said, "Who preached at you? Who gave you the message of salvation? Who got you saved?" No one ever told me the message of salvation. No one ever preached the true gospel to me. Jesus Himself came, met with me, and personally led me through a sinner's prayer. He alone made it happen and 'got me saved'. I said, "You did. No one on earth did it. You did it all Yourself". He replied, "Then don't you think I am able to reach your family and save them too? I am the one who does it and I will arrange it all. I will save and restore them". What freedom and rest I received! The heaviness lifted and complete trust came into my heart (I had evidence that God could do it for them because He did it for me).

The peace that surpasses all understanding filled my heart and life and I never worried again. One of the things that happen to many people is that they do not understand the reality of the peace that surpasses all understanding and, therefore, reject it. This peace is completely supernatural and we need Kingdom mentality to grasp it. This is the best and only way I can explain it: The peace that surpasses all understanding makes you feel almost like you do not care anymore about the situation. It is a strange feeling because you do care, but you no longer have the concern or the heavy burden. Many people think that if they do not worry about the situation then that means that they do not care. Somehow we have equated worry and anxiety with caring. Funny isn't it? Caring and worrying are two different things. We can care but have complete rest and be worry free.

I remember, many years ago, I used to worry about our finances and Ivan did not worry at all. Ivan has always been very responsible and hard working, so it was not that he was irresponsible. He has never been, but many times financial crises would come which caused me to worry. In those times I used to get upset thinking that Ivan did not care about our situation and about me really, because if he did he would show concern. For me to know that he cared I needed him to worry. That is the way I understood it. That's what I saw my parents do. However, he would tell me, "Honey I care. I really do, but I have complete peace in my heart because I know my Father will take care of us. He will help us and everything will be just fine". Well, that was not good enough for me. I was hurt for a long time by this attitude. Then later, when God started changing me, I realized what was happening. Ivan had this supernatural peace that surpasses all understanding and could trust God completely, which was foreign to me. In time, as I got closer to my Father and got to know Him better, healing came to my heart and I too began to receive that supernatural faith. When challenges would arise and fear or concern tried to come in, I simply told myself, "It's OK. I do not need to worry anymore because my Father has been faithful before, is faithful today, and will surely be faithful tomorrow". I would then look at the evidence, which was undeniable, and ponder on it. As a result faith, peace, and rest would come. I still do this and constantly see the change in how I react to circumstances. God is faithful indeed!

AMANDA

Some years ago our daughter had a major swimming accident. It was the last day of school and they had a pool party at the local swimming pool. There were almost 300 kids playing in the pool and someone hit her on the head, knocking her unconscious under the water. There were life guards there, but in that ocean of heads who is going to notice one child missing? Finally, a younger child noticed that she was missing and began to look for her. He saw a body at the bottom of the pool and a sixth grader pulled her out of the water. She was already blue when they found her and the lining of her lungs had come out. The doctors told us that when the lining of the lungs comes out people die and that she was about 60 seconds away from complete and absolute death when they rescued her. They rushed her to the hospital and, of course, we immediately went to meet her there.

When I walked into the ER I froze at the sight. She was hooked to five or six machines and there was a team of six to eight doctors and nurses working on her trying to keep her alive. They were all fighting for her life. At that moment I had the biggest déjà vu of my life. I knew I had been there before. Exactly one year before, I had a dream in which I saw this all happen. In the dream she was hooked to the machines just the same and the doctors and nurses doing all they could to keep her alive and Ivan and I were by her side fighting for her life. It was bad for a while but at the end of the dream, she was fine and we bonded completely as a family. We became a real family as a result, and we were all happy.

We adopted Amanda from Guatemala when she was seven years old. She came out of much abuse, rejection, and destitution. Her family situation was not good and she suffered very much. When we adopted her she told me right out, "Lady, what is your name? I want to call you by your name. I am not calling you Mom because you are not my Mom. I have a mom of my own back home and I do not need another one. Besides, I will not be staying long with you. I will go back soon to my mother in Guatemala". We did our best to explain to her that she now had two mothers, one in Guatemala and one here, and that we were now a family forever. Ivan asked her to call me Mom and not by my name. She did, but it was an empty word, which was actually quite painful for me. She did not accept me and did not want anything to do with me. She adored Ivan because she never had a Dad and, more than anything in life, she wanted to have a Daddy of her own. Life was not easy. She had many behaviour problems because of her background, which also added to our trials. The school could not handle her and she was on permanent notice of expulsion for a year and a half. They said that she was one of the four greatest bullies in the whole school. She would beat and kick children and teachers alike.

Because she did not speak any English at the time I had to translate everything for her including all discipline issues, which made me, look like the 'Wicked Witch of the West'. Even when Ivan disciplined her the three of us would sit together and I translated for him, but much later she told me that when that happened, in her mind she was sure that I was lying and that her Dad never said any of those things. She would tell me, over and over, that she wanted to get rid of me so she could have her Dad and go back to her real Mom. She, of course, did not know that she had been given away three times to other people before we came into the picture, and we were number four. She knew her mom and, regardless of the circumstances, she loved her as it should be. Many times she would tell me how her 'real mom' desperately wanted her back but that I was in the way keeping them apart so she was on a campaign to get rid of me. She did all she could to break us up and, through that, we learned how strong our marriage really is.

When she came into our lives, all her issues awakened some hidden issues of my childhood that I was not aware of and opened up a much deeper layer of the hurt, caused by the abuse and rejection I had suffered from my own mother. I thought I had dealt with it all, but like with the onion, there are many layers to our healing process. So, besides the circumstances with our child, I was also dealing with all the brokenness that suddenly arose in me and, without realizing it, I put up some walls to protect my heart. Also, I was protecting myself from the rejection of the child. Ivan, bless his heart, was the instrument of God holding things together. Pain is pain and is not pretty, but thank God that He has provided healing and freedom. As I became aware of my pain I began to deal with it and got much prayer ministry, which set me free.

After all, Jesus came to set the captives free and I am proof of that. Things at home continued stormy with our child. One day, two and a half years after she came to us, she had one of the biggest outbursts against me and told me again that she did not want me in her life, that she wanted the Dad without me and so on. She then took all the photos she had of the two of us when we met in Guatemala and got rid of them in front of me. It was very painful. Ivan said, "Honey, we are dealing with the hurt of the child, not with the heart of the child. We must continue praying and trusting the LORD because one day, when the hurt in her gets healed, the heart that is within will come out, and everything will change". We decided to continue believing that one day things would change.

The next day we were in church and I decided to make an extra effort to minister in the 'opposite spirit'. It is very common, when faced with difficult situations and attitudes, to react in the same way that we are treated. For instance, if someone has issues of rejection they act in a way that causes people to reject them. Normally people react according to the spirit behind the action. If someone reacts out of anger, that spirit causes people to respond in anger too, and so on. Therefore, we must pay attention to the spirit behind the action and, once we recognize it, then we can choose to respond in the opposite spirit. For instance, if the spirit behind the action is rejection, responding with love and acceptance will diffuse the rejection. I remember one particular time Amanda was misbehaving and I was getting upset. She began to speak louder, which bothered me and I responded by raising my voice too, which then caused her to get angrier. She got really out of sorts and, as I went to respond, suddenly I heard myself say, "Honey, just come here". Something amazing happened. As I said, "Honey", my voice softened because it is a term of love and endearment, which caused me to become calm and feel love for her. She heard it and reacted in the same manner. She stopped, looked at me and softened her voice, which allowed us to work things out without anger. What an amazing key this is!

So, that Sunday at church, I decided to minister to her in the opposite spirit. I made an extra effort to show her love and acceptance. She began to soften a bit and allowed me to get closer to her. The next day, Monday, I did it again all day. Tuesday was her last day of school and I knew that she was really excited about the swimming party. I made an extra effort to come and wish her a wonderful day. She seemed to appreciate it and gave me a hug. That was the day of the swimming accident. The next time I saw her she was on that table, at the ER, fighting for her life. I was frozen in that room seeing the condition she was in. The doctors told us that there was not much they could do for her as her condition was beyond their training and ability. They contacted the nearest Children's Hospital, which was one hour away and had a nurse permanently on the phone getting instructions from them, in order to help Amanda, while a specialized team came for her. They told us that they could not transport her in their ambulance because they did not have the equipment to keep her alive during the trip.

As I heard all of that, I then remembered the end of the dream and I decided to focus on that. I thought, "If the first part of the dream came to pass surely the end will too". I decided to fix my eyes on the promise at the end of that dream, no matter what my physical eyes were seeing and, as a result, peace came to me and the presence of God filled me. As soon as Amanda became conscious she began to fight them. She was in survival mode and was quite feisty. She was pulling out the tubes she had in her nose and mouth and all the other needles she had in different parts of her body, so the doctors had to give her a strong drug to paralyze her body. This was so hard because she was conscious but her body was paralyzed. The doctors told us that this was emotionally difficult for her but that we should not worry, because one of the other medications would erase her memory, so she would not remember what happened on that table. As Christian counselors we knew that it would not be so easy because the trauma of that event would be registered in her subconscious and eventually it would come up, but she would not know why, because the memory was erased. At the same time we were grateful to know all this so we can help her at the right time. Unfortunately, she kept on fighting the paralyzing drug and they had to keep giving her more, until they said that they could not give her any more. We were standing on the side praying and the doctor asked me to come and talk to her so I could calm her down. She could hear so they thought that hearing Mom's voice would do wonders for her. I knew that hearing me would probably make it worse because she did not want me near her. However, I was not going to try and explain that to the doctors and nurses, so discreetly I asked Ivan to go and talk to her and she calmed down as soon as she heard his voice.

A few hours later, Ivan had to go out for a while and suddenly Amanda had another fit. The doctor looked at me and said very firmly, "Mom, you have to come and help us. Talk to her and calm her down". I had no choice but to go. I talked to her but not in the mushy way the doctors wanted me to. I said to her, "Amanda, this is Mom and I am here to help you. These doctors are working hard to help you as well, and you have to stop fighting them and let them do their work. Dad and I will protect you but you have to behave". The doctor was staring at me with a puzzled look on his face. However he noticed that all her vital signs went down immediately. She calmed down completely and, from that moment on, she did not fight them anymore. Since she was paralyzed and could not fight me either, I decided to get close to her and touch her. I rubbed her hair and her face, kissed her and began to tell her that I loved her and other nice mushy things. Immediately, I felt this rush of love come up from deep within me and, at that moment, all my walls crumbled to the ground. I knew right there and then that I was 'her mother'. It was the most amazing feeling ever. For the first time I felt what it was like to be a mom, and my heart connected with that child completely, from that moment on, every time they poked her with needles (which they did every three to five minutes) I could feel the poking. Every time she twitched or reacted I felt it deep in my soul. I had become a Mom!

A while later, the specialized team came to take her and they told us that she was alive and would probably live but, due to the length of time she was without oxygen, it was very likely that she had serious brain damage and could be a vegetable or be seriously impaired. They wanted us to brace ourselves for what was to come. I heard that and, for a moment, I panicked and began to cry. It was a horrible feeling of hopelessness. Then I remembered the dream and decided once again not to focus on the circumstances but to focus on the ending of the dream and to believe it. Instantly, the peace returned and I was fine again. I relived the ending of that dream over and over and over and as I did faith arose within me.

We drove to the Children's Hospital, where Amanda was hooked to even more machines and had a nurse sitting by her side watching all the monitors and her every breath. We were with her a few hours and prayed much for her. Many of our friends and family were also praying for her. Finally, by midnight, the nurse noticed that her lungs were responding, which was absolutely amazing. She was unconscious so the nurse encouraged us to go home and rest for a few hours. At 7:00 the next morning we got a call from the hospital. Amanda was awake and off all the machines except for the oxygen, which was a complete miracle. She was coherent and chatting with the nurses and doctors (she was bossing them, they said), and ate breakfast. We decided that in order not to upset her Ivan would go in the morning and I would go in the afternoon with him. I thought that seeing me would be upsetting to her. I was her mom now, but adoption is a two-way street and she had to accept me too. Ivan got to the hospital and as soon as she saw him, she asked for 'Mom'. For the first time ever, she wanted me not just her Dad.

When I got to the hospital she was unwell with a very high fever and still had a lot of water in her lungs. She was curled up in a little ball on the bed and barely talked. I got next to her on the bed, held her, kissed her, and simply loved-up on her. She allowed me to do it but more than that she was able to receive love from me and, slowly, as she received love from me, she began to improve. Within just over an hour, she was sitting up chatting and looking so much better. Two hours later we were playing games and the doctor was shocked seeing the incredible improvement in her. The next morning the neurologist checked her and said that, against all odds, she had not suffered any damage and could go home. She was home before lunch. Imagine! And just like in the dream, from that moment on, we became a family. Her walls also came down that day in that ER and she became my daughter.

She accepted me as her Mom and slowly started trusting me, beginning to believe that I would not give her away like it had happened in the past. Slowly 'Mom' was not just a word she had to say. The emptiness of it went away and there was feeling and love behind it. Ivan was right. In time, as healing came and the hurt went away, her heart came out and it is precious. She is a very happy child. Today we have a wonderful relationship. She has the most amazing prophetic anointing and great passion for the LORD and His people, just like we do. She carries God's love in her heart and it flows out of her. We really are a family and can truly join Joseph in saying that, "What the enemy intended for evil God turned into good" (Genesis 50:20). And the promise of the dream came true! God is indeed faithful to His words!!

SECTION SIXTEEN

DISSECTING PROPHECY

When receiving prophecy it is common to feel overwhelmed by it all because we see it as a whole. There is so much in a prophecy and we need to learn to break it down. Dissecting prophecy makes it possible. Now that you know all the steps described in this book you will look at your prophecies differently and will understand them better. This is a simple guideline to dissecting your prophecies:

Make different columns for each section:
- Identify all the promises of God and write them down in one column. Remember to keep them handy as these are weapons to fight well in the LORD'S battles.
- Identify all the gifts that are released into you through the prophecies spoken over you. What new things were spoken over you and then do something about them so they get activated. Remember, do not neglect them.
- Identify all blessings spoken over you and take ownership of them.
- Identify all the impartations you have received and start investing.
- Identify your Kingdom identity, embrace it and start aligning your life accordingly and changing your mindsets. Develop Kingdom mentality
- Identify the mandates God has given you and choose to act on them.
- Plan a strategy for your prophetic destiny and road map your prophecies.
- Reverse engineer your prophecies and then start taking the steps to get you there

• **Please listen for repetitions.** This is very important. In Genesis 41 Joseph is interpreting Pharaoh's dream and in verse 32 he says: "Now as for the repeating of the dream to Pharaoh twice, it means that the matter is determined by God (has been decreed by God), and God will quickly bring it about". We have paid attention to this through the years and realized that it is true. Most people think that when God repeats something in prophecies, it simply is confirmation. Yes, it is confirmation, but, that is not all there is to it. Repetition also means, "Listen because it has been decreed by God and it will happen quickly!" We often hear people casually say, "In the last while, this has been prophesied over me three times, funny how people get the same thing". Let me tell you, that is huge, and it is God shouting and blowing the trumpet saying: "Get ready because it is near. The rain is about to fall". Write down every repetition and the date when it was spoken. Sometimes people say, "Wow that was prophesied over me ten years ago." The fact that it is now being repeated simply means that the time for it to be fulfilled is finally coming, and God wants to alert you so you can prepare. This is a great key to help us discern the timing of events and be ready for them. May you have ears to hear, and may your harvest quickly come.

One of our friends was going through a hard time and could not focus on her destiny at large. She attended one of our conferences and became interested in understanding strategy. We taught her how to dissect her prophecies and then set up a strategy for each area. Two weeks later she told us that everything had changed in her life after she had done what we suggested. She was finally able to understand, and see how it could be possible. As a result, her heart was set on fire for God's plans for her. She changed the direction in which she was going and is now walking into the destiny she was born for.

To get you started we have provided some pages at the back so you can start working on dissecting your prophecies.

Remember that it is not by the strength of the horse but by the might of the LORD that the battles are won. The hardest battle you will ever fight is for your destiny and our challenge to you is to be strong and very courageous.

Do not be afraid, because it is your Father's great delight to give you His Kingdom today!

WORK PAGES TO DISSECT YOUR PROPHECIES

Use these pages to start making the prophetic road map to your destiny.

First, write down your prophecies in full, then break them down according to the guidelines on page 245. Once you have done that, start applying the keys given in this book and walk towards your goal. Be courageous and very strong because the violent take the Kingdom by force (Matthew 11:12).

Remember that, "The land which we passed through to spy out is an exceedingly good land. If the LORD is pleased with us, then He will bring us into this land and give it to us–a land which flows with milk and honey. Only do not rebel against the LORD; and do not fear the people of the land, for they will be our prey. Their protection has been removed from them, and the LORD is with us; do not fear them" (Numbers 14:7-9)

Much love, hugs, and blessings,
Ivan & Isabel

www.ivan-isabel.com
www.hcm-stratford.org

Promises	Gifts	Blessings	Impartations	Kingdom Identity	Mandates	Strategy

Promises	Gifts	Blessings	Impartations	Kingdom Identity	Mandates	Strategy

Strategy	Mandates	Kingdom Identity	Impartations	Blessings	Gifts	Promises

Promises	Gifts	Blessings	Impartations	Kingdom Identity	Mandates	Strategy

Promises

Gifts

Blessings

Impartations

Kingdom Identity

Mandates

Strategy